I0121759

Needlework, Affect and Social Transformation

Needlework, Affect and Social Transformation

The Everyday Textures of Feminist Activism

Katja May

BLOOMSBURY VISUAL ARTS
LONDON • NEW YORK • OXFORD • NEW DELHI • SYDNEY

BLOOMSBURY VISUAL ARTS

Bloomsbury Publishing Plc, 50 Bedford Square, London, WC1B 3DP, UK
Bloomsbury Publishing Inc, 1385 Broadway, New York, NY 10018, USA
Bloomsbury Publishing Ireland, 29 Earlsfort Terrace, Dublin 2, D02 AY28, Ireland

BLOOMSBURY, BLOOMSBURY VISUAL ARTS and the Diana logo are
trademarks of Bloomsbury Publishing Plc

First published in Great Britain 2023
Paperback edition published 2025
Copyright © Katja May, 2023

Katja May has asserted her right under the Copyright, Designs and Patents Act, 1988,
to be identified as Author of this work.

For legal purposes the Acknowledgements on p. vii constitute an extension
of this copyright page.

Cover design: Holly Capper
Cover image © Benjavisa Ruangvaree/Adobe Stock

All rights reserved. No part of this publication may be: i) reproduced or
transmitted in any form, electronic or mechanical, including photocopying,
recording or by means of any information storage or retrieval system without
prior permission in writing from the publishers; or ii) used or reproduced in
any way for the training, development or operation of artificial intelligence (AI)
technologies, including generative AI technologies. The rights holders expressly
reserve this publication from the text and data mining exception as per
Article 4(3) of the Digital Single Market Directive (EU) 2019/790.

Bloomsbury Publishing Plc does not have any control over, or responsibility for,
any third-party websites referred to or in this book. All internet addresses given
in this book were correct at the time of going to press. The author and publisher
regret any inconvenience caused if addresses have changed or sites have
ceased to exist, but can accept no responsibility for any such changes.

A catalogue record for this book is available from the British Library.

A catalog record for this book is available from the Library of Congress.

ISBN: HB: 978-1-3502-8358-9
         PB: 978-1-3502-8362-6
      ePDF: 978-1-3502-8359-6
     eBook: 978-1-3502-8360-2

Typeset by RefineCatch Limited, Bungay, Suffolk

For product safety related questions contact productsafety@bloomsbury.com.

To find out more about our authors and books visit www.bloomsbury.com
and sign up for our newsletters.

Contents

Illustrations

Acknowledgements

Little did I know that this book is where the journey would lead me when I first joined a local quilt group at the age of eighteen. I am deeply grateful to all the women in the quilt groups I have attended over the years and who have taught me so much about the craft. Their creative practices have inspired much of this research!

I would also like to express my heartfelt thanks to the organisations and individuals with whom I have worked throughout this research. This book would not have been possible without their unwavering support, cooperation, enthusiasm and generosity: Chawne Kimber; Marsha MacDowell and the Michigan State University Museum; Sara Trail and the Social Justice Sewing Academy; Pascale Goldenberg and Guldusi; Gillian Travis; Assiya Amini from the Afghan Academy International; Hannah Hill; Margo Smith and the Kudzu project; and the Building the Anti-Racist Classroom Collective (BARC).

My utmost thanks and gratitude also go to my PhD supervisors, Stella Bolaki and Carolyn Pedwell, for their unconditional support with this research, and to my examiners, Jennie Batchelor and Ben Highmore, for their useful feedback. A huge thank you to my writing and thinking buddies who have sustained me over the last few years by always providing encouragement and support (and for reading drafts!), especially, Ellen Fowles, Katalin Halasz, Danne Jobin, Adele Mason-Bertrand, Faten Khazaei, Betsy Porritt, Julia Rosche, Sobia Ahmad Kaker. Finally, a big thank you to my brilliant coach, Vinita Joseph, for helping me to get all of this done and to the London Writers' Salon for holding space.

Introduction: The Affective Politics
of Needlework

When in the spring of 2020 countries across the world went into lockdown as a result of the Covid-19 pandemic, many people suddenly found themselves spending much more time at home. They were faced with the emotional, financial and physical aspects of living life in a pandemic of unprecedented proportions. Loneliness, grief and anxieties about the future and the well-being of loved ones became defining features of this experience for many as they juggled new work and household dynamics. During these difficult times, many found solace in creative practices, in making things with their hands (Sullivan 2020; Wellesley-Smith 2021). For experienced makers as well as novices, practices of needlework became a powerful way to process their experiences of life in a pandemic. Making with needle and thread, or yarn and hook, offered an embodied way of soothing the mind in a time of heightened global distress. In combination with digital networks, practices of needlework also offered makers a way to connect with others and share experiences at a time marked by isolation and a lack of the everyday interactions as part of going to the office, the supermarket or the gym.

In response to these developments, the @covid19quilt founded by Australia-based artists Kate Just and Tal Fitzpatrick offers people across the world a targeted platform to creatively express and share their experiences of the pandemic including feelings of fear, anger, loss and loneliness. Started in April 2020, the initiative encourages makers across the world to create a textile piece in any style or technique and to submit a square picture of it along with a text about their experience of the pandemic. These images are then shared on the initiative's dedicated Instagram account to create a digital quilt made of a mass of individual pieces submitted by different people from different places. Just and Fitzpatrick see the initiative as part of their commitment to 'engage communities in thinking through, and making art about complex social and political issues' (Just n.d.). As active participants in the contemporary craftivism movement that brings together craft and activism, Just and Fitzpatrick have previously used practices of needlework, like knitting and quilting, for community organizing and political activism to address social justice issues like sexism, racism and climate change. They consciously tap into the long gendered activist practices connected to needlework as well as their celebrated mental health benefits and combine it with networked digital technologies.

To this date, the @covid19quilt consists of over 500 entries from at least thirty countries. While some entries reflect personal experiences of illness and loneliness, many entries explicitly address injustices like: racism; environmental pollution, increased through expanded use of personal protective equipment (PPE); underfunding of the healthcare sector; or the heightened risk for those deemed clinically vulnerable. An embroidered piece by Rubina Singh from India, for example, in red lettering on a black background with a virus molecule stitched in the middle, states: 'Corona didn't break the system, Corona exposed a broken system'. Some of the entries also show in almost a humorous fashion how the pandemic has changed people's relationship with everyday habits and objects, such as toilet paper, which all of a sudden became for a while a highly coveted item. According to Just, the textile contributions 'reflect a sustained engagement with textile processes that address the diverse range of issues people around the world are facing' (n.d.). They provide a window into people's different experiences of the pandemic. Some of the online viewers of the digital quilt may share these experiences and the concerns expressed, to others they may appear rather alien. For Just and Fitzpatrick, the project is a means of 'asserting that we can reclaim our connection to each other by continuing to make things with our hands and by sharing stories that highlight our shared humanity' (Fitzpatrick n.d.). It is about connecting people digitally, materially and affectively through practices of needlework.

Needlework, Affect and Social Transformation explores the affectivity – the un/ conscious emotive capacities – of practices of needlework in the context of feminist political activism. It examines how practices of needlework may move people to relate, think and feel differently about themselves and others. The book focuses on affect as that which involves identifiable emotions like anger or despair but also 'embodied and non-conscious ways of experiencing, knowing and remembering' (Kolehmainen, Lahti and Kinnunen 2022: 3). As a result, I offer a nuanced theoretical framework for understanding the political potential and meaning of practices of needlework for different people. This research pays attention to the assemblages of meaning that have formed around needlework in relation to race, gender, class, sexuality and nation and how these relate to the personal positioning of makers, viewers and readers. What narratives dominate popular understanding about the meaning of practices of needlework? Whose stories are the most prominent? How does this reflect larger inequalities? What are the implications of this for the role of textile crafts to feminist activism? Needlework is political. From embroidered suffragette banners to the knitting installations on the fence of Greenham Common Women's Peace Camp and the famous Pussyhats worn at the Women's March – practices of needlework have long been tied with feminist activism. Whether one sews for a living or just knits for fun, in the privacy of one's home or as part of a craft group, practices of needlework are deeply tied to conceptions about femininity, work and leisure, art and materiality. Consequently, practices of needlework and their narrative representations may reproduce structures of power which marginalize and oppress people.

Attention to affect offers important insights into the seemingly more subtle and under-the-radar workings of power and social hierarchies in ways that conventional analyses, for example, of financial inequalities, cannot (Ahmed 2004; Boler 1999; Kolehmainen, Lahti and Kinnunen 2022). At the same time, attention to affect also opens up new ways for understanding how political resistance and solidarity might emerge (Cvetkovich 2003, 2012; Love 2007; Pedwell 2014, 2021). I conceptualize needlework as affective social practices of meaning making, that is, as routine activities invested with feelings and entangled with concrete material and social conditions, in order to attend to needlework's complex political potential. My analysis focuses on various textured encounters with, in and between texts, textile artefacts and practices of textile making to examine how these encounters orient people affectively and politically. Texture as a concept, a materiality and a framework for analysis is ideally suited to exploring practices of needlework and their narrative renderings as affective social practices of meaning making. Meaning making is neither a smooth nor a linear process but can involve multiple iterations and getting stuck; it is a textured process because it is multifaceted in the same way that the meaning of practices of needlework is not monolithic. In this sense, the types of affective meaning making that I am interested in in this book do not necessarily require specific agency and intention from the maker.[1] Rather, what is of greater importance from an affect studies point of view is 'the relational, dialogic and distributed aspects of meaning-making' that are entangled in the texture of everyday life (Wetherell 2012: 53).

Through the study of individual and collective practices of textile making that range from the activist quilting practices of contemporary African American quilter Chawne Kimber to literary representations of the private sewing activities of

London immigrant homeworkers, I explicate the complex affective transnational entanglements that are part of contemporary performances of needlework and their narrative representations. Inspired by Ann Cvetkovich's concept of an 'archive of feelings', I attend to a variety of cultural text(ure)s as affective archives 'which are encoded not only in the context of the texts themselves but in the practices that surround their production and repetition' (2003: 7). I explore how the meaning of practices of needlework is shaped through the links between affect and personal and cultural narratives, literary representations and dominant discourses about needlework and feminist politics. The key contention of this book, then, is that practices of needlework make possible a politics of embodied orientation. They move people physically and affectively towards new everyday imaginaries of social transformation and may point towards different kinds of social and affective relations. In other words, making with one's hands or engaging with other people's accounts of making can be a first step towards envisaging more just social relations.

This book does not offer an account of what such relations may look like. There are certainly lots of practical and important changes that can be made in the interest of social justice, for example, concerning legislation for racial justice, or trans people's rights, and, particularly in the context of textile crafts communities, regarding the visibility and support of makers of colour (Hewett 2021; Patel 2020). Yet, because of the unequal flow of power – the workings of which I trace throughout this book – certain voices and accounts are more likely to be heard than others. Therefore, a prescriptive vision for social change or a more just future is likely to further marginalize certain people and groups. I follow the critical traditions of affect studies, prefiguration and anti-authoritarian organizing (Coleman 2020; Deleuze and Guattari 1987; Dixon 2014; Manning 2016; Massumi 2002; Pedwell 2021). Thus, I find it more generative to focus on the continuous unfolding of new relations to allow for the shifting dynamics of power. I regard practices of needlework as part of a prefigurative politics of experimentation that attempts to craft and remake a new world from the midst of our current one (Fitzpatrick and Kontturi 2015; Yates 2015). The unequal flow of power may of course also be felt within these spaces of experimentation. It is, therefore, important to recognize how white supremacy and patriarchy function as overarching structures of governance of much of the current world (Hunter and van der Westhuizen 2022; Perry 2018). They penetrate the most intimate spheres of everyday life, and it is important to consider what affective attachments and habits they produce to understand not only how power works, but also how to envisage social transformation (Pedwell 2014, 2016, 2021; Sullivan 2006). Like other artistic practices, the literary also provides a space in which to creatively experiment and practice such new politics and to offer alternative accounts of what constitutes change. *Needlework, Affect and Social Transformation*, in this context, explores how practices of needlework may 'offer ways of knowing, imagining and critiquing that counter ongoing colonial realities and contribute to cultural shifts' (Black and Burisch 2020: 8).

I suggest that practices of needlework and their narrative representations may provide a texture through which new forms of transnational feminist solidarity may emerge that are not based in supposedly shared experiences of gendered oppression that regularly privilege the experience of white (and often middle-class) women in the Global North. Instead of looking to textile crafts and its connotations with comfort, warmth and care to overcome tensions between women from different backgrounds, I point to the ways that practices of needlework present a generative way of being with these affective tensions which include discomfort, anger, defensiveness and disappointment. They may help to initiate a transnational feminist solidarity which recognizes these affective tensions as foundational *and* generative to transnational feminist politics (May 2023). As such, this book contributes to contemporary debates about the long and contested history of the meaning, purpose and potential of so-called women's craft in the context of transnational feminist solidarity politics. It does not offer a teleological account of how practices of needlework can be used to support a 'good' or 'bad' feminist politics – nor do I think that such an account is possible or indeed beneficial (May 2020). Rather, through a diverse set of case studies including literary texts by African American women writers as well as contemporary craftivist initiatives like the Pussyhat and Kudzu projects, I explore what political acts or tendencies practices of needlework and their narrative renderings make possible. Through the different case studies, I develop a substantial and illuminating analysis of contemporary women's texts and textile practices, offering a 'big picture' synthesis that moves across disciplines, theoretical frameworks, geographical contexts and social movements.

Through my case studies, I hope to define the terrain of a contemporary politics of making with fibres by exploring how textuality and materiality interact as part of this politics. In this context, storytelling and narratives are important because they not only enable people to give an account of their life, but also make the co-existence of a variety of accounts possible (Couldry 2010; Harding 2004). The multiplicity of the accounts of lived experience can then serve as a building block for social justice work committed to dismantling hierarchies of power and the unequal distribution of resources and opportunities. Thus, my selection of materials for this research is purposefully diverse, as are the interpretive frameworks I use to make sense of them in recognition of the entangled nature of everyday life, and the difficulty of capturing these entanglements in the research process (Highmore 2002b; Hine 2007; Law 2004). My archive includes: novels and short stories; displays of textile works in galleries and quilt shows; the digital in the form of websites, online newsletters and social media; makers' testimonies; and moments of direct political action like the Women's March on Washington.

The everyday gendered domestic context, in which much textile making takes place and in which the finished object is often used or displayed, plays a pivotal role in my analysis. By focusing on the everyday performance of practices of needlework and the way the practice is part of the texture of everyday life, and, consequently, of narratives about the everyday, I explore how needlework serves as a tool for meaning making in the context of a transnational struggle for social justice and feminist solidarity. In addition, I trace any potential shifts in meaning as practice and object leave the domestic sphere and travel into and through the public and digital domain without shrugging off the connection to the home.

Both texts and textiles, as I argue throughout this book, can generate moments of disruption as well as affective attachment, as they move from the personal sphere of the home into the public as part of quilt shows, gallery exhibitions, online platforms and also through direct action. These encounters between people and material objects are part of the affective, social and political entanglements through which the status quo is perceived and reconfigured. A quilt may cause disorientation through its design, background story or the context in which it is created and displayed. For instance, as I discuss in chapter one, Chawne Kimber sews her quilts at home, but posts about the process online and many of her quilts eventually hang in art galleries or quilt shows to be seen by sometimes thousands of people. Ethnographic novels like Monica Ali's *Brick Lane*, which I analyze in chapter two, are consumed in private as well as public settings. Such novels are often presented as providing insight into the personal homemaking practices of marginalized groups like Bangladeshi immigrant women in London. Yet, the concept of 'authentic' representation is deeply problematic as it implies the possibility for an unmediated experience of the world.

The featured case studies are diverse and exciting and have never before been covered alongside each other in one comprehensive study. As each chapter looks at a specific type of needlework – quilting, dressmaking, embroidery and knitting – the breadth and depth of textile crafts are highlighted. Yet, each chapter also draws out the subtle differences between these techniques and how they become construed within larger narratives about gender, race, class, sexuality and nation. Importantly, they each demonstrate how practices of needlework can be turned into vehicles for individual and collective meaning making with a range of socio-political implications.

Everyday life 'is a thoroughly relational term' that cannot be definitively fixed (Highmore 2011: 2). In this sense, theories of the everyday and theories of affective practice are both marked by their attention to relationality. Like the everyday, 'the concept of affective practice stretches to encompass both conventionality and unconventionality' and it embraces the multiplicity and contingency of feelings (Wetherell 2012: 117). By implication, both are notoriously difficult and complex realms of study as they include a multiplicity of areas for analysis and points for entry. Yet, as my discussion of each case study aims to show, it is precisely this multiplicity that makes the everyday and affective practices such generative categories for research into processes of personal and social transformation. This multiplicity allows for a particular attunement towards different kinds of assemblages and the ways such figurations might manifest themselves or change, not just on a grand scale but also in the minor key – through gestures, tendencies, habits, orientations and modes of dwelling (Cvetkovich 2012; Manning 2016; Pedwell 2021).

Practices of needlework and their narrative renderings are affective processes of meaning making through which the self and its affective relationships to others and the world can be explored. The following section outlines some of the key discussions in relation to the meaning of practices of needlework, femininity and feminist politics and how the ambiguity of these meanings is negotiated in the realm of the literary. I flesh out how the supposedly inherent connection between needlework and femininity established during the nineteenth century has effectively influenced perceptions about needlework in relation to gender, class, race and labour until today. By extension these links have shaped ideas about the possibility of subversion of social norms in and through needlework. The literary, then, can provide a space in which the entangled meaning of practices of needlework can be negotiated.

Needlework, Women's Writing and Feminist Activism

The @covid19quilt I mentioned at the beginning of this chapter, according to sociologist Marybeth C. Stalp, 'uses (mostly) non-threatening femininity and humor to encourage us to think more critically and deeply about difficult and troubling things' (2020: 356–7). It is because of these links to 'non-threatening femininity', to which Stalp refers, that the relationship between needlework and feminist politics and activism has always been marked by much contention. The connection between practices of needlework and femininity gained prominence in the Global North in the nineteenth century. As Rozsika Parker shows in her seminal *The Subversive Stitch* (1984), embroidery, particularly, was used to inculcate women into the Victorian white, middle-class feminine ideal of a demure and nurturing housewife. Yet, at the same time, according to Parker, it also offered women 'a weapon of resistance to the constraints of femininity' (1984: 1).[2] Of course, as Joseph McBrinn (2021) shows, men have also always been involved in needlework. Yet, men's creative endeavours with needle and thread, especially from the nineteenth century onwards, are also viewed in light of needlework's connection with femininity often in an attempt to brandish these men as effeminate.[3]

This resistance to the feminist ideal through practices of needlework, that Parker refers to, shows in myriad, and often seemingly small ways. For example, pictorial nineteenth-century embroidery frequently displayed scenes of estrangement between men and women (Parker 1984; Quinn-Lautrefin 2018). A more exceptional example is the asylum uniform densely embroidered by Austrian seamstress Agnes Richter with snippets of autobiographical information. Today, the jacket provides a singular account of a late-nineteenth-century woman's experience of madness and incarceration (Hornstein 2012). Across the Atlantic in the New World, quilts became a rare medium through which women could actively express their political allegiance by embroidering their name on a quilt in order to signify support, for example, of the temperance movement or for a presidential candidate (Kiracofe and Johnson 1993; Sapelly 2019). The suffragettes tapped into the popular associations of embroidery and femininity in their campaign for the women's vote, but fashioned femininity as a source of strength rather than weakness (Parker 1984; Tickner 1987). They appliquéd and embroidered large banners with political slogans and took them to their marches, out in public for everyone to see, thus making practices of needlework an active part of direct political action. During the First World War, knitting so-called 'comforts' for soldiers, for some women, was an intentionally patriotic act and turned knitting into a 'vehicle for gender appropriate political expression' (Strawn 2009: 248; Bruder 2019).

Women's writing offers interesting insights into the relationship between needlework and femininity and the way needle and thread facilitate acts of resistance (Gilbert and Gubar [1979] 2000; Hedges 1991; Koppy 2021; Parker

1984; Showalter 1982). Nineteenth-century writers like the Brontë Sisters, George Elliot, Elizabeth Gaskell and Emily Dickinson drew on needlework's deep connection to femininity not only to negotiate their female characters' relation to Victorian ideals of femininity, but also their own identity as writers which often clashed with precisely these ideals (Gilbert and Gubar [1979] 2000; Moers 1978; Showalter 1982). To write, that is, to think and create, was considered unfeminine behaviour and a transgression into the male sphere. Likewise, the value of women's writing was contested in the same way that needlework was relegated to the position of craft and not art; a debate that is certainly not yet over (Buszek 2011). In many novels, the occupation with needlework served female characters as a way to contain and mask their passion and amatory feelings (Okumura 2008; Parker 1984; Rudgard-Redsell 2007). The alacrity with which women swung the needle 'invariably functioned as a barometer of female emotions' (Rees 2018: para. 1). In the context of one of the most famous literary knitting women, Madame Defarge in Charles Dickens' *A Tale of Two Cities* ([1859] 2003), the practice is openly linked to power and women's resistance to the feminine ideal. Madame Defarge, an active schemer during the French Revolution in Paris, secretly encodes the names of people to be guillotined in her knitting. In the United States, Black abolitionist Sojourner Truth, on the other hand, used knitting in her photographic portraits from the 1860s to demonstrate respectability. Pictured in a chair next to a small table with her knitting in hand, the image served to establish Truths' middle-class femininity in order to legitimize her abolitionist and Black women's rights advocacy (Bryan-Wilson 2017).

'New Woman' authors of the 1890s to the 1920s, along with earlier women writers of 'sensation novels', attempted to counter the Victorian feminine ideal by focusing their writing on a new type of woman less concerned with decorum and propriety than with gender solidarity, sexuality and the wish to shed the constraints of the feminine ideal (Heilmann 2000; Ledger 2002; Pykett 1992). Many of these authors and those following in their wake display downright antagonism to practices of needlework. When American writer Sylvia Plath passed away in 1963, she left a substantial body of work in which needlework was not only representative of the confines of domesticity and femininity, but also physically damaging to women as the needle pricked women's fingers and could be transformed into a stabbing weapon (Hedges 1991: 347–8). In contrast, the new emerging literary figure of the amateur female detective made cunning use of the needle. Sitting, supposedly focused on their knitting, became a successful way for the likes of Agatha Christie's Miss Marple to blend into the background and go unnoticed when, in reality, they were actively eavesdropping on the conversations around them (Rees 2018).

The Women's Liberation Movements of the 1960s and 1970s in the Global North put a new spotlight on 'women's work', including practices of needlework (Dunn 2014; Parker 1984; Robertson 2011). Second-wave feminism in North America and Western Europe openly questioned the century-long exclusion of much of women's creative productions and especially needlework from conceptualizations and representations of high culture and the arts (Pollock 1987). Black feminist artist Faith Ringgold, whose work I discuss in more detail in chapter one, likewise, drew on the medium of textiles, more specifically quilts, to portray African American women's identity struggle within a patriarchal and racist society. Her quilts are unique in that they are 'story quilts' that include text and tell of the struggles of African-American women and their communities. Conversely, due to their fragmented nature and epistolary format, the novels *Beloved* by Tony Morrison and Alice Walker's *The Color Purple*, which I also analyze in chapter one, arguably, structurally mirror the layers and pieced nature of a quilt (Daniel 2000; Dunn and Morris 1992; Falling-rain 1994). In these creative practices, by utilizing text and textile, personal experience was given an outward form in the same way that poets and critics of the time like Audre Lorde, Cherríe Moraga and Adrienne Rich, were attempting to 'find language to express oppressions and liberations that had no name' (Reed 2005: 89). Many viewed practices of needlework as a generative mode of female creative expression in relation to women's genealogies, agency and questions of sisterhood.

Second-wave feminists and subsequent liberation movements deliberately took practices of needlework outside the home space by incorporating them as part of public instances of direct action, such as the Greenham Common Women's Peace Camp in the United Kingdom in the 1980s. The women protesters knitted practical items such as scarves or socks in the peace camp (Robertson 2011; Titcombe 2013). In addition, they placed fibre installations on the wire mesh fence around the airbase in ways that pre-empted contemporary practices of yarn bombing which I discuss in more detail in chapter four. Highlighting knitting, with all its stereotypical connotations of domesticity and femininity, as part of life at camp emphasized the deep connection between the public and the private in relation to patriarchy's and militarism's impact on people's lives. In addition, staging the protest as a permanent campsite where the women lived and performed mundane practices such as cooking, childcare and personal hygiene, powerfully demonstrated how any extraordinary type of direct action is always also necessarily surrounded and quite often sustained by everyday activities (Kauffman 2017). The women reiterated verbally and showed practically how the personal and the everyday are political in multiple ways – also a key point of contention of this book.

During the Pinochet dictatorship in Chile, which lasted from 1973 to 1990, women started making *arpilleras*, pictorial appliquéd and embroidered textile pieces, to chronicle the terror and human rights violations that had become part of their everyday lives (Bryan-Wilson 2017; Franger 2009). As small, easily foldable objects and supposedly unassuming textile creations made by women, *arpilleras* offer a powerful way to circumvent the censorship of text and to share experiences with the world. Another prominent example for the use of practices of needlework in political activism is the AIDS Memorial Quilt, which was first displayed in its entirety on the National Mall in Washington, DC, in 1987. Conceived by queer rights activist Cleve Jones, the project aimed to provide a tangible memento to the lives lost to HIV/AIDS and a powerful visual marker of the scale of a disease that public officials refused to acknowledge. Creating a quilted panel for a deceased person, which would then be displayed with thousands of other panels, was also intended to provide mourners with a creative and calming outlet for their grief (Stormer 2013; Tanner 2006). To this day, parts of the quilt continue to travel the world and remain a testament to one of the most devastating health crises. At the same time, it is a tangible piece of evidence of the way a needlework-based initiative, in combination with more traditional grassroots organizing spear-headed by the group Act-Up, made the national spotlight and, ultimately, forced the US government to attend to the health crisis (Gould 2009).

In the 1990s, with the advent of what came to be known as third-wave feminism, questions of femininity, domesticity and women's crafts received renewed attention. The third wave can broadly be characterized as united by an apparent wish in younger women to distinguish themselves and their experiences from feminists of the previous generation (Gillis, Howie and Munford 2007). Scholar Elizabeth Groeneveld (2010) locates a general drive for reclaiming a new domesticity as significant for specific discourses about the reclamation of needlework. On the other hand, crafting practices are also presented as a means of forging connections with older women, but not necessarily in a politicized context that considers class, consumption and feminist solidarity (Chansky 2010; Clarke 2016; Gajjala 2015; Groeneveld 2010; Newmeyer 2008). Rather, as Wendy Parkins (2004) argues, one may locate a nostalgic wish for a supposedly de-politicized, 'slower' and 'better' past in twenty-first-century discourses about the reclamation of needlework. Chris Land, Neil Sutherland and Scott Taylor

(2019) also note a nostalgia for a supposedly lost cultural authenticity in the contemporary popularity of traditional craft practices that range from home sewing to DIY beer production. In this sense, this return to craft can also be understood as a political response to the neoliberal capitalist order of the Global North and the negative affects it produces such as an alienation from work (Dawkins 2011; Hackney 2013; Hochschild [1983] 2003; Luckman 2013). As a result, the amateur crafter is framed as having successfully reclaimed the meaning of work. Using the hands to manually perform practices of needlework is framed as a more embodied or connected way of working than people commonly experience as part of their paid employment (Luckman 2013; Sennett 2008).

In addition, crafting is figured as an alternative to capitalist consumption (Williams 2011), although the flourishing global craft industry is also a testament to how craft practices resemble alternative consumption practices as opposed to an alternative to capitalist markets (Cvetkovich 2012: 171). As I shall flesh out in chapters two and three in my analysis of Monica Ali's novel *Brick Lane* and the Afghan–European embroidery initiative, Guldusi, such claims about needlework often emanate from the Global North and rarely consciously attend to the ways these amateur practices are entangled with the global labour market and especially the South East Asian textile industry. Likewise, as I discuss in chapter four in the context of the Pussyhat and Kudzu projects, race is overlooked as a contributing factor to perceptions about the efficacy of women's craft-based forms of activism, especially in relation to ideas of non-threatening femininity which is ultimately a white femininity (Close 2016; Hahner and Varda 2014).

Cultural theorist Ann Cvetkovich (2012) regards crafting as a generative practice which allows people to tune in to their experiences of depression and despair. She identifies these feelings as part of a shared negative response to the capitalist status quo, as opposed to conceptualizing depression as an individual psychological disorder. Indeed, practices of needlework have gained prominence in the last decade in relation to health and well-being initiatives as effective tools for reducing stress and improving mental health (MacDowell, Luz and Donaldson 2017; Pöllänen 2013, 2015; Wellesley-Smith 2021). This can be observed also in the large number of popular craft books available with titles such as *Knit Yourself Calm: A Creative Path to Managing Stress* (Rowe and Corkhill 2017) or *Craftfulness: Mend Yourself by Making Things* (Davidson and Tahsin 2018). Contemporary writers like Anne Boyer have also picked up on this connection between health and needlework. In her short collection of lyric prose, *Garments Against Women* (Boyer 2015), she aligns writing and sewing as part of an exploration of women's experience of time and the illness-ridden female body. In these contexts, as I outline in more detail in chapter one, resistance is linked to individual care work and to looking after oneself during difficult times.

Discourses about needlework and well-being also regularly stress the practice's value to building community. Something that is also reflected in bestselling so-called women's fiction such as Jennifer Chiaverini's Elm Creek Quilts series (2008–19). Practices of needlework allow people to knit or sew in the privacy of the home, but also in the company of others and as part of a large transnational community of needlewomen, linked through digital platforms like Ravelry and social media sites like Facebook and Instagram. The digital has become an important fact in accounts that stress the generative potential of practices of needlework for forging new relationships (Bratich and Brush 2011; Gauntlett 2011, 2018; Hackney 2013; Hackney, Maughan and Desmarais 2016; Minahan and Cox 2007; Orton-Johnson 2014). As with the @covid19quilt, the digital has come to take up a key role in many craftivist initiatives and I shall discuss this and its implications for political organizing more generally in chapter four. According to Shannon Black, craftivism can be conceptualized as the 'broader political movement' that emerged from the renewed interest in textile craft alongside digital technologies at the beginning of the current century (2017: 700). Embracing a 'gentle form of activism' (Corbett 2017), craftivism is aimed at people who might not be comfortable with more confrontational forms of protest, thus consciously engaging with popular gendered perceptions about needlework that frame it as non-threatening (Greer 2014).

It is this long-standing and often ambiguous connection between needlework, femininity and feminist politics that I have outlined above that has made textile crafts such a rich area for research. Looking at practices of needlework in a global context, analyses usually focus on regional and cultural differences in the execution of a particular type of needlework as well as the role of identity and belonging, often within the critical framework of postcolonial theory (Hemmings 2015; Jefferies, Conroy and Clark 2016; Mandell 2019; Sharrad and Collett 2004). In general, scholars and practitioners continue to be challenged by how to grapple conceptually with the ambiguity of needlework beyond binary categories of subversive/oppressive, art/craft, un/successful activism, good/bad feminism (Gilson and Moffat 2019; Jefferies, Conroy and Clark 2016; Mandell 2019; Robertson 2011, 2016). To avoid this, some have suggested viewing the relationship between needlework and feminism on a continuum model to capture makers' diverse political investments (Amos and Binkley 2020; Black 2017; Pentney 2008; Turney 2009). Others have succinctly pointed out the importance of staying with the messiness of these perceived divisions (Bryan-Wilson 2017; Cvetkovich 2012).

Affect, as I demonstrate throughout this book, offers a particularly salient way for attending to this messiness and complexity. Conceptualized as thoroughly relational, as that which 'arises in the midst of in-between-ness: in the capacities to act and be acted upon', affect is always brimming with potential (Seigworth and Gregg 2010: pos. 50). Throughout *Needlework, Affect and Social Transformation*, I highlight moments of affective potential that develop through practices of needlework to attend to the entanglements of the discursive with the material and affective to explore how they shape knowledge about needlework and its perceived efficacy for feminist politics. Through my diverse archive of texts and textiles I am able to engage with the everyday textures of affective social practices of meaning making and to trace the 'lines of flight' (Deleuze and Guattari 1987) that emerge as meaning is produced, blocked, destroyed and revived. A focus on texture and its entanglements makes it possible to avoid essentialist categories and instead enables me to follow different trajectories of meaning making across the textured web of everyday feminist lifelines, situated not in an abstract realm, but in concrete material and affective experiences. The following section outlines in more detail my understanding of texture as an entangled dynamic concept, materiality and interpretive framework.

The Texture of Analysis

'Text', 'textile' and 'texture' are etymologically linked through the Latin noun *textura*, a weaving, and the verb *texere*, to weave (OED n.d.). While well into the nineteenth century 'texture' referred to a kind of woven cloth, the term has also come to denote 'any natural structure having an appearance or consistence as if woven' (OED n.d.). As such, it could be any kind of tissue or web, for example, that of a spider. Texture also delineates the specific properties of fabric, such as being coarse, plain or ribbed as a result of the specific way it has been woven out of individual threads. The term 'line' can be linked to linen, a type of fabric made through the weaving together of individual flax threads into a cloth. By extension, texture may also describe 'the constitution, structure, or substance of anything with regard to its constituents or formative elements' (OED n.d.). It can be applied to concrete tangible matter such as fabric, but may also invoke the immaterial as it refers to someone's disposition or character. Thus, texture implies a connection between the social, the (im)material and the affective while, at the same time, acknowledging the impossibility of fully separating any of them from each other. Texture is 'a zone of entanglement ... to which there are no outsides, only openings and ways through' (Ingold 2016: 106). Practices of needlework but also other processes of creative making enable 'practitioners [to] bind their own pathways or lines into the texture of material flows comprising the lifeworld' (Ingold 2010: 91).

Storytelling, according to anthropologist Tim Ingold, is a means of travelling along some of these textures without fixing them in place. As a process of meaning making, storytelling makes it possible to consider different kinds of meaning that others have created. It is also mindful of already existing meaning and narratives created by other travellers – to stick with Ingold's imagery. There is no obligation to include or adhere to dominant narratives, as one is free to traverse along different paths (Ingold 2016: 77). Meaning is created and 'knowledge integrated' (Ingold 2016: 94) as the story unfolds and one travels along a narrative as well as the physical and affective world of the storyteller or listener. According to Ingold, 'there is no point at which the story ends and life begins' (2016: 93). Therefore, textuality is more than the narrative or material properties of the text; it refers also to the phenomenological and affective practice of telling or reading a story with meaning being forged as part of the practice (Ingold 2016: 94; see also Grattan 2017; Stockwell 2009).

In line with Ingold's conception of storytelling as an unmarked map open for exploration, critical feminist legal scholar Imani Perry is committed to developing modes of narrating and making sense of the past and the contemporary moment in ways that are critical of concepts, terms and legal formations such as personhood, property and sovereignty (2018). These concepts are regularly used in everyday contexts of governance but often without recognition for how they are part of patriarchal and white hegemonic structures of authority spread across the world during the age of empire (Perry 2018; see also Hunter and van der Westhuizen 2022). I locate narratives of feminist resistance and creative making as part of these practices of storytelling to which Ingold and Perry refer, and I explore throughout this book the different ways in which they are part of a transnational feminist politics. For feminist theorist Clare Hemmings, 'a series of interlocking narratives of loss, progress and return' are indicative of Western feminists' struggle with gender essentialism, identity politics and intersectionality (2011: 3). These narratives are tied to problematic power structures. They not only oversimplify the complexity and multiplicity of feminist theory (or theories), but also bring to the foreground the experiences of Western feminist subjects as the tellers of these stories. Rather than offering a corrective narrative, however, following Perry (2018), Cvetkovich (2012) and Hemmings (2011), I suggest that attention to the texture of narrative – to the stories we tell in text and textile to make sense of the world and to the plethora of practices that surround the creation and reproduction of these stories – makes it possible to attend to a radical feminist imaginary that is continuously in the making.

Textiles and practices of needlework are ubiquitous in everyday life from the cradle to the grave. Making and using textiles is 'also mak[ing] narratives of time spent, of mental space, of taste, of family, of pleasure, leisure, necessity, luxury and thrift' (Turney 2019: 158). Furthermore, textiles and practices of needlework are part of transnational assemblages that connect bodies, economies, cultures and societies on multiple levels (Ong 1999; Tsing 2004). The North American production of cotton was based around the transatlantic slave trade for cheap labour supply; textiles played a large role also in the creation of the British Empire (Skeehan 2020). European settlers to the New World brought with them practices of needlework like quilting that would be refashioned to become a constitutive feature of the foundational myth of the United States in the form of the American quilt (Kiracofe and Johnson 1993; Mazloomi 2015). Indeed, quilting and sewing skills were important tools used by American missionaries to 'civilize' the Indigenous population of Hawaii (Kimokeo-Goes 2019). Today, discount fashion chains in the Global North are able to operate successfully because of the availability of cheap garments from South East Asia often produced under highly exploitative and dangerous working conditions (Anguelov 2016). At the same time, a large number of development-aid initiatives for women in the Global South are centred around utilizing women's needlework skills in order to generate a small income, for example, by training them as tailors or by producing local traditional textile crafts to be sold to tourists or in the Global North (Jones 2019).

My selection of case studies attempts to reflect this ubiquity of textiles and practices of needlework, as well as the diversity of textile practices, and highlights links between the mundane and the extraordinary. In chapter one, I look at the connection between African American quilting and Black women's writing in the United States, tracing a genealogy between writing and quilting as generative practices in Black women's social justice work. Reading the works of contemporary Black women writers alongside the textile practices of contemporary Black women quilters and the work of the US-based youth organization, the Social Justice Sewing Academy (SJSA), the chapter examines how creative textile practices may contribute to a shared anti-racist womanist politics. Chapter two considers Monica Ali's novel *Brick Lane* (2003a), which chronicles the lives of Bangladeshi garment factory worker Hasina and her sister, Nazneen, who is a homeworker for a London sweatshop. The novel is loosely based on economist Naila Kabeer's qualitative study about Bangladeshi women in Dhaka and London working in the garment industry (2000). It raises questions about the affective and generative properties of dressmaking in the context of the international labour market, Bangladeshi diaspora and East London immigrant life. Chapter three explores the German-based, Afghan-European embroidery initiative, Guldusi, whose mission is to use embroidery to help rural Afghan women generate an income while, at the same time, preserving the country's rich embroidery heritage and creating a space for a cultural encounter between Europeans and Afghan embroiderers. Lastly, in chapter four, I analyse the Pussyhat project, the knitting initiative that developed in 2016 as part of the Women's March on Washington, and the Kudzu project, a yarn-bombing initiative inspired by these events, in the context of the twenty-first-century craftivism movement and white privilege.

These examples have in common that they are about making connections, or, in other words, about creating entanglements between individuals, communities, cultures, materials, narratives, affects and across feminist genealogies. They are a part of past and present efforts in the transnational collective fight for social justice and individuals' everyday efforts towards social change. They all navigate the gendered history of needlework and the stories attached to it, but also enable new trajectories of meaning making as they operate within and beyond the constraints of this history. Though all case studies emanate from the Global North and are often connected to a particular place, for example, a country, city or individual home space, each is transnational in orientation to varying degrees. The anti-racist work of US Black radical women writers and quilters is not only grounded in the legacy of the African diaspora and the Black Atlantic, but, like the work of the Pussyhat and Kudzu projects, also in the recognition that social justice issues connected to race, gender and the environment are of both global and local significance. They are transnationally networked in their creative activist efforts through the use of digital technologies like social media. In this sense, they are also profoundly intersectional as they recognize the ways in which race, class, gender and other forms of oppression converge (Collins 2019; Crenshaw 1991). *Brick Lane* grounds the global garment industry and its multi-million-dollar economy in the capital cities of Dhaka and London as well as a small rural Bangladeshi village and a decrepit English council flat (Ali 2003a). At the same time, the novel is caught in the transnational politics of cultural authenticity and its representation as it draws inspiration from an ethnographic scholarly study. While part of Guldusi's mission is to build a bridge between

Afghan and European cultures, the initiative is shaped by the geopolitics of a US-led War on Terror and the way it frames perceptions of Afghanistan in the Global North.

I put close readings of key passages of the literary works in conversation with literatures on craft research, feminist theory, affect, critical race theory and social movements. Furthermore, I provide analyses of quilts and other textile artefacts. I use interviews I conducted and testimonials by makers to substantiate my analysis, but also to decentre my own white, cis-gendered voice in the case of my discussion of Black women's resistant practices.[4] Refocusing towards modes of storytelling that travel along the textured histories of a transnational feminist struggle as opposed to across a fixed set of discourses that privilege the narratives of white, cis-gendered women in the Global North is a crucial critical move. It allows for a highlighting of the entangled and interwoven nature of meaning and knowledge. As a result, assumptions about commonality between women based on a shared identity as needlewomen can be bypassed. Thus, I aim to complicate narratives that centre and privilege experiences of white (and often middle-class) Western women. As a white, western European woman myself, I do not claim to give voice to the experiences of women of colour in the Global North nor to the meaning of practices of needlework to women from the Global South. Clearly, such a project would reproduce the very structures I critique by framing me as the knowledgeable researcher, speaking on behalf of marginalized groups (Alcoff and Potter 1993).

Conscious of such acts of epistemic violence (Madhok and Evans 2014; Spivak [1988] 1994), I hope to address the variety of women's experiences and the apparent lack of representation of this diversity within the context of transnational feminist struggles for liberation. I draw attention to the unequal power structures that value certain knowledge more than others and prioritize certain bodies as the producers of knowledge, as opposed to 'simply' attempting to fill a representational gap, though this gap most certainly exists and needs to be addressed (Hewett 2021; MacDowell 1997). I am committed to a feminist citational practice that highlights the critical voices of women and purposefully refrains from privileging straight white male theorists, in an attempt to avoid the re-inscription of a white male intellectual genealogy (Ahmed 2013, 2017). For example, while I find Ingold's work useful and intellectually stimulating, and also see resonances between my own research and his, as well as the work by theorists of everyday life like Michel de Certeau (1984) and Henri Lefebvre ([1992] 2004), I am mindful not to over-emphasize their work and place them in conversation with work by feminists, queer scholars and critics of colour.

The purpose of drawing on an inventive archive, as I do, is not to untangle, straighten or smooth out the textures of everyday life, but to attend to the potential of 'temporary grouping of relations' (Coleman and Ringrose 2013: 9; see also Ahmed 2006b). In each of my case studies, I consider the multiplicity of this potential which may, on the one hand, serve to reproduce existing structures of knowledge. On the other hand, it may also point towards new meanings, collective formations and ways of being. Participating in a sewing competition organized by the Afghan-European embroidery initiative, Guldusi, for instance, may provide a space for European women to 'do good' without having to question their own complicity in the reproduction of unequal structures of power. However, it may also stimulate their engagement with this complicity. More importantly, it provides an income for the Afghan women that may enable them to envisage different ways of living. In sum, attending to textures is not about trying to codify or fix meaning in place, but about mapping potential and, as such, involves 'attending to the social and cultural world as mobile, messy, creative, changing and open-ended, sensory and affective' (Coleman and Ringrose 2013: 1; references omitted).

Everyday Affective Potential

Needlework, Affect and Social Transformation attends to the mundane and quotidian as the setting in which practices of needlework are performed and narrative representations of the practices are produced, consumed and circulated. Drawing on various feminist understandings of the everyday by, for example, Rita Felski (1999) and bell hooks (1991b, 1995), the everyday is also where I locate the potential for personal and social transformation. Clearly the mundane cannot be avoided because, even when attempting to define prolonged states of exception and extraordinariness – for instance, during times of war – such evaluations of the situation are shaped by prior assumptions about what is ordinary and normal. Thus, the everyday is also the realm in which I locate the potential for individual and, ultimately, social change, because it is often on the level of everyday personal, but also collective, experiences that one comes up against the unequal flow of power and feels its impact, sometimes strongly and at other times less so (Stewart 2007). This is not to disregard the ways in which people might suddenly be pushed to take action and participate in vigils or demonstrations because, for example, witnessing an elementary school become the site of a mass shooting has changed a person's view about gun control (Metzl 2020).

Yet, my concern is about how on the level of meaning making, everyday acts of creative making reverberate with the potential for larger social transformation. This is, of course, not to suggest that small-scale political gestures will invariably be followed by large-scale acts of social transformation or, indeed, need to be followed by such acts in order to be validated. Rather, I am interested in the entanglements of the personal and the political, the local and the global, of affect and structure. In this sense, my account of practices of needlework and the way it connects everyday making and contemporary social justice movements echoes cultural studies scholar Carolyn Pedwell's 'ontology of transformation in which the revolutionary and the routine are perpetually intertwined and minor gestures and tendencies may be just as significant as major events' (2021: 6).

Following Cvetkovich, my analysis is attuned to 'forms of affective life that have not solidified into institutions, organizations, or identities' (2003: 9). I am curious about how these 'forms of affective life' connect people in and across diverse communities. In addition, I am interested in how they link preceding and future generations in ways that make it possible to persevere in the present moment while also becoming able to imagine not simply a more equitable future, but one that completely reconfigures existing power structures (Kelley 2002; Sharpe 2016). Focusing on practices of needlework on the level of embodied practice, that is, as a slow repetitive hand movement, I examine a 'politics of feeling that is manifest not just in overt or visible social movements of conventional politics but also in the more literal kinds of movement that make up everyday life practices or forms of cultural expression' (Cvetkovich 2012: 199). I attend to quilting and textile artefacts as the everyday life practices and cultural forms of expression that Cvetkovich (2012) mentions alongside literary texts to show how they are all part of a politics of feeling which connects ordinary practices to activism and visions of social transformation.

My focus is on how practice and object orient people, as well as the narratives we tell about them, individually and collectively, in the world. According to cultural studies scholar Sara Ahmed, orientations 'are about starting points' (2006a: 545). To be oriented always implies being oriented towards an object. This object, however, does not have to be a physical object, but may also be 'objects of thought, feeling, and judgment, and objects in the sense of aims, aspirations, and objectives' (Ahmed 2006a: 553). Yet, a shared characteristic of these objects is that they shape our experience of bodily surfaces through contact with them; they leave 'impressions' as part of our encounter with them that entrust the subject, that is, us, with a sense of the materiality of our body and the space it occupies (Ahmed 2004: 24–6). These impressions can be literal in the sense that a physical object comes into direct contact with the skin or can be more 'sensational' in the form of affects that we encounter on an everyday basis (Ahmed 2004, 2006b; Brennan 2004; Golda 2016). What we are oriented towards, and, consequently, what is in our foreground, is the result of histories of power struggles which, through acts of repetition and force, have imprinted certain orientations as the norm (Ahmed 2006a: 552).

The contested meaning of needlework is firmly embedded in these power struggles and efforts to make normative that which reproduces patriarchy and white supremacy as society's overarching structures (Walker 2020). I am interested in how points of intersection between text, textile and texture allow for moments of affective realignment and reorientation and, as such, may offer a space for alternative imaginaries to heteronormative and patriarchal structures of government. I conceptualize making as a form of encounter that connects not only materials, but also people and affects, and thus I attend to the ways intimate attachments to structures can be unsettled and reshaped. Encounters – or, in other words, coming face to face with something other than the self – are 'mediated, affective, emotive and sensuous' (Wilson 2017: 465). They are also relational, in that they imply the coming upon, or becoming oriented towards, something. As such, they can resemble an opening of sorts, but also serve to maintain relations of difference and hierarchy, for example, in the colonial encounter. It is precisely this ambiguous nature of encounter that makes it a useful analytical category when attempting to think outside binary logics. An attunement to the texture and temporality of encounters, what cultural and social geographer Helen Wilson calls a 'focus on the doing of encounter' (2017: 464), can reveal instances in which encounters shift relations and enable different kinds of orientation. It is in these reorientations, and even disorientations, that I locate generative moments of dwelling in a potential that can foster personal and social transformation (see also Manning 2016; Muñoz 2009).

Due to its etymological link to weaving, texture, as a concept, is already firmly grounded within histories of femininity, women's work and practices of needlework. As a result, it orients the critic towards exploring the textured nature of feminist politics that is deeply entangled with issues of power, protest and personal and social transformation. Textures are types of entanglements that invite an engagement with the individual threads and the knots they form outside of binary judgements (Sedgwick 2003). As such, they invite exploration of 'where they might go and what potential modes of knowing, relating, and attending to things are already somehow present in them in a state of potentiality and resonance' (Stewart 2007: 3). Though messy, they are entanglements that can orient the maker, the viewer and the critic alike as they follow their directions and '"do things" with' them as part of everyday modes of being (Ahmed 2006a: 550, 552; Stewart 2007). As a result of being open to becoming oriented differently through tracing the entanglements of different practices and modes of thinking, new encounters become possible while others are blocked or moved out of reach (Ahmed 2006a: 552). For example, the European participants in the Guldusi embroidery initiative are nudged towards considering the lived experience of their Afghan counterparts. However, I also show how participation in the initiative is not a guaranteed pathway for transnational feminist solidarity.

Practices of needlework involve movement in the sense of 'moving and being moved as a form of labour or work, which opens up different kinds of attachment to others' (Ahmed 2004: 201). In this sense, crafting is closely connected to conceptualizations of creativity as an embodied process and a 'feeling' (Gauntlett 2011: 17). In this vein, Cvetkovich claims:

> Defined in relation to notions of blockage or impasse, creativity can be thought of as a form of movement, movement that maneuvers [sic] the mind inside or around an impasse, even if that movement sometimes seems backward or like a form of retreat. Spatialized in this way, creativity can describe forms of agency that can take the form of literal movement and are thus more e-motional or sensational or tactile.
>
> 2012: 21

This literal movement can be the guiding of a needle through a piece of cotton fabric or a pair of shears cutting up an old sheet. Theorized as an embodied practice, quiltmaking, for example, becomes a form of 'making' which involves a creative process as well as the repetitive interaction between a physical body and a physical world. The body, then, is not only moved by the material, but also 'follow[s] the forces and flows of material' (Ingold 2010: 97).[5] More so, I argue, these bodies – as complex somatic and affective assemblages – may be stirred towards new directions and openings.[6]

Moments of gesturing and orienting towards new ways of being are not fully developed acts of resistance but signify an opening up to resistant modes of being (Muñoz 2009; Manning 2016). Indeed, 'becoming resistant' is often a rather slow process in the same way that substantive social change which affects everyday structures of oppression takes time as new habits and practices need to form (Pedwell 2016). Moments of gesturing or orienting indicate the potential of the future as opposed to providing a blueprint for a different way of life (Muñoz 2009). They are indicative of a prefigurative politics committed to the collective development of another world in the shell of the old (Dixon 2014; Ishkanian and Saavedra 2019; Swain 2019). As such, relationships and structures of power in the social and cultural world are being reworked as part of the process of becoming and being resistant within an unequal and oppressive system. Dwelling, in this context, refers to a state of inhabiting the body and noticing how its contours are shaped by feelings and the way they affect perceptions of what is inside or outside (Ahmed 2004). The act of dwelling, then, is important to the doing of encounter as it offers a starting point for becoming oriented differently and for reshaping these contours (Ahmed 2006a: 545). Yet, dwelling is not about linear practices of working through or overcoming the potentially disorienting or discomforting state of encounter. Instead it offers the opportunity to be in and stay with the complexity of the encounter and to make (re) orientation, and, by extension, transformation, a possibility. Due to the form of repetition, it requires – inserting the needle into the fabric from the top, pulling it through and taking it back into the material from behind before the whole process starts over again – needlework may foster a habitual dwelling in the potential of new encounters and orientations (Cvetkovich 2012: 189).

Crafters, like storytellers, 'participate from within the very process of the world's continual coming into being' as their creative practices lay out new routes for meaning towards which others may become oriented and thus 'contribute to [the world's] weave and texture' (Ingold 2016: 83). These new routes for meaning may develop into what social psychologist Margaret Wetherell calls 'affective ruts' (2012: 14), which form as a result of the affective involvement in the repeated performance of practices of needlework. It is in these affective ruts, intertwined with the vibrancy of significant events like protest marches, that I locate the potential for being oriented differently. Practices of needlework provide the opportunity to dwell in a state of potential that is open to a different, more just future without being prescriptive of what such a future may look like (Cvetkovich 2003; Fitzpatrick and Kontturi 2015). Rather, it is about modes of dwelling that allow crafters to remain radically open to the shape of this future as well as using practices of needlework as a way of prefiguring the kind of relations that might be foundational for such a future (Coleman 2020; Fitzpatrick and Kontturi 2015). As I discuss in chapter four, this resonates also with one of the central tenets of the contemporary craftivism movement, which cherishes craft practices for their ability to provide a space in which people can express their dissent, but also actively practice the new relations they would like to see in the world. In this sense, it is also about 'developing another way of *doing* politics' (Dixon 2014: 89, original emphasis) that neither reproduces patriarchal and white-supremacist structures nor orbits around the kind of individualism that has dominated neoliberal and so-called post-feminist discourses (Banet-Weiser 2018; Phipps 2020; Hunter and van der Westhuizen 2022).

Chapter Overview

I opened this book with a description of the @covid19quilt initiated by Australian-based craftivists Kate Just and Tal Fitzpatrick. In text and textile, digitally and tangibly, the @covid19quilt tells many stories of life during a pandemic of unprecedented scale. It connects people but also may repel others because of the political weight that some of the pieces carry. It is a texture through which the affective political potential of practices of needlework materializes. *Needlework, Affect and Social Transformation* is a texture in its own kind. In the following chapters, through its diverse range of case studies, the book provides insights into the affectivity of practices of needlework and the potential of new orientations and relations connected with them. Chapter one, 'Quilting Black Resistance: Slavery's Afterlives, Creativity and Social Justice', engages with African American women's practices of historical redress of official histories of slavery and its legacy through texts and textiles. Reading Toni Morrison's novel *Beloved* (1987) and Alice Walker's *The Color Purple* ([1982] 2004) as well as her short story 'Everyday Use' ([1973] 1994), alongside the activist quilting practices of Faith Ringgold, Chawne Kimber and the Social Justice Sewing Academy, I argue that the writers and quilters participate in creating alternative affective archives of Black women's experiences in the United States. Quilts and quiltmaking and the narrative representation of them may provide an opportunity for an engagement with slavery and its afterlives, focused on celebrating Black women's lives, without covering up the effects of racism and patriarchy. They are a testament to African American women's commitment to social justice work and self-care as radical strategies for survival. In this context, the home space functions as a site where radical creative practices are performed as beautiful quilts are created not only for functional purposes, but as part of generative practices of care and resistance. Yet, these practices also emanate outside through digital technologies, public exhibitions and in response to large-scale acts of social grassroots organizing, such as the formation of the Black Lives Matter movement. In this sense, quilting may also orient people towards an awareness of lived realities of oppression different to one's own. Thus, this chapter illustrates how quilting may serve as a generative practice which allows for an attunement to the potential of a more just world that values Black life.

Chapter two, 'Sewing Desire: Homework, Gendered Agency and Bangladeshi Diaspora', provides a close reading of Monica Ali's novel *Brick Lane* (2003a). I consider the novel's relationship with scholar Naila Kabeer's qualitative study about Bangladeshi garment workers in Dhaka and London (2000) and engage with critiques of the novel that perceive it in the context of 'authentic' ethnographic fiction. I contend that such a focus is problematic because it views the literary as representative of 'true' experience as opposed to recognizing its potential as a creative experiment to trace how individuals can become oriented differently through everyday practices of housework and paid piecework for a local sweatshop. Theoretically, the chapter brings together the work of practice theorists and scholars of affect to explore some of the object/subject/affect assemblages connected to practices of needlework (Knudsen and Stage 2015; Reckwitz 2002; Stewart 2007; Wetherell 2012). I discuss the protagonist Nazneen's paid piecework in *Brick Lane* in relation to second-wave and neoliberal feminist narratives of women's liberation through paid work and contemporary understandings of meaningful leisure practices. I analyse how sewing serves as an important affective social practice of meaning making that has a significant effect on Nazneen's personal development. Sewing, I argue, becomes part of Nazneen's everyday home routine and, because it is representative of the emerging relationship with her young lover Karim, it is deeply tied to the slow recognition of her own desires and ultimately also to her ability to express those wants. I demonstrate how the physical movement implied in repetitive machine-sewing affectively orients Nazneen towards a different and more assertive sense of self. As such, the chapter highlights some of the possibilities and limits of practices of needlework in relation to women's agency, emotion work and paid labour.

Chapter three, 'Stitching Transnational Solidarity: Textile Crafts and Cross-Cultural Encounters', explores the Afghan–European embroidery initiative Guldusi in the context of textile-based, feminist-solidarity initiatives and a contemporary resurgence of Orientalism. The chapter engages with various materials including the initiative's website and online newsletter, short publications by and about Guldusi, makers' testimonials, an interview with its founder and an analysis of various textile artefacts by Afghan and European women produced in response to the initiative. I critically examine Guldusi's objective to facilitate cultural understanding between European and Afghan needlewomen by sketching out the limits of feminist solidarity grounded in claims of a shared identity as needlewomen. Building on the work of transnational feminist cultural scholars (Grewal and

Kaplan 1994; Mankekar 2015; Ong 1999) and post-/decolonial theory (Bacchetta, Maira and Winant 2019; Farris 2017), I contend that narratives about the power of practices of needlework to foster solidarity between women from the Global North and the Global South often privilege the stories of white Western women. I trace how these narratives and the textile artefacts created by women from the Global North in response to the Afghan embroideries often reproduce contemporary Orientalist discourses that have regained new prominence through the political and media rhetoric accompanying the US-led War on Terror. However, by placing these discourses in relation to the affect and materiality of practices of needlework, my analysis also identifies openings for the reconfiguration of the unequal power structures between needlewomen. Through attending to the transnational affective entanglements of everyday practices like stitching, tea drinking, cooking and gardening, I show how making provides a way of connecting not only materials but also bodies and affects in ways that generate new opportunities for feminist solidarity.

Chapter four, 'Knitting Feminist Politics: Craftivism and Affective Tension', examines the contemporary craftivism movement through an analysis of the Pussyhat and Kudzu projects, bringing together a well-known large-scale initiative with more localized action directly advocating for the removal of Confederate monuments across the US South. Conceptualizing the Pussyhat project as a figurative and literal texture, I engage with critiques of the Pussyhat project as trans-exclusionary, vulgar as well as white-centric and view it as representative of a wider ongoing struggle for intersectional transnational feminist solidarity. I turn to the Kudzu project, which was inspired by the Pussyhat project, to follow some of the affective possibilities of these critiques. Drawing on the concepts of 'fabriculture' and platforms for creativity (Gauntlett 2011, 2018; Minahan and Cox 2007), I outline the initiatives' entanglements with digital modes of organizing and creative making. I argue that the act of making serves to orient people towards new affective avenues for meaning making that may move them towards a different politics that questions and, at times, actively subverts, the white supremacist and patriarchal status quo. The Kudzu project, in this context, is of particular interest because it uses craftivism as the supposedly more gentle form of activism to openly address issues of whiteness and white privilege. Rather than focusing on common ideas about craftivism as gentle and comforting, I draw on theories of prefiguration and social change in the minor key (Dixon 2014; Fitzpatrick and Kontturi 2015; Manning 2016; Pedwell 2021) to flesh out how practices of needlework can offer a generative way for embracing affective dissonance and tension (Hemmings 2012; May 2023). I argue that the resulting forms of affective dissonance can serve as a generative starting point for a shared feminist political imaginary that values Black lives and advances understandings of feminist solidarity.

Finally, 'Coda: Un-making Whiteness' recaps the various strands discussed throughout the book in relation to the affectivity of practices of needlework. It also pushes the ideas of texture and affective tension developed throughout *Needlework, Affect and Social Transformation* to point towards the way in which practices of needlework may offer a generative theoretical and practical medium for anti-racist theory and practice. I connect African American philosopher George Yancy's concept of 'un-suturing' with a brief analysis of Tayari Jones' novel *An American Marriage* (2018) and the work of contemporary British embroiderer Hannah Hill. Becoming 'un-sutured', for Yancy (2014, 2018), describes the process by which people racialized as white become aware of whiteness as a power formation. This involves recognizing how one's own whiteness is implicated within larger social, political, economic and cultural structures. In these processes of un-suturing, in my opinion, practices of needlework have the potential to be more than a metaphor. They may percolate in the transformative possibilities of affective tensions as sutures, seams and stitches may be undone, sewn shut, dropped, unpicked and entangled. This opens up exciting new areas of research through which to address some of the pressing problems in certain popularized anti-racist approaches to whiteness in relation to white fragility, white catharsis and progressive narratives of 'overcoming' bad feelings (Yancy 2018; Hunter and van der Westhuizen 2022). This coda is a call to action for attending to these entanglements in more detail.

1

Quilting Black Resistance: Slavery's Afterlives, Creativity and Social Justice

Bright and colourful, with tiny pieces of blue, green, red, yellow, purple and pink randomly stitched together in a variety of shapes – the haphazard design of the quilt reminds the viewer of a basket of small fabric scraps being emptied out and floating through the air. As the viewer's gaze glides further down, it comes to rest at a banner of words towards the bottom of the quilt. Spanning the width of the quilt, the banner states: 'In essence, I am a sophisticated cotton picker.' The quilt was made by Chawne Kimber in 2015 and exhibited at Quiltcon, the annual show of the Modern Quilt Guild in the United States, as well as part of a range of other exhibitions in art galleries. The sentence on the banner is from the biography of African American singer Eartha Kitt. For Kimber, the phrase resonates in many ways with her own experience as a Black woman in the contemporary US and with her family's heritage. Kimber's ancestors laboured in the cotton fields and in the mills of rural Alabama and many of the women in the family, including her grandmother, where quiltmakers just like Kimber. Cotton, as raw material, work clothing, or creative medium in the form of fabric has in one way or another played an important role in each of their lives. Cotton was also central to the institution of slavery in the US, the legacy of which continues to shape the lived experience of Black people today.

This chapter explores contemporary practices of quiltmaking by African American women alongside Black women's narratives about these practices.[1] Quilts play a significant role in narratives of African American resistance and provide a tangible repository of the past whilst also sparking an engagement with the affective legacy of this past. Drawing on text and textile, I flesh out the relationship between different kinds of textualities and the ways they become entangled in the efforts of African American women to redress official records about the affective legacy of slavery and Black women's embodied experiences of racism and sexism. I outline a trajectory from nineteenth-century quilts made by slaves to the creative practices of contemporary Black women writers and quiltmakers all the way to the Black Lives Matter movement. Examining individual and communal quilts alongside makers' personal testimonies, as well as quilting practices featured in literary texts, my analysis participates in a tradition of feminist epistemology that challenges dominant notions of archive and methodology, but also notions about what constitutes resistance (Ahmed 2017; Harding 2004; Lorde [1984] 2007; Madhok and Evans 2014). I look at Toni Morrison's novel *Beloved*, Alice Walker's *The Color Purple* and her short story 'Everyday Use', as well as Faith Ringgold's story quilts, because all three artists are publicly committed to Black projects of historical redress. In addition, I examine the resistant quilting practices of modern quilters like Chawne Kimber and the Social Justice Sewing Academy (SJSA), a US-based youth organization committed to social justice education, through their blogs, media publications, videos and personal interviews. As I shall discuss in more detail throughout this chapter, I do not view these quilting and writing practices in the context of essentialist and problematic ideals of an 'African American aesthetic'. Rather, I am interested in how quilts *made by* African American makers participate in particular affective economies shaped by the material and affective legacy of slavery and systemic racism in the US. Throughout this chapter, I am interested in how practices of quilting and creative critical writing including blogging become part of everyday practices of meaning making that are ways of telling stories about the past, the present moment and a more just future outside official records.

Recognition for a representation of history from the view of people of colour has been central to anti-racist, feminist liberation movements over the past century. Part of this effort has included a challenge to what constitutes an official archive or, rather, what materials are seen as providing meaningful insight into past experiences and their effects on the present (Hartman 2007; Sharpe 2016; Sheller 2012). Contemporary liberation and decolonizing movements like Black Lives Matter emphasize the importance of rewriting official historical records in ways that decentre the perception of white people, but also acknowledge the material and affective consequences of settler colonialism and slavery in North America (Bacchetta, Maira and Winant 2019; Hesse and Hooker 2017). Turning to the affective and embodied legacies of slavery, colonialism and racism in the context of literature and postcolonial theory has been one way of challenging the official archive (Fanon [1952] 2008; Hartman 2007, 2019; Sharpe 2016). Indeed, for radical Black feminists, to achieve recognition for the challenges of Black women, in general, and Black working-class women, more specifically, a revision of official history as recorded primarily by white middle- or upper-class males was imperative. They argued that history written by members from the group of the oppressor, that is, history written by white people, could not account for 'the way Black identity has been specifically constituted in the experience of exile and struggle' caused by the institution of slavery (hooks 1991b: 29). In particular, these accounts, which have come to dominate popular and state-sanctioned official discourses, could not adequately represent Black women's affective experiences of intersecting forms of oppression like racism, sexism, ableism and classism.

Recognition of the legacy of slavery for Black people in the US is a central tenet to many African American anti-racist and social justice practices. Black Lives Matter and the prison abolition movement both explicitly link the disproportionately large marginalization of African Americans in the US to the aftermath of slavery and post-slavery segregation (Davis 2016; Dixon 2014; Sharpe 2016). According to the website of Black Lives Matter, the movement, founded by Patrisse Cullors, Opal Tometi and Alicia Garza in 2013, is 'rooted in the experience of Black people [in the US]' and, as a result, in the history of these people (n.d.). Sparked by the vigilante killing of Trayvon Martin in the same year and fuelled by the subsequent police killings of Mike Brown, Tamir Rice, Sandra Bland and Eric Garner, to name but a few, the movement regards these events not as isolated incidents, but as symbolic of institutionalized racism and systemic state violence that disproportionately affect African Americans (Lowery 2017: 16). In this rhetoric, racism and social injustice are direct consequences of the institution of slavery 'in an attempt to manage free Black people,' as veteran Black feminist activist and scholar Angela Y. Davis puts it (2016: 117). The contemporary struggles of African Americans in the US and elsewhere are historicized within the legacy of slavery, and the acknowledgement of its impact is framed as imperative to the creation of a more just and equal society (Black Lives Matter n.d.).

Texts and textiles, along with personal and collective narratives, play a prominent role in discourses and affective practices surrounding the cultural trauma of slavery. Through mixing text and textile, literally, by including one in the other or, figuratively, by drawing on its etymological history, new modes of knowledge are forged as official records and archives are rewritten by African American writers, scholars and artists (see also Skeehan 2020). This happens on a public scale, but also through more private actors within communal settings. Textile artefacts like quilts, in this context, are of particular interest because of the connection between their primary material, cotton, and African American history. Slaves were put to work on the cotton plantations and, after the abolition of slavery, picking cotton or working on the cotton gins remained a key source of employment for many African Americans, as was the case with Kimber's relatives. On the cotton plantations in the American South, the connection between African American identities and cloth took on a new level of meaning as slaves bled and sweated in the fields and toiled on the cotton gin. For scholars Melanie McKay and Maaja Stewart quilts, therefore, 'keep alive not only the stories of ancestors, but the very bodies of those who suffered in indigo fields and around indigo vats, or labored in the jeans, overalls, aprons and shirts' that would eventually be turned into quilts (2005: 165). As the clothes are cut up and reassembled into a quilt they participate in the 'affective economies' (Ahmed 2004) of mediating African American experience, which I shall unpack in more detail in the following sections.

This process of redress, of course, is ongoing in the same way that the struggle for liberation for people of colour is. In the following sections, I flesh out in detail the importance of everyday practices of quiltmaking for the reworking of dominant narratives about slavery and its legacy. Black women quilters and writers can be viewed as part of a radical Black feminist tradition grounded in everyday practices of creative making that emerge from the realm of the home space. They employ practices of quiltmaking in order to craft counter-narratives which offer alternative histories of African American experience as private acts of making are intertwined with official histories and contemporary events. These practices of making provide a mode for dwelling in the possibility of a more just future. They provide a space in which to consciously inhabit the present while engaging with the past and its painful legacy. In addition, this space allows for an orientation towards radical social imaginaries that value Black life.

The Affective Economies of Quiltmaking

Black quilting and writing – like any creative practices – need to be considered within the context of their production and in relation to how product and practice become entangled not only in discursive formations, but also in what cultural studies scholar Sara Ahmed calls 'affective economies' (2004: 46). Ahmed employs the term to highlight how feelings 'do not reside in subjects or objects, but are produced as effects of circulation' (2004: 8). It is only through circulation and through being 'sticky' with affects that quilts as material objects can participate in African American identity politics as carriers of memory and as a means to transmit cultural knowledge to future generations. Alice Walker illustrates this in her short story, 'Everyday Use' ([1973] 1994). The story follows an unnamed mother and her daughter, Maggie, as they welcome Maggie's older sister, Dee, for a short visit. During the visit Dee asks for some family heirloom quilts, which she would like to display on the wall of her house as a memento of her African American heritage. By simply looking at the two quilts, the viewer cannot gather the meaning of their individual scraps and fragments. It is only through Mama explaining to Dee the trajectory of each individual piece of material that the significance of the quilt in relation to her family's history and wider African American history becomes accessible to Dee and the reader. For example, Mama explains that 'one teeny faded blue piece, about the piece of a penny matchbox', in one of the quilts came from the uniform of Dee's great-grandfather Ezra who fought in the Civil War (Walker [1973] 1994: 32).

The quilts also connect Mama to her matrilineal heritage as they had been sewn and quilted by her mother and her sister, Big Dee, who in turn had been taught by the women in the family how to sew and quilt. Following the example of her own mother and sister, Mama passed this knowledge on to her daughter, Maggie. However, Dee had refused to learn how to quilt because she believed it to be backwards (Walker [1973] 1994: 32). The quilts in question had been promised to Maggie, but Maggie claims that she does not need them as a way to remember her ancestors because she feels connected to them through her knowledge of the practice of quiltmaking. Mama appears to share this sentiment: to her, wearing out the quilts through everyday use does not represent a carelessness in the handling of a family heirloom, because, like Maggie, she knows how to make a quilt (Walker [1973] 1994: 33). Dee, who now prefers to be called Wangero in a symbolic attempt to free herself from the lineage of the white slave owners who had named her ancestors, accuses her mother and sister of a lack of appreciation for the history of the items. The items she requests, to Dee, are symbolic of a past during which Black people were unfree and economically destitute and quilts had to be sewn by hand because of a lack of sewing machines. Dee had previously shown little interest in her family history, but this appears to have changed through her involvement with the Black Arts Movement of the 1960s and early 1970s. This movement was concerned with establishing an authentic Black identity free of any influence or connection with the white oppressor but, as such, was also 'fundamentally essentialist' as it 'dismissed all forms of cultural production by African Americans that did not conform to movement criteria' (hooks 1995: 68; see also Byerman 1991: 810–1). The movement centred around an 'abstract idea of cultural heritage, with links back to an imagined Africa and an abstract America, where the formal identity of citizenship and the romantic identity of cultural heritage were held in a tension filled unity' (Eyerman 2001: 63).

For Dee, the quilts are a '*priceless*' reminder of slaves' ability to provide for themselves and make do in a violent environment (Walker [1973] 1994: 33, original emphasis). She accuses Mama and Maggie of being unable to value this heritage through the recognition and display of everyday objects as precious artefacts from a horrible past. The material object, for Dee, is representative of this past; but, more importantly, as an artefact, it is also symbolic of the progress of the present moment. She insists that times have changed and 'it's really a new day for us [Black people]', dismissing her mother's affective attachments to the objects which bear the marks of the people who both made them and interacted with them on a daily basis (Walker [1973] 1994: 43). In contrast to that, Mama and Maggie value 'the functional nature of their heritage and [imply] that it must be continually renewed rather than fixed in the past' (Christian 1994: 130). To make quilts and to use them in the home, to include the beautiful in the everyday, is for them to appreciate the creative legacy of their ancestors while also acknowledging the horror of slavery (Boudreau 1995: 453). The affective investment in this legacy manifests itself in Mama and Maggie's quiltmaking practice, which shapes their own identity in relation to their heritage. As the women cut, sew and quilt fabrics they are invariably confronted with their own heritage as well as the history of the people whose clothes they might be upcycling or who have taught them the craft. They are moved by the material while simultaneously moving the material.

For Mama and Maggie, quilting is a means to connect with their ancestors through a 'bodily epistemology of knowledge'; they are linked to them through the embodied practice of quiltmaking (Tanner 2006: 6). Thus, quiltmaking becomes an embodied mechanism to interrogate the categories within which African American experience is framed through different public discourses such as those of the Black Arts Movement and institutionalized historical records. In the end, Mama takes the quilts from Dee and 'dump[s] them into Maggie's lap' in acknowledgement of her younger daughter's commitment to her heritage (Walker [1973] 1994: 34). With 'Everyday Use', Walker provides a written record of Black experience which, at the same time, is also evidence of an unofficial affective archive filled with cultural texts such as quilts that function as 'repositories of feelings and emotions, which are encoded not only in the content of the texts themselves but in the practices that surround their production and repetition' (Cvetkovich 2003: 7). Knowledge about the self, but also its relationship with others, is developed in response to an engagement with these written and stitched records and the affective repositories and practices that surround them.

Because slavery and its legacy are perceived as an all-encompassing force that literally affects every part of life, cultural texts like textile artefacts become caught up in the official and private, material and psychic, as well as social and personal processes involved in the 'dialectics of remembering and forgetting' the trauma of slavery and its afterlife (Eyerman 2001: 130; see also Del Rosso and Esala 2015; Smelser 2004). The affective structures thus produced 'constitute cultural experience and serve as the foundation for public cultures' committed to recognizing the long-lasting effects of slavery on the experience of African Americans (Cvetkovich 2003: 11). As I shall show in more detail below, however, Walker's and Morrison's literary works, like Faith Ringgold's story quilts and the quilts of Chawne Kimber and the Social Justice Sewing Academy, provide a foundation not only for public trauma cultures, but also for cultures of resistance against white supremacy and patriarchy. As such, they also highlight the entanglement of personal and public experiences as well as between affect and structures of power and governance.

Legacies of Everyday Creative Resistance

In her landmark essay 'In Search of Our Mothers' Gardens' ([1983] 2004), Walker explicitly links the legacy of African American quiltmakers to contemporary African American women writers and critics attempting to rewrite discourses of Black experience. She identifies quiltmaking as an important tool in Black women's resistance against slavery, racism and patriarchy alongside practices of creative critical writing. Although Black slave women and their descendants may not have referred to themselves as artists and their work was not recognized as such, Walker insists that these women are the artistic and spiritual forerunners of African American women today (Walker [1983] 2004: 23; see also hooks 1991b; Mitchell 2020). She laments how the grandmothers of many African Americans were deprived by their white oppressors of the right to be artists and to express themselves creatively and critically (Walker [1983] 2004: 234). Slaves were forbidden to read or write as well as denied access to the materials needed to become a sculptor, painter or inventor. Quilting, however, was one of the very few creative practices to which slaves had access (Mazloomi 2015; Walker [1983] 2004). Scraps of used cloth could be salvaged from the master's home and old clothing was used as an additional source of material. Slaves made quilts in order to keep themselves and their families warm, but the small number of surviving slave quilts is also a testament to their creative and aesthetic investment in the practice.

According to quilt and folk historian Carolyn L. Mazloomi, these quilts and their descendants are evidence of how slaves managed to preserve and pass on their African heritage through reference to traditional designs and patterns, as well as the inclusion of symbols popular in African cosmology and mythology, such as the snake. As such, the slave quilt 'became a covert expression of resistance within the context of storytelling', even before it became employed in the Underground Railroad, a secret network that helped Black people escape to the free North (Mazloomi 2015: 7). It was a means to counter the suppression of the cultural traditions and knowledge of their African homeland and to pass them on to descendants. Some quilts were narrative in their appliqué designs which, like a picture book, offered a pictorial representation of a story: for example, the famous story quilts by the enslaved Harriet Powers. With other quilts, African American history was more covertly embedded in the choice of material or the abstract design that required the explanation of someone versed in the meaning of the symbols and cloth. For Mazloomi, this practice echoes the narrative tradition of the African griot or oral historian as the quilts 'tell stories of family leaders, moral and spiritual values, and social concerns' (2015: 7).

Up until the 1980s, Black quilters were notoriously absent from traditional American quilt histories (Hood 2001; Klassen 2009; Mazloomi 2015). It was only then that quilt scholars began to investigate more closely African Americans' participation in the American quilting tradition as part of broader practices of rewriting histories of African American experience and cultural production (Benberry 1980, 1992; MacDowell 1997; Mazloomi 2015; Scheper-Hughes 2004). In 1999, Jacqueline Tobin and Raymond Dobard's publication on the Underground Railroad sparked public and commercial interest in the topic ([1999] 2000). Yet, the white quiltmaker in her role as active abolitionist is regularly placed in the foreground in these narratives, as opposed to the plight of the slave and the detrimental conditions of slavery and racism that necessitated the creation of the Underground Railroad. In fact, contemporary quilt patterns in homage to the network are often marketed to a white audience alongside Civil War reproduction fabrics (Brackman 2006). Popular narratives about the network by bestselling authors like Tracy Chevalier (2013) likewise appear to romanticize the experience of escape for the slave, as well as the involvement of white abolitionists, in the journey of African Americans to the free North.

In 2002 the first exhibition of the now famous Gee's Bend quilts in the Fine Art Museum in Houston and subsequent exhibitions, publications and documentaries established African American quilting traditions in the spotlight of the American and international quilting community and generated new public and academic interest. The quilts made by descendants of former slaves living in the remote and impoverished community of Gee's Bend, Alabama, were heralded nationally and internationally for their apparent African American aesthetic which centred around improvisation, asymmetry and bold colour choices (Arnett 2002). The women and their quilts gained fame only when a white folk-art collector 'discovered' them and they became associated with the works of white, male masters of high modernism. The international art scene and the modern quilt community more broadly celebrated the women and their works 'through [a] racial nostalgia that denies the reality of exploitation and poverty as an American tradition' that affected the Black community in particular ways (Cooks 2014: 354). The cause of the material reality of dire poverty and social exclusion in which the women lived and made their quilts, as well as 'the continued exploitation and structural inequality in Gee's Bend and beyond', is mostly ignored (Cooks 2014: 59). Instead, the quilts are framed as the 'untutored expressions of a Western art-world aesthetic', while, at the same time, the makers become exoticized as 'carriers of a unique local tradition' (Klassen 2009: 320, 322). Indeed, a *Guardian* article in anticipation of the very first display of the quilts in the United Kingdom in the spring of 2020 echoes this rhetoric as it refers to the quilts as 'miraculous works of modern art' (Brown 2019: n.p.).

While Mazloomi does not deny that African Americans developed a unique quilting style 'drawing on their African past', she criticizes how this aesthetic is used to position quilts made by African Americans outside mainstream American quilt histories (2015: 7). Currently, the International Quilt Museum at the University of Nebraska–Lincoln identifies the contemporary American quilter on its website based on a survey from 2014 as 'female, 64 years old, well educated, and affluent' and, by extension, white – since it informs the reader a few lines further on that 'men also quilt, as do African Americans' (n.d.).[2] Contemporary Black quilters like Chawne Kimber repeatedly find their works entangled within dominant assumptions about a so-called African American aesthetic. Indeed, she has been told by white people that her quilts 'aren't African American quilts', because they break with assumptions about a supposed African American aesthetic (Hewett 2021: 148). Whiteness, in these contexts, is identified in opposition to being 'ethnically marked', implying that the maker's non-white ethnicity is somehow reflected in the artefact, for instance, in the form of a clearly discernible aesthetic (Dawkins 2011: 268). In this framework, the white, supposedly unmarked, aesthetic is once more placed as the default mode and the works by makers of colour are defined in relation to this standard and, as a result, become placed outside the mainstream. The quilt as a material object, as featured in traditional mainstream American quilt histories, is thus also exposed as a tool, which has served to 'reaffirm existing social relations and ... established values' in favour of the status quo, which subjects Black people to racism, systemic oppression and exclusion from American society (Klassen 2009: 327). For Kimber, the focus on the essentialist African American quilting aesthetic is about 'them [white people] trying to make you fit their mold for what a Black person's allowed to do' (Hewett 2021: 148).

Walker insists that African American women have always managed to find creative outlets such as quiltmaking, singing or, in the case of her mother, the planting of beautiful flower gardens. As such, these women have left a creative legacy for contemporary African American women writers and critics from which to draw inspiration (Walker [1983] 2004). While writing *The Color Purple*, Walker purposefully took to working on a quilt as a form of meditation, during which the characters would 'come to her' and the story would begin to unfold as her quilt began to grow (Walker [1983] 2004: 358). In commemoration of her grandmother, who was an avid quilter, Black feminist critic bell hooks claims that she inherited the 'legacy of commitment to one's "art"' from her grandmother and she 'proudly points to ink stains on [a] quilt [made by her grandmother] which mark [her own] struggle to emerge as a disciplined writer' (1991b: 121).

African American artist Faith Ringgold appears to reference this tradition of creative critical practices in her famous story quilts that feature text written onto the fabric to form a collection of short stories or, as Ringgold says, a 'mini novel'. These narratives are referenced in other parts of the quilts where Ringgold has drawn images on the fabric and then embellished them through quilting stitches. Indeed, Ringgold refers to her series of story quilts, *The French Collection* (1991), as being 'like [her] first novel' (Ringgold, Freeman and Roucher 1996: 26). With *The Purple Quilt* (1986), Ringgold even created a story quilt inspired by Walker's novel, *The Color Purple*. It features the novel's main characters as the quilt's centrepiece, which is framed by panels with excerpts from the novel. For Ringgold, the piecing together of fragments of personal and historical experience in the same manner that material scraps are pieced together is critical to her artistic practice (Ringgold, Freeman and Roucher 1996). As African American writers and artists flesh out Black people's experiences from the early days of the slave trade to the contemporary United States, they provide alternative histories of African American experience. According to Ringgold's daughter, cultural critic Michelle Wallace, it is imperative for Black women's liberation to produce such alternative histories because 'knowledge of "the past" determines power in "the present"' ([1978] 2015: 22). Wallace values creative and critical histories steeped in personal experience as opposed to supposedly objective factual history which does not provide space 'for taking into account contradictory voices and interpretations' ([1978] 2015: 25). In this context, for Ringgold, text and textile works by African American women become art works outside the dominant financial and institutionalized systems of the art world, as she identifies art as 'based on something you know about and have experienced' (Ringgold, Freeman and Roucher 1996: 14; see also Graulich and Witzling 1994). Her own painted quilts are 'an expression of the African-American-female experience', as are the works of many other African American quilters, and the material object cannot be separated from this experience (Ringgold, Freeman and Roucher 1996: 10).

According to Walker, those early quilters 'handed down respect for the possibilities – and the will to grasp them' ([1983] 2004: 242). To find space for the creative engagement with fabric and thread amidst the continuous abuse and degradation the majority endured at the hands of their masters, for Walker, is an act of resistance against a form of systemic oppression that aimed to extinguish any kind of spirit, and consequently also creativity, among Black people. Bell hooks refers to this attitude as an 'aesthetic of existence' characteristic of the African American experience:

> many displaced African slaves brought to this country an aesthetic based on the belief that beauty, especially that created in a collective context, should be an integrated aspect of everyday life, enhancing the survival and development of community, these ideas formed the basis of African-American aesthetics … rooted in the idea that no degree of material lack could keep one from learning how to look at the world with a critical eye, how to recognize beauty, or how to use it as a force to enhance inner well-being.[3]
>
> 1995: 66

In this aesthetic, the homeplace and the everyday are placed at the core of a radical politics of survival. As the space removed furthest from the control of white supremacy, the homeplace simultaneously becomes the space in which resistance can flourish and dehumanization can be resisted (hooks 1991b: 42–4).[4] Walker recounts how her mother always planted very 'ambitious gardens' no matter where they lived or the size of her mother's general workload ([1983] 2004: 241). These gardens with their colourful and beautifully arranged selection of flowers, according to Walker, are a powerful expression of her mother's creativity as she, like many quilters, 'left her mark in the only materials that she could afford' ([1983] 2004: 239).

Similarly, in Ringgold's story quilt, *The Sunflower Quilting Bee at Arles* (1991), a group of famous African American women (including Sojourner Truth, Harriet

Tubman and Ella Baker) gathered around a quilting frame, affirm in the presence of famous modernist artist Vincent Van Gogh: 'We are all artists. Piecing is our art. . . . We did it after a hard day's work in the fields to keep our sanity and our beds warm and bring beauty to our lives. That was not being an artist. That was being alive' (Ringgold, Freeman and Roucher 1996: 37). In this way, Ringgold questions dominant definitions of art and links women's everyday practices of quilting to those of high art in an attempt to 'explore the significance of the everyday in [the lives of African-American women]' (Graulich and Witzling 1994: 18). Indeed, in an essay about her mother and her artwork, Wallace recounts how Ringgold's art practice was part of everyday family life with the dining room functioning as Ringgold's studio. The large dining table provided a surface on which to lay out the quilts for the whole family to admire and discuss while Ringgold's mother assisted with some of the sewing (Wallace 1990; Ringgold, Freeman and Roucher 1996).

In her story quilts, Ringgold not only defies institutionalized definitions of art, she also affirms a connection between beauty and the mundane practice of quiltmaking with social change and activism. She says about *The Sunflower Quilting Bee at Arles*: 'I put the women together as quilters to say that they are piecing together freedom in this country' (Ringgold, Freeman and Roucher 1996: 37). In the story quilt, as the sun sets and the women are no longer able to continue with their quilting, they claim: 'Now we can do our real quilting, our real art: making this world piece up right' (Ringgold, Freeman and Roucher 1996: 32, 37). The women are not only in charge of creating textile artefacts; they are also portrayed as active participants in international social justice movements and as advocates for women's rights, voter registration, civil rights and much more. Quiltmaking is thus depicted not as separate from these engagements, but as a vital part of them in its affirmation of life and beauty. As Mysha Priest argues in relation to Ringgold's works, the quilt becomes a 'metaphor for cultural creation and a mode of redress for oppression enacted on the Black female body' (2014: 463). However, this relation is not only metaphorical, but is also felt. As Priest claims: 'The quilt is a process of self-recognition embodied' (2014: 468); the material object moves the body while the body moves the material. For hooks, this makes quiltmaking part of an aesthetics that is 'more than a philosophy or theory of art and beauty' but a phenomenological way of being in the world, that is, 'a way of inhabiting a space, a particular location, a way of looking and becoming' (1995: 65; Checinska 2018). As such, the practice of quiltmaking provides a way of dwelling in the current state of being as part of an embodied sense of self that recognizes this experience as a starting point for new becomings.

Creativity, thus, is part of everyday life and presented as essential for survival. Drawing on Black writer and activist Audre Lorde's work, Ahmed argues that, for those 'never meant to survive', creativity is, in fact, necessary in order to survive (2017: 236). It becomes a means to forge a living and to develop creative ways to support one's existence in a world in which this existence is constantly under attack. In such an environment, to claim a space for making and to leave one's mark in material, be that fabric or paper, is always a political act. Making then is not only a conscious refusal of ready-made products but also of existing social structures. More so, creative practices can generate resilience in makers to enable them to continue facing the oppressive structures they are working to redefine. In this sense, works by Walker, Lorde, Ringgold and hooks have anticipated the emergence of scholarship and discourses that stress the positive effects of practices of needlework and other creative crafts for mental health and well-being. The following sections look at Morrison's *Beloved* and Walker's *The Color Purple* to show in more detail some of the connections between quiltmaking, resilience, well-being and (personal) care work in the context of African-American women's experiences.

Mediating the Horrors of Slavery through Text and Textile

Both Morrison and Walker regard their work as part of a wider anti-racist project of rewriting history and they interrogate the marginalization of cultural works by African American women. In addition, they place their own acts of rewriting within the context of the cultural trauma of slavery and attempt, as Morrison puts it, to 'disentangle received knowledge from the apparatus of control' (1989: 8). This entails not only the representation of history from a Black point of view, but also the unearthing of how previous records by African Americans were shaped and amended within the dominant narratives of an unequal and racist society. For example, Black women's traumatic experiences of slavery, until well into the twentieth century, had frequently been confined to the tradition of the slave narrative (Hartman 2007; Luckhurst 2008). These narratives were 'instructive, moral, and obviously representative' and aimed to provide 'fuel for the fires [set up by] abolitionists' (Morrison 1995: 87). Representation of the slave experience by Black writers had to be sanctioned by white patrons before publication. Yet, much of that experience was also deemed 'too terrible to relate' to the reader and omitted under a veil of silence (Morrison 1995: 91). Black women's affective experiences of slavery were essentially censored and placed outside official archives.

Morrison consciously participates in the recovery and sustaining of an affective archive of African American history. In her fiction, she attempts to connect the past with the present as she 'journeys to a site to see what remains were left behind and to reconstruct the world that these remains imply' (1995: 92). Morrison sees it as her duty as an author to attend to this archive and to relate what she calls the 'interior life' of Black people and, as such, 'fill in the blanks that the slave narratives left' (1995: 93–4). Thus, *Beloved* follows the life of three generations of Black women – Baby Suggs, Sethe, Denver and Beloved – and their journey from slavery in the South to life in the free North. Walker, likewise, claims that African American women authors have the opportunity as well as 'the great responsibility ... to give voice to centuries not only of silent bitterness and hate but also of neighbourly kindness and sustaining love' ([1983] 2004: 21). According to Walker, the experience of being Black, female, poor and Southern makes for a 'way [of] seeing the world [that] is quite different from the way many people see it' (quoted in Davis 1994: 106). This is not to suggest, however, that there is such a thing as a Black 'essence'; rather, it is a call to recognize how African American identities have been specifically constituted through this experience (hooks 1991b: 29). In this vein, Walker's novel *The Color Purple* portrays the development of the main character, Celie, from silent and demure victim of racism and patriarchy to a successful businesswoman who has managed to patch up her relationship with her own community, including her abusive ex-husband and stepson.

In *Beloved*, a quilt with two orange patches is a subtle, but constant, point of reference throughout the novel, as different characters engage with it to varying degrees in the house at 124 Bluestone Road. The quilt often recedes into the background along with the ordinary interior of the home, the pots and pans, jelly jars and the smell of leftover food from the restaurant at which Sethe works. Linked to slavery and racism, the quilt serves as a reminder of a traumatic and terrible past, while, at the same time, encouraging engagement with this past. It is connected with Sethe's mother-in-law, Baby Suggs, and the latter's withdrawal to her deathbed in the keeping room where she 'will end her days defeated by slavery's cruelty' (Soon 2011: 238). After Baby Suggs spends eight years 'ponder[ing] color', she concludes that 'there is no bad luck in the world but white folks' (Morrison [1987] 1997: 201, 89). Once Baby Suggs has died, the quilt with the two orange squares, which stand out starkly in-between the 'scraps of blue serge, black, brown and gray wool' and against the muted and dark interior of the home remains a reminder of Baby Suggs and her life which was marked by slavery and racism (Morrison [1987] 1997: 38). In addition, the quilt acts as a silent witness to the events in the home from the disappearance of the ghost of the baby girl (whom Sethe had killed to spare from a life of slavery) to Beloved's appearance at the doorstep of the family home. As such, it also connects three generations in this family, namely Baby Suggs, Sethe, Beloved, and Denver as they all turn to the quilt as a token of a past that throws its shadows on their present life.

In Sethe's case, the quilt prompts her meditation about Baby Suggs' withdrawal and her need to ponder colour, which eventually leads Sethe to face her own traumatic past. This includes the abuse Sethe suffered at the hand of her slave master and his students, and her killing of her own baby girl. According to Rafael Pérez-Torres (1999) and Florian Bast (2011), the contrast between the lack of colour in the home, in general, and the two bright orange squares in the quilt is symbolic of the lives of Baby Suggs and other characters, marked by deprivation expressed as a lack of colour. Indeed, Sethe describes herself becoming as 'color conscious as a hen' from the day of the funeral of her baby girl, which could be attributed to the 'effect of chronic shock' from the trauma she has suffered (Morrison [1987] 1997: 38–9; McKay and Stewart 2005: 162). Sethe's need to face the past is 'catalyzed' by the appearance of the teenage Beloved – possibly the baby girl's ghost – and heightened through the girl's fixation with the quilt (Krumholz 1999: 115). Likewise, in reading the character of Beloved not only as an incarnation of the dead baby girl, but also as symbolic of the 'Sixty Million and more' Africans killed on the middle passage to America to which Morrison dedicates the novel, the necessity for Sethe to face her past is turned into a more general need for all American people to face the past. A past, which, as suggested in the last chapter of the novel, is one that is difficult to narrate and remember. 'It was not a story to pass on', that is, a story that should be retold and 'passed on' but, rather, one to be avoided, 'passed on' (Morrison [1987] 1997: 274–5).

The change in Sethe's attitude to her past, at the end of the novel, is mirrored in the refashioned appearance of the quilt. The dark and muted colours have been replaced and it is now a quilt of 'merry' and 'carnival colors', while the house is decorated with 'ribbons, bows, bouquets' and scattered with 'brightly colored clothes' (Morrison [1987] 1997: 240, 271, 272). Yet, the quilt, as a physical object within the home, continues to be a reminder of the persistence of the cultural trauma of slavery, in the same way that Sethe cannot fully overcome her individual trauma or be fully reconciled with the past. Once she faces her past, Sethe becomes an invalid, emotionally and physically unable to care for herself and Denver, and she comes to rely on the support of the community. As such, the reworked quilt is also symbolic of the process of redress to which Morrison herself is committed: one that 'remembers at the site of rupture [but] does not cast away the ravished body or the memory of injury, but finds them central to re-creation' (Priest 2014: 475). Through the quilt, Sethe manages to approach a past, which she struggles to put into words, on an affective level that is less structured than that of language or narrative. The quilt is affectively charged with memories, 'smelling like grass and feeling like hands – the unrested hands of busy women: dry, warm, prickly'; as such, it provides an entryway 'to recreate what happened, how it really was' for Sethe, Baby Suggs and the sixty million more affected by slavery (Morrison [1987] 1997: 78). It is only after this repeated contact with the past through the quilt that Sethe becomes able to articulate how her own experiences as a slave led to the killing of her baby girl. Yet, Sethe has difficulty expressing herself in the form of a coherent linear narrative: she circles the topic in the same way she literally circles her friend Paul D and the kitchen table as she is trying to tell her story. While the quilt propels Sethe to face and tell her story, it is also representative of the continuous haunting of it.

Stitching as Self-Care

In the last decades, occupational therapy and mental health research has highlighted the calming and stress-reducing effects of crafting on people's general sense of well-being (Burt and Atkinson 2012; Hackney, Maughan and Desmarais 2016; MacDowell, Luz and Donaldson 2017; Pöllänen 2015; Wellesley-Smith 2021). Crafts are described as 'a way to remove negative emotions', because the 'lengthy process of craft making can enable negative feelings to be confronted and worked through by doing with hands' (Pöllänen 2015: 95). Specific research into quiltmaking shows that the engagement with colourful textiles appears to have an 'uplifting effect on the mood' (Burt and Atkinson 2012: 54). In addition, makers value the freedom of choice their crafts provide (Burt and Atkinson 2012; Pöllänen 2013, 2015). Handling materials and equipment as well as performing the necessary techniques produces 'a feeling of control' that might not be present in other areas of life; it is empowering and 'offers a sense of agency' (Pöllänen 2013: 223; hooks 1995: 71). The Black slave woman was controlled by her white master in more or less every aspect of her life, including her sexuality. Piecing quilts out of scraps of material, which she was able to secure from her master's house or from discarded clothing, was one of the few areas in which she could take control of her actions.

For Celie, the protagonist in Walker's *The Colour Purple*, it is this creative activity that keeps her going, and keeps her mind occupied, amidst her hardships.

When she finds out that for years her husband Albert had kept her sister's letters from her, it is the taking up of a 'needle and not a razor' that prevents her 'right there in [his] house from killing [him]' (Walker [1982] 2004: 133, 224). Creative practice, in this context, becomes a means of working around an impasse and, in Celie's case, a means of dealing with her grief and anger. As Celie's friend and lesbian lover Shug suggests: 'Times like this, lulls, us ought to do something different. . . . Let's make you some pants' (Walker [1982] 2004: 132). Through her quilting and sewing practices Celie manages to connect with other women like Shug and Sofia, the wife of her stepson, and through these relationships she slowly changes from passive victim to active agent of her own well-being. Used to the continuous abuse suffered at the hands of men, Celie had adopted an attitude of numbness because, as she puts it: 'What good it do? I don't fight, I stay where I'm told. But I'm alive' (Walker [1982] 2004: 22). Towards the end of the novel, this attitude has changed and Celie stands her ground against her husband: 'I'm pore, I'm black, I may be ugly and can't cook, a voice say to everything listening. But I'm here' (Walker [1982] 2004: 184). In this spirit, she leaves Albert and accompanies Shug to Memphis to start a successful sewing business. On her return to her community, Celie reconciles with Albert in the process of teaching him how to sew and quilt.

In *The Color Purple,* quilting and sewing are practices of survival, a means to hold 'a needle and not a razor in the hand', but also symbols of female and communal connection. This 'aesthetic of existence', to use hooks' term, is ultimately a Black feminist – or 'womanist', to use Walker's term – aesthetic in its 'commit[ment] to survival and wholeness of an entire people' (Walker [1983] 2004: xi). Quiltmaking, sewing and writing become united within Walker's womanist prose that 'celebrat[es] Black woman's insistence of living' (Christian 1994: 37).[5] It becomes evidence of the 'outrageous, audacious, courageous or wilful behavior' of a womanist, a Black feminist and descendant of millions of Black women who have endured the unendurable and not given up on themselves (Walker [1983] 2004: xi–xii). Creative making and resistance go hand in hand. Indeed, everyday creative practices and their finished objects are foundational to the individual and collective orientation towards resistance.

In a hostile environment, habitual acts of making are political because they facilitate survival. Ahmed describes racism as an 'attack on the cells of the body, an attack on the body's immune system' (2017: 238). It is an all-encompassing force that penetrates and permeates the personal and the political, the private and the public, and exposes the deep entanglements between these realms (Cvetkovich 2012: 120). According to Ahmed, 'being poor, being Black, puts your life at risk' and one has 'to work out how to survive in a system that decides life for some requires the death or removal of others' (2014: n.p.). In *Beloved*, the psychological and physical effects of racism are exemplified through Baby Suggs' retreat to her deathbed, where she finally succumbs to the fact that there 'was no bad luck in the world but white people [because] they don't know when to stop' (Morrison [1987] 1997: 104). For Celie, on the other hand, quiltmaking and sewing become ways of dealing with trauma, not necessarily because they offer a form of escape, but because they allow for a dwelling in (negative) affect that is not fixed around a teleological end goal such as working through or overcoming. Instead, stitching offers her the possibility of forging an existence in which she is neither incapacitated by the horrors of her own past nor denies its effects on the present.[6] Once Celie has embraced sewing as a regular activity she tries to forge as many opportunities for sewing as she can. It sustains her in moments when she feels low, as well as during the happy times she spends with family and friends, when she is 'so much in the habit of sewing something [she] stitch[es] up a bunch of scraps, try to see what [she] can make' (Walker [1982] 2004: 252).

Making and Dwelling in Potentiality

As I outlined briefly at the beginning of this chapter, contemporary African American quilter Chawne Kimber draws explicitly on the rich relationship between quilting and the African American experience in her textile works. Quilts from old clothing by her great-grandmother, who laboured on a plantation, were a constant in Kimber's home when growing up. In line with their original purpose, the quilts were utility objects used to keep family members warm and, because of tight finances, had been patched up many times (Appendix 2017: Skype interview). Today, as Kimber explained during our interview, quilting, for her, is a way to affectively connect with her great-grandmother:

> I feel I have to commune with the things that I make. It's about the process of the feel of cotton in your hands. It's about the sound of pulling thread through cotton very slowly. These are the best things. It's a full-body experience. The smell of [the material] when you first press it – it's just so crisp and earthy in a really delicious way. . . . I think it's important to slow it down. It isn't social media. It's not immediate gratification; it's not that instant message. . . . I want to know what it felt like for my great-grandmother to make a quilt. . . . I'm communing with her in a way through these [hand-piecing] projects.
>
> Appendix 2017: Skype interview

The tangible properties of the material are essential in this process as they have become part of the sensory and affective experience of present and past. Kimber has barely any memories of the design of her great-grandmother's quilts, but she remembers very well the weight of these quilts heavily stuffed with cotton fluff and she connects them with fond memories of family and home (WJRH 2017: n.p.).

For Kimber, it is important to value the process employed by her great-grandmother. Like her, she has created quilts from the clothing of family members. She also values the gathering of relatives' clothing and sewing pieces of it together to form a quilt as a powerful act of community building. Like her great-grandmother, Kimber feels that she is 'kind of pulling together all these different aspects of members of the family through the fabrics' (Appendix 2017: Skype interview) and, thus, joining not only cloth, but also people. However,

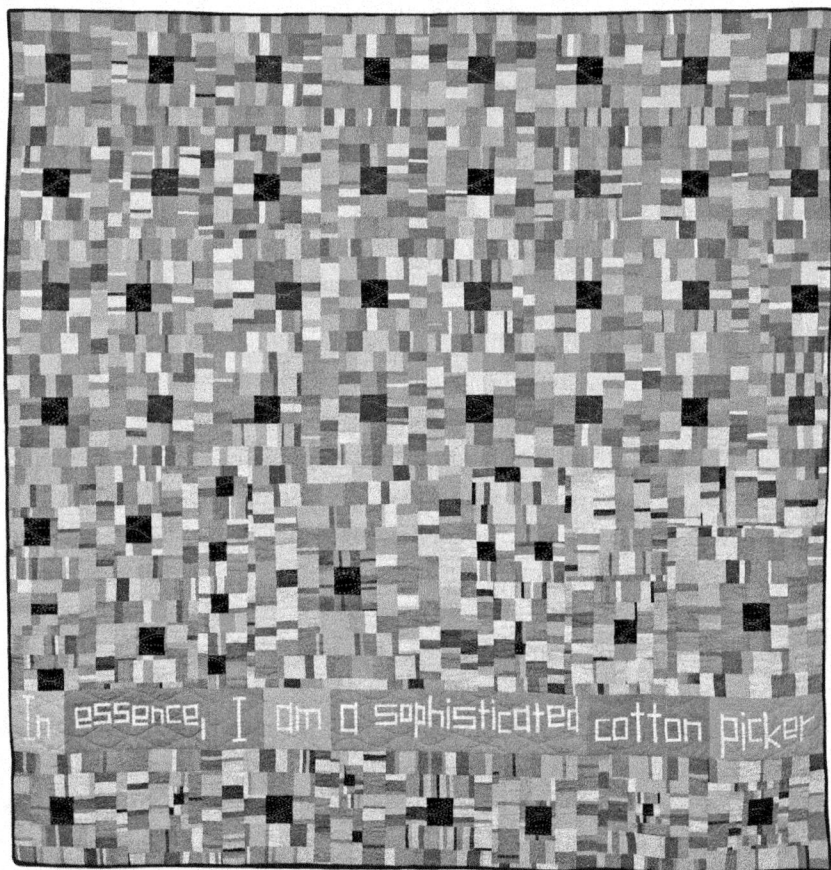

Figure 1.1 *Cotton Sophisticate*, 2015, Chawne Kimber. (Photo by Clay Wegrzynowicz for Lafayette College Communications; © Chawne Kimber).

Kimber's own quilting practice is also marked by an awareness of the stark differences between her own situation as a tenured maths professor at an American university and that of her great-grandmother. Conscious of the limits of shared processes of making to forge connections between generations and between people with different lived experiences, she notes: 'How do you represent the kind of privilege that I do have now? I do face all sorts of discrimination, but I have to admit that the kind of education I have achieved [and] the job I have allow me even more [than my father and his generation]' (Appendix 2017: Skype interview).

Some of Kimber's quilts reflect this tension through the choice of material as well as the textual elements employed. *Cotton Sophisticate* (2015, figure 1.1), the colourful quilt I described at the opening to this chapter, is one such example. Through the phrase: 'In essence, I am a sophisticated cotton picker' on the quilt, Kimber plays with the ways text can be open to interpretation. She explains:

> As a sense of thinking about my family, it [the phrase] resonates very well with me. It's a statement about slavery, a statement about the results of slavery, of course, because it didn't just end with the emancipation. At quilt shows many people [just] respond to [the many fabrics and colors used in the quilt]. They believe it's about someone who has a very large stash [of fabrics]. It's a way to avoid the other more serious issues of that statement.
>
> Appendix 2017: Skype interview

These reactions are symptomatic of the mainly white (and middle-class) audience of quilt shows. It reflects not only most people's unwillingness to engage with the relationship between race and social justice, but also how their whiteness provides them with the privilege to do so. It is easy to ignore or feign ignorance about the way in which others are systematically discriminated against if one is not directly affected by these acts of oppression. Scholars in critical race theory (Hunter and van der Westhuizen 2022; Phipps 2020; Sullivan 2019) and anti-racism activists (Dabiri 2021; Eddo-Lodge ([2017] 2018) have identified this ignorance and demonstrations thereof by white people as part of the machinations of race and white supremacy. Hunter and van der Westhuizen poignantly sum up this phenomenon as part of the 'fundamentals of whiteness' which includes '[whiteness's] wilful ignorance as a not-knowing accompanied by absolution of responsibility for racism and its effects' (2022: 9). Or, in the words of Black British journalist and activist Reni Eddo-Lodge: 'White privilege manifests itself in everyone and no one. Everyone is complicit, but no one wants to take responsibility' ([2017] 2018: 157). White privilege, for Eddo-Lodge, 'is the fact that if you're white, your race will almost certainly positively impact your life's trajectory in some way. And you probably won't even notice' ([2017] 2018: 150).[7]

By now, Kimber is a household name in the quilt world with a large online following and a busy schedule of teaching quilting all over the United States alongside her day job at university. In 2016, her quilt *The One for Eric G* (2015), in response to the death of Eric Garner at the hands of New York police, was awarded first prize in the Improvisation category at QuiltCon, the annual convention of the Modern Quilt Guild (figure 1.2). QuiltCon 2023 featured the first retrospective of Kimber's work. Yet, the quilt world is still wary of quilts that include strong political messages, particularly on topics related to racism. Works like Kimber's tend to cause highly charged debates about appropriate subject matter for quilts. Kimber notes:

> People were saying you shouldn't do this on a quilt: 'It's our sacred space. . . . Please do not come in and corrupt our world.' But it's really also playing up white privilege. People have the privilege [of] not noticing the news, not paying attention to what's going on. They hate it when you point out that shit happens in the world.
>
> Appendix 2017: Skype interview

Quilts, then, are a powerful medium for drawing attention to social issues because, as I fleshed out in the Introduction, of their inherent connotations of domesticity, femininity and comfort. Outrage, anger, defensiveness, discomfort and upset are all feelings regularly displayed by white people upon being confronted with the reality of white supremacy and their invariable, though perhaps (un)conscious, complicity with these structures (Eddo-Lodge [2017] 2018; Sullivan 2014, 2019; Yancy 2014, 2018).[8] As Black American philosopher George Yancy and others (Ahmed 2004; Sullivan 2014) have argued, these affective (and often highly performative) responses, regularly serve to 'distance the white self from the charge of racism and, indeed, that one can be implicated in its perpetuation' (Tate and Page 2018: 151). Nonetheless, the affective charge these situations carry may also be a starting point for new reflections and increased awareness of personal background. 'Catching people off guard is a great way to have a profound effect and stick in memory', asserts Kimber, 'They're gonna remember and ask more questions. They're gonna have . . . more intense emotions about it too' (Appendix 2017: Skype interview). However, Kimber is also conscious that people can also be put off by the intensity of the feelings that such an engagement generates (Appendix 2017: Skype interview).

Figure 1.2 *The One for Eric G*, 2015, Chawne Kimber. (© Chawne M. Kimber/Michigan State University Museum).

It can take up to two years for Kimber to complete a quilt. As a result, the original event or incident that inspired the making of a specific quilt may no longer be present in people's minds. For this reason, Kimber 'tries to make sure that [her] quilts all have a context beyond the incident itself' (quoted in Allen 2017: para. 4) and, as such, speak to different people on different levels of meaning. Her online blog and Instagram feed serve as a channel to document the different stages of making from conception to finished product without revealing too much of the final message (Kimber, Appendix 2017: Skype interview). For Kimber, the time spent working on the project allows her to reflect on the incident that inspired a specific quilt and its broader context – such as the shooting of Trayvon Martin or the election of Donald Trump: 'Working on that project is the time for me to meditate and do more reading and think through what I am going to be putting out as the ultimate message' (Appendix 2017: Skype interview). On her blog, she may list some of those readings or other types of media through which people can learn more about topics such as race, social injustice and women's rights. Kimber explains:

The blogging is my opportunity to catch someone. They come through the quilting . . . that's why I don't filter in the politics constantly because I don't want to turn people off. But the final reveal is when I get to blast out, for example, 'Hey, let's go read more about rape culture.' My quilts are my voice. They are me speaking out. So, I obviously have an intent of educating the audience, affirming the experiences of those who have similar experiences to me.

Appendix 2017: Skype interview

Kimber participates in the rewriting of official records that traditionally exclude or marginalize experiences of Black women, just like Walker, Morrison and Ringgold. They all assert the specificity of their experiences in the context of the legacy of slavery and pervasive racism and sexism, and yet, also draw strength from these shared experiences of persistence and resistance in a hostile environment.

Connecting People through Affect

The Social Justice Sewing Academy (SJSA), a non-profit organization, which delivers social justice education through quiltmaking, similarly participates in this project. Founded in the United States in 2017 by Sara Trail, a young Black woman and Harvard graduate now in her mid-twenties, the small grassroots organization has gained national recognition beyond the quilt world and counts thousands of volunteers amongst its number. Through a range of different programmes, which include short- and long-term workshops for young people and exhibitions for the general public, SJSA, in its own words, 'is designed to raise awareness of a topic most Americans are uncomfortable discussing: social justice and systemic racism' (Trail and Wong 2021: 12). Workshops are aimed at allowing young people to 'explore, discuss and express modes of oppression, lived experiences and creativity' (SJSAcademy n.d.). The specifically developed social justice curriculum 'draws on concepts taught in history, ethnic studies, education and sociology' as a means of making students 'aware of systemic injustices' and their historic legacies, while at the same time equipping them with the ability to become active participants of social change (SJSAcademy n.d.). Materials in this section may include 'readings from Angela Davis, bell hooks, Kimberly Crenshaw, Toni Morrison, Patricia Hill Collins, Maya Angelou, Audre Lorde and others' (Hazlewood 2017: n.p.). They are intended to counter American public schools' standard history curriculum which, according to Trail, 'is not inclusive, ostracizing hundreds of thousands of Black and Brown people whose history lies outside of the dominant American narrative' and does not acknowledge 'today's social, educational and economic inequality as remnants of that history' (quoted in Britex Fabrics 2016: n.p.). Like many Black feminists (hooks [1981] 1987, 2000; Sharpe 2016; Walker [1983] 2004; Wallace [1978] 2015), Trail implies that the reclaiming of Black history and understanding of how it was and is being shaped through Western Eurocentric discourse is imperative to social justice.

Students design and make their own appliqué quilt blocks to reflect social justice issues important to them or their lived experience of a range of injustices related to, for example, racism, sexism, violence and environmental issues (Hazlewood 2017: n.p.). The blocks are then mailed to volunteers across the United States who embroider and embellish them before they are sewn together into a community quilt (figure 1.3). For Trail, fibre is an appropriate medium

Figure 1.3 SJSA community quilt. (© Sara Trail, Social Justice Sewing Academy).

through which to address social justice not only because of its deep connection with African American history, but also because of its etymological links to concepts of weaving and storytelling which connect people and tie them together. Stories, for Trail, are an essential part of social justice activism, because she believes that they enable 'people to feel hooked to an issue. You have to experience things on an individual level to feel motivated to act on a systemic level' (Appendix: unpublished video footage).

Hosting many workshops in different parts of the United States, Trail was struck by how students' experiences differ regionally (Hazlewood 2017: n.p.). Concerns around social justice for teenagers in private schools are more likely to centre on issues such as climate change or ending animal abuse; whereas young people in inner city areas in Oakland and Chicago were concerned with police and gang violence, as well as drug abuse, because many of them had been directly affected in their immediate environment (Hazlewood 2017: n.p.). Through sending the blocks across the country to be finished off by volunteers, people for whom social justice is 'a far more "removed" concept/theory/issue', as opposed to those for whom it is a 'lived reality', come into direct contact with these experiences (Trail, quoted in Hazlewood 2017: n.p.). As a result, Trail explains, 'for some volunteers, this project helps to foster a deeper understanding of how systems within society – disproportionately and often negatively – affect marginalized communities' (Trail and Wong 2021: 9). For Trail, 'the community aspect is key' to this (Hazlewood 2017: n.p.). She is convinced that 'by bringing the two fabric artists together through sewing, a common ground of understanding and empathy is found', which hopefully may motivate people to become activists of social change (Trail, Appendix: unpublished video footage).

In addition, SJSA's Instagram feed and website offer a glimpse of the many creations as have various exhibitions, more recently also as part of large national quilt shows such as QuiltCon 2019. People's reactions to the quilts are similar to the kind that Kimber's quilts evoke. While some are positively surprised to see these issues addressed within the quilt world, others strongly criticize the so-called politization of quilting. Expressions of white defensiveness are common with the latter group, as are demands for people to 'just be nice to each other', which dismiss the need for a collective and individual engagement with racial injustice (Trail and Wong 2021). In these instances, the affective response that the quilts trigger is often perceived as negative, unsettling or offensive – a common reaction in white people upon being confronted with their white privilege and (though perhaps unconscious) complicity with white supremacy (Phipps 2020; Sullivan 2014, 2019; Yancy 2014, 2018). On the other hand, the quilt blocks and finished quilts can be the starting point for an affective investment in social justice as they help to orient people towards certain affects connected with the lived experience of others. They can point viewers towards considering, for example, the fear of the violent consequences of racist profiling that accompanies Black adolescent men and their families in their everyday life. Some SJSA students also create individual art quilts the size of small lap quilts. One by Bryan Robinson, a teenager, features the torso of a Black man with a gun held by a white hand to each side of his head (figure 1.4). The names Tamir Rice, Trayvon Marten [sic], Oscar Grant and Eric Garner are appliquéd in large letters around the torso. The piece is titled *Born a Crime* (2016) and the teenager explains: 'At first I couldn't think of any social justice issue to sew that would directly relate to me until I realized the value of my experience as a young Black male in society. In an effort to bring awareness to an epidemic of killing unarmed Black men, I carefully situated as many names as I could on the quilt' (SJSAcademy n.d.). According to Cvetkovich, 'affects that become an index of how social life is felt become the raw material for cultural formations that are unpredictable and varied' (2012: 48). It is in this unpredictability and variety that I locate the potential for unexpected and diverse practices of resistance to take shape.

SJSA's creative practices redefine what counts as art in the same manner that Ringgold and Walker claim their own conceptualizations of art outside institutionalized discourse. Instead, emphasis is place on personal aesthetic validation. 'Good art makes you feel something', says Trail, which is why she is also wary of any hierarchical distinctions between art and craft which regularly place textile works and quilting in the latter, supposedly inferior, category (Appendix: unpublished video footage). The Social Justice Sewing Academy is open to all genders and sewing is presented as a medium of creative expression accessible to anyone, notwithstanding its often-pejorative connection to women's culture and femininity (Hazlewood 2017: n.p.). For Trail, using fibre and particularly quilting, resembles a form of resistance not only because of the social justice issues that the students address in their works, but also because it attempts to 'incorporate forms of knowledge that come from people of colour ... that are not necessarily part of the western Eurocentric narrative of what is art. [It's] really that idea of making our own definitions of what is valuable rather than listening to other people's definitions' (Appendix: unpublished video footage).

Insistence on the relevance of personal lived experience is part of the process of redefinition by which the personal is made political. Black and women's liberation movements first introduced this connection in the 1960s and attempted through consciousness-raising groups to identify systemic structures

Figure 1.4 *Born a Crime*, 2016, Bryan Robinson. (© Sara Trail, Social Justice Sewing Academy).

of oppression alongside women's subjugation in the private sphere (Reed 2005: 77). For veteran Black feminist activist Angela Y. Davis, 'there is a deep relationality that links struggles against institutions and struggles to reinvent our personal lives and recraft ourselves' (2016: 106). By insisting on the homeplace as a space for resistance, it becomes politicized as it radiates with beauty and life amidst real material hardships and life in a racist system. Walker recounts: 'Because of [my mother's] creativity with her flowers, even my memories of poverty are seen through a screen of blooms' ([1983] 2004: 241). The inclusion and appreciation of beauty in everyday life for both hooks and Walker resembles a commitment to an aesthetic of existence. Lorde ([1984] 2007) and Ahmed (2017) similarly speak of creative techniques of survival with regard to the painstaking and continuous work of crafting a life within a normative system that does not acknowledge the value of life outside that norm. For Ahmed, this work is essentially political and a form of protest as opposed to creative activity being mere self-indulgence (2017: 227–37). In this sense, quilts are 'more' than simply material objects for adornment or practical use. The material object as well as the practices of making and narrating it are entangled in a legacy of political warfare on the side of African Americans. Both are part of Black women's struggles to forge their existence and to recognize how African American identity has been implicated by the legacy of institutional slavery and its aftermath. 'Quilting becomes an act against oppression. It is a way for our participants, which tend to be those belonging to a minority or marginalized group, to share their untold stories', affirms Trail (quoted in Hazlewood 2017: n.p.). Ultimately, the SJSA hopes to 'create conscious art activists who will use their creativity to change their world one stitch at a time' (SJSAcademy n.d.). This means that participants, it is to be hoped, not only reflect on the way in which they are personally affected by social injustice, but also become leaders and organizers in their communities who will work actively to address and change these issues.

Towards a Different Future

In all the examples discussed in this chapter, the everyday, the beautiful and the critical/radical are connected through the creative practice of making, which is about more than the material production of artefacts. Creative making is a radical practice that, through its performance, 'enables communities to envision what's possible' (Kelley 2002: 7). A commitment to an aesthetic of existence is expressed in an attitude, which requires one to notice beauty in the everyday, because, as Shug Avery puts in *The Color Purple*, 'it pisses God off if you walk by the color purple in a field somewhere and don't notice it' (Walker [1982] 2004: 165). Through insisting on the homeplace as a site of resistance, everyday practices of making in text and textile are politicized in their potential to affect and change structures beyond the personal home space. Routine everyday practices therefore become 'enabling of both compulsive repetition and creative becoming' (Pedwell 2016: 2). Consequently, practices of needlework are always brimming with the possibility for a change in orientation, or at least a gesture towards such transformation. In this sense, textile practices also echo the double nature of the home space, which I shall discuss in more detail in the next chapter, as a space that can be oppressive, but also the realm in which resistance takes shape.

However, regular practices of creative making are certainly no guarantee for transformation on either an individual or collective level.[9] Nor are the moments of intensive feeling that Kimber observes in viewers of her quilts necessarily connected to a dynamic model of 'becoming activist'. Indeed, like Pedwell, I am suspicious of the progressive narratives that connect social change to a radical 'rupture of consciousness', which supposedly leads to a rethinking of personal and collective politics and a commitment to transformation (Pedwell 2016: 4). Trail's hope of mobilizing people into activists on the basis of having them connect on an emotional level with the lived experience of a marginalized people, echoes this narrative to a certain extent (see also Trail and Wong 2021). Yet, she also speaks of changing the world, and by extension the people in it, 'one stitch at a time', thus indicating the necessity of continuous engagement with the practice and the problems it hopes to address (Trail, Appendix: unpublished video footage). I contend that there is more value in conceptualizing routine practices as a way to manifest a consciousness or awareness that can lead to active political engagement and eventually social change because, as T.V. Reed states, 'surrounding the drama of social change, there takes place much undramatic day-to-day activity that alone can consolidate the work of movement's "ritual public displays"' (2005: xix). In this way, the personal and the home space become once more implicated in the political. Indeed, for Black historian and author Robin Kelley, it is 'in the poetics and struggles and lived experience, in the utterances of ordinary folk, in the cultural products of social movements' that it becomes possible to imagine different ways of being and living together (2002: 9–10). As such, everyday practices cannot only prefigure another, more just world, but they are, indeed, essential to the practice of prefiguration itself (Dixon 2014; Swain 2019; Yates 2015). They make possible modes of dwelling in which new futures, or new ways of relating to each other, can be imagined and practised on a small scale. This includes 'challenging everyone to do more to value all lives' (Trail and Wong 2021: 74) and, in particular, those of people of colour, in the way that the SJSA hopes to do through its recently started Remembrance Project. Here, makers, who live within a few miles of where a victim was murdered and many of whom may never directly have experienced racial or gender-based violence, are asked to create textile portraits to memorialize the victims of such crimes and their lives. The mundane practice of making a quilt block is not a definitive tool for individual or social transformation; but it may serve as a generative starting point for new affective relations and attachments that may prefigure larger modes of change.

When Kimber first took up quilting at the age of thirty, she did so because she 'needed something to occupy [her] mind' (Appendix 2017: Skype interview). The projects she committed to at the start were a means of learning various techniques and her work was focused on precision piecing as she copied various available patterns. She only switched to more improvisational and artistic works after the sudden death of her beloved father: 'I kind of went back to sewing thinking that the meditative effect of making would help me through. But it felt really futile to make that precision patchwork and so I had to find meaning in what I was making' (Appendix 2017: Skype interview). Improvisational quilting has become a generative practice for Kimber not because of the aesthetic qualities of the finished product, but because of the way in which improvisational piecing allows for meaningful forms of dwelling marked by uncertainty:

> I often do not know what my quilts look like until that final unveiling after they're done. . . . I don't have a design wall [on which individual sections would be laid out before sewing them together] because I don't want to encourage self-doubt, you know, just constantly moving around little tiny pieces that won't have a very huge effect in the large scale. I often work very small modules and then combine them to make bigger. And I have had some failures where at that unfurling I go, 'Uuhh, what just happened?'. But it's about accepting those results.
> Appendix 2017: Skype interview

Given that it can take a couple of years for Kimber to finish a quilt, the process is just as important as the end product. Some of her improvisational piecing is as small as a quarter of an inch, which not only means that it takes many pieces in order to get to a substantial size, but also makes it a rather fidgety process. 'It's not about doing the same thing over and over again', explains Kimber (Appendix 2017: Skype interview), but about dwelling in a state that is not prescriptive of the future. It is about the opportunity to pause, reflect and realign and about consciously inhabiting this space.

In this sense, the process of quiltmaking, for Kimber, is also a metaphor for life and political activism (Appendix 2017: Skype interview). With her explicitly political quilts, Kimber does not intend to 'give direction on what to do necessarily' and, indeed, she is critical about people approaching her and asking for advice about how to foster change and provide support (Appendix 2017: Skype interview). Since injustice and oppression are the result of white hegemonic social structures and not caused by people of colour, Kimber identifies this line of questioning as another manifestation of white privilege: 'My people didn't cause the problem. . . . So, to assume that the solution should arise from within [the African American community] is actually really a kind of denial' (Appendix 2017: Skype interview). Rather, Kimber hopes that through her work and blog she is 'poking at people to learn more so that they then can start generating the solutions on their own' (Appendix 2017: Skype interview). The poking becomes a way of orienting people towards the possibility of imagining a 'different future in the present' that values Black life (Kelley 2002: 9).[10]

These practices of 'poking', for Kimber, are firmly embedded in legacies of Black resistance reaching from her great-grandmother's quiltmaking as a means to keep a large family warm to the current Black Lives Matter movement who, by the time Kimber had finished *The One for Eric G*, had since popularized the slogan 'I can't breathe' through its activism. Through constantly placing herself as a successful Black middle-class woman in the contemporary United States in dialogue with the historical legacy of slavery and social injustice, Kimber highlights the intersectional nature of the struggle. At the same time, by not fixing meaning on the level of text, textile or narrative representation, her works allow for an understanding of 'the concrete differences in context, experience and oppression' (Black Lives Matter n.d.) that African Americans and other marginalized groups experience. The works become a means of 'reading the relation between affect and structure, or between emotion and politics' that places an individual's struggle within a collective context that is not static but open for transformation (Ahmed 2004: 174). In this framework, creativity and creative practices such as quiltmaking and their narrative renderings become a means to attend to these relations without insisting on fixing them in place.

Literal and figurative practices of quiltmaking and their accompanying objects, in the examples discussed in this chapter, are imbued with a sense of potential that cannot be fixed in the present as cultural heritage and knowledge are preserved and continually renewed. As scholar Mysha Priest says, evoking Walker's flower garden analogy: 'The quilt is the mother's garden that makes possible' (2014: 468). Quiltmaking, in this sense, becomes an active verb that is 'about doing and moving forward' in a state of continuous potential (Jefferies 2011: 232). Further, it resembles a radical politics that insists on a non-prescriptive future which recognizes a multitude of experiences as opposed to one single official discourse. In *The Color Purple*, this potential is represented in the novel's possibly utopian ending, which is marked by reconciliation and reunification. In *Beloved* and 'Everyday Use', as well as the works of Faith Ringgold, Chawne Kimber and the SJSA, potential is entangled in the non-prescriptive nature of the works as they 'attempt to enhance our attunement to ... mind–body–environmental assemblages and understand "progress" as an experiential possibility in the present' (Pedwell 2016: 22). As such, this potential is also part of a radical practice that, as Kelley argues, 'takes us to another place, envisions a different way of seeing, perhaps a different way of feeling' (2002: 11) that is grounded in the affective experience of the unequal flows of power of the present moment. Thus, it has the potential to be transformative as part of everyday entangled modes of being that connect the affective, the social and the political.

As quilts are usually connected to comfort, warmth and familiarity, expressive quilts like those by Chawne Kimber or the community quilts of the Social Justice Sewing Academy challenge normative perceptions of the meaning of practices of quiltmaking through their outright confrontation with questions of gender, race and identity. Along with the story quilts of Faith Ringgold, and the literary works of Toni Morrison and Alice Walker, they examine how these categories are implicated in the lived experience and political struggle of African Americans. As a result, the quilts and the literary works offer counter-narratives to official records about Black women's experiences of the legacy of slavery and the pervasive effects of racism and sexism. In addition, they generate resistant modes of being grounded in a generational legacy of creativity and self-care. Committed to processes of historical redress, the writers and quilters discussed in this chapter use quiltmaking and narrative representation of this practice to create space for the affective dwelling in the potential of a different, more just future. They actively challenge the status quo and particularly white people's affective attachment to it as people are 'poked' (to use Kimber's word) to confront a range of injustices.

2

Sewing Desire: Homework, Gendered Agency and Bangladeshi Diaspora

Chronicling the life of the sisters, Nazneen and Hasina, Monica Ali's debut novel *Brick Lane* (2003a) tells two different stories about Bangladeshi women working in the global garment industry: Nazneen as a homeworker in London and Hasina as a factory worker in Dhaka. For Nazneen, sexual desire and sewing are closely linked. A close reading of the novel makes for a useful and surprising speculative engagement into the links between practices of needlework, desire and processes of global capitalism, labour markets, exploitation and migration. Through its unique setting in the United Kingdom and Bangladesh, the novel allows for an exploration of practices of needlework, particularly garment sewing, alongside questions of agency, political consciousness and the everyday politics of domesticity and paid labour within a transnational diasporic context. Home dressmaking has regained popularity over the last two decades, especially across Western Europe, Scandinavia, Britain and North America. The practice is often framed as the more sustainable response to the prevailing culture of fast fashion, its disastrous effects on the environment and the dangerous and exploitative working conditions sweatshop workers face in the Global South. These discourses, however, are often fairly limited with regard to the type of maker they envisage and do not sufficiently engage with the ways that class, race and locality intersect as part of transnational flows of power.

Through reading *Brick Lane* with a focus on the performance of sewing homework, I show how the novel illustrates the complexity of women's experience of paid and unpaid work in the realm of the home space. I consider how these practices are entangled with affect and unequal structures of power, thus highlighting the complexity of women's experiences of labour. As a result, conceptualizations of women's homework, particularly in relation to sewing and piecework in the global garment industry and a feminist politics of the everyday, are complicated. Through my focus on manufacturing homework and housework, this chapter also speaks to contemporary concerns about how the new rise in (digital) homeworking practices as a result of the Covid-19 pandemic may further entrench gender inequalities in labour markets (Chung *et al.* 2021). My analysis draws attention to manufacturing homework (as opposed to office work performed on a computer) and points to the ways in which many women have been performing homework alongside housework prior to the pandemic.

Having grown up in a rural Bangladeshi village, Nazneen comes to England as a young woman because of her arranged marriage to the older Chanu, a first generation immigrant who has been living in London for some years. As Nazneen tries to settle into her new married life in England, her sister Hasina also leaves their home village behind but follows her lover against her father's wishes to the capital Dhaka and attempts to make ends meet without any family support network. While Hasina joins the ranks of the 'garment girls' in Dhaka's factories, Nazneen eventually takes on paid piecework that she performs from her council flat in London's Tower Hamlets. With the sewing work, a love interest also enters Nazneen's life along with new financial and personal opportunities.

My discussion of *Brick Lane* does not aim to position the literary text as a 'transparent vehicle for conveying the "truth" of another's experience' (Whitehead 2017: 2) even though the novel is, in fact, loosely based on a qualitative ethnographic study by economist and social theorist Naila Kabeer (2000). Nor do I see the text as representative of all women's experiences. I do, however, find the literary to be a useful medium through which to become attuned to individuals' particularized experiences and the rich texture of their lives. The literary can generatively complicate cultural narratives, for example, about the meaning of practices of needlework and paid work for women, precisely through providing an account of lived experience marked by 'ambivalence, contradiction and paradox' that cannot be folded into neat binaries (Potter and Stonebridge 2014: 7; Whitehead 2017: 139). As such my analysis also avoids reductive readings of the novel that are overly concerned with Ali's Bangladeshi heritage and her background as an ethnically marked author. As Ali puts it, often her 'brown skin is the dominant signifier' along with her foreign-sounding name for the assessment of her literary work, which becomes overly focused around questions of authenticity and representation, instead of on the literary merits of the text (2003b: paras 14–15). Viewed as an imaginative literary experiment, *Brick Lane*, powerfully 'facilitate[s] our understanding of global women at work' through its particular fictional setting and characters and the detailed exploration of these (Marx 2006: 22). Grounded in the everyday life stories of Nazneen and Hasina, the novel gives texture to dominant narratives about identity, domesticity and women's employment in a transnational context.

Attention to the texture of the everyday life of the characters in the novel enables the tracing of the entangled trajectories that constitute the quotidian. It becomes possible to zoom in on a variety of object/subject/affect assemblages, that are part of everyday affective practices, and to explore their effects on the self and the relationship with others. The novel raises questions about what it means for different women from various backgrounds to work in London and Dhaka's global garment industry and it negotiates questions of identity and agency on an individual and collective level, thus responding to the larger questions about subjects' potential journeys to becoming political that are at the heart of *Needlework, Affect and Social Transformation*

Bringing together the work of practice theorists and scholars of affect, my focus is on 'processes of developmental sedimentation, routines of emotional regulation, relational patterns and "settling"' (Wetherell 2012: 22). I understand such processes as always embedded with potential and therefore as promising starting points for research into the dynamics of personal and social change. As routines settle into place and affective attachments form, the potential for things to be otherwise and for new subjectivities to emerge always lingers. Thus, my focus is on the affective social practices of homemaking and sewing that make up Nazneen's everyday life. Through them, I trace Nazneen's development from submissive housewife to paid homeworker and extramarital lover on to employed single mother.

First, the chapter explores Hasina's experience of factory work in relation to Kabeer's research, household gender roles, the Bangladeshi diaspora and Nazneen's journey to taking up homework. The next section offers a synthesis of the work of social psychologist Margaret Wetherell, alongside that of other practice theorists and scholars of affect, to provide a detailed theory of affective social practices of meaning making which I shall subsequently use to trace the impact of Nazneen's home-sewing practice on her development of self. I show how, through needlework, Nazneen is confronted with her own desires and ultimately moved towards following their pull. Her coming to consciousness is grounded within the texture of her everyday life shaped by housework, emotion work and homework for the sweatshop. As such, this chapter explores how personal, and, by extension, possibly social, transformation is not necessarily (and certainly not solely) founded on a 'radical rupture of consciousness' (Pedwell 2016: 4) but is steeped in the politics and textures of everyday practices of making.

Labour, Liberation and Literary Imagination

Kabeer's (2000) research into the labour-market decisions of Bangladeshi women was initially inspired by the apparent paradox of these choices. It appeared that in Bangladesh more and more women from mixed age groups and social backgrounds and of different marital status, were leaving the home space in order to work in factories. On visits to Bangladesh Kabeer observed that these developments were taking place irrespective of Bangladesh's strong tradition of female seclusion, or so-called purdah, which was a prominent practice in the workers' communities and family structures. Within Bangladeshi communities in Britain, however, a significant number of women evidently turned to home-based work 'at a time when research based on official statistics in the UK had declared that manufacturing homework was a "relative rarity"', not compliant with contemporary economic trends and Britain's long tradition of women's factory work (Kabeer 2000: vii–viii).

In *Brick Lane*, for Hasina, the initial encounter with paid work takes place outside the home and work is perceived as very liberating. Indeed, as literary studies scholar John Marx argues, the novel represents work as having an extraordinary effect on Hasina's sense of her place in the world' (2006: 21). Paid work in the garment factory empowers Hasina not only financially, but also on a personal level as she comes to feel part of a community in which she is valued, based on her skill as a machinist. Hasina claims that working is a 'cure' to the monotony of everyday life because 'sewing pass the day and I sit with friends. As actual fact it bring true friendship and true love' (Ali 2003a: 113). Like the Dhaka garment workers Kabeer interviewed for her study, Hasina and her colleagues seem to develop a 'new sense of identity and self-worth' through their work. However, this does not rule out an awareness on the side of the women of their often problematic and difficult labour conditions (Kabeer 2000: 189; see also Kabeer 2004). Intra-household relationships often changed significantly for the women as a result of their occupation and the stories of Hasina's colleagues echo accounts by Kabeer's participants. In *Brick Lane*, for example, Aleya uses her wages to send her children to school. Though her husband has consented to her working, he walks her to and from the factory and insists that she wear a burqa in order to safeguard her purdah. Shahnaz, a young unmarried colleague of Hasina, echoes Kabeer's findings in her questioning of the traditional practice of dowry to be paid by the bride's family when she states: 'Why should I give dowry? I am not a burden. I make money. I am the dowry' (Ali 2003a: 112).

However, Hasina's situation changes dramatically once she becomes romantically involved with her male co-worker, Abdul. Her positive descriptions of men and women working alongside each other like 'brother and sister', with women's purity secured because they 'keep purdah in the mind [where] no one can take it', change as her colleagues begin to shun her (Ali 2003a: 114). The women are concerned about Hasina's reputation and their own as both might be tarnished by gossip about the supposedly promiscuous nature of the so-called 'garment girls'. Ultimately, Hasina is fired from her position and Abdul rejects her, while their boss makes allowance for Abdul's behaviour because young men 'have to get a little practice in before marriage' (Ali 2003a: 120). Subsequently, Hasina is forced to resort to prostitution as a means to support herself until she eventually finds a position as a maid in a rich Bangladeshi household.

In contrast to the findings from Dhaka, Kabeer's study concludes that, in London, 'women's homeworking activity had a fairly limited impact on gender relationships within the household and in the wider community' (Kabeer 2000: 306). The homework has to be worked around the many other demands the women face in terms of hospitality, child rearing and household management – a dynamic with which many women are all too familiar since the pandemic-induced lockdowns (Chung *et al.* 2021). In the London Bangladeshi migrant community that Kabeer studied, homework provided a practical opportunity for the women to earn a small wage while, at the same time, observing their community's expectations of women with regards to purdah and domesticity. The women's income was generally very small, the stupendous and repetitive 'flat' machining they performed was regarded as unskilled women's work, and the broader family's involvement in this work was high because it took place within the home (Kabeer 2000: 280, 285). Yet, the majority of the women did share the 'view that women's capacity to earn was critical to the respect that they received within their families' (Kabeer 2000: 301). Nevertheless, this respect was limited, because the decision to perform homework had to be negotiated with regard to 'various anxieties related to the boundaries of gender, culture, and class' (Kabeer 2000: 238).

In contemporary industrialized and neoliberal capitalist societies working is framed as an inherent quality of the supposedly 'natural order' in which every individual is meant to earn a living through participation in the labour market (Weeks 2011: 3). As such, working is 'part of what is supposed to transform subjects into the independent individuals of the liberal imaginary' and not merely an economic necessity but a social one as well (Weeks 2011: 8). As 'a central component of daily life rather than an outcome', people may be worn out and frustrated by the rhythm of work, but also inspired by and pleased with what they do (Weeks 2011: 18). What counts as work is, of course, not only connected to the 'privileged model of waged labor', but also varies across time and is heavily gendered and classed (Weeks 2011: 14, 19; see also Glucksmann 2000). Women's work inside the home often goes unrecognized, is regarded as unskilled and – with the exception of the labour provided by domestic maids or servants – is usually unwaged. Paid domestic work engagements are often precarious, and the (mainly) lower-class and immigrant women working in the sector are often not protected by labour law due to a lack of employment contracts and social security (Chang 2016). Practices of needlework, as I outlined in the Introduction, inhabit a peculiar position within this dynamic of unwaged housework. Regarded as women's leisure activities as well as part of the clothes-care work women perform for the family, practices of needlework, even when remunerated, are often not recognized as work (Dawkins 2011; Stalp 2007).

Indeed, concerned about his status as head of the household and male provider, for Chanu, Nazneen's husband, paid piecework for the sweatshop only becomes an acceptable activity only once he realizes that the extra income would be useful to his plan for moving the family back to Bangladesh. While he used to be concerned that the additional work would interfere with Nazneen's household and childcare duties, the paid homework is reframed as an act of selfless devotion to the 'family project' of relocation even though Chanu is the sole proponent of this plan. Chanu compares the monotonous piecework to the 'old and honourable craft of tailoring' popular in Bangladesh and, in the process, elevates it from unskilled to skilled labour (Ali 2003a: 154). The sewing work is not framed within the exploitative context of sweatshop work and the global textile industry, but as reclaiming Bangladesh's rich textile history, which, according to Chanu, had been ruined by British colonialism through the implementation of tariffs on textile goods from Bangladesh and India (Ali 2003a: 236). Like Nazneen's housework and emotion work for the family's wellbeing, the paid homework is relegated to the background of day-to-day family life and is not part of a straightforward journey towards liberation. However, as I show in the remainder of this chapter, in the form of the routine practice of sewing, the paid homework also functions as a starting point for Nazneen's orientation towards resistant affects like her increased unhappiness with her situation and her budding desire not only for Karim, but also for a different way of being.

Novelist Diran Adebayo locates the power of the contemporary postcolonial novel in its ability 'to tell universal truths from a different angle that's been less explored' (quoted in Ali and Adebayo 2004: 350). A radical claim to imagination then becomes a powerful tool for marginalized groups to claim authority: the authority to imagine and tell stories that naturally oscillate between personal experience and imagination, and need not be fixed by conventional expectations of realism and literary genre. For bell hooks, fiction is a means of defying power because it can be reflective of an imagination suffused with resistance (1991a; see also Brochin and Medina 2017). As hooks suggests, 'critical fictions disrupt conventional ways of thinking about the imagination and imaginative work, offering fictions that demand careful scrutiny [and] resist passive readership' (1991a: 56). For example, Alice Walker's and Toni Morrison's literary works, as I have shown in the previous chapter, provide powerful counter narratives to state institutionalized discourses about slavery. *Brick Lane* represents an entanglement of different meanings and no singular truth can be extracted through a normative reading practice. Instead, the practice of reading itself serves to orient and move the reader, not in the sense that contemporary fiction is necessarily a vehicle for mutual understanding or empathy, but in the way it stages a confrontation with the unequal flows of power that are invariably part of encounters between different subjects (Davis 2016; Whitehead 2017). Thus, fiction, as novelist Luisa Valenzuela puts it, can stimulate 'the imaginary expression of desire' (1991: 82) and, as such, functions as a 'progressive force that underlines movement [and] resists interpretation and any final closure' (Gorton 2008: 1). With Walker's and Morrison's work, as I discussed in chapter one, it provides moments for dwelling in the possibility of a differently arranged future in which new kinds of entanglements form and, thus, prefigures more just ways of living together that value Black life. A close analysis of the housework and paid homework that Nazneen performs for the sweatshop then becomes a productive way of critically examining dominant narratives about domesticity, paid work, women's self-liberation as well as the meaning and potential of home dressmaking.

Housework, Affect and the Fashioning of the Self

For Nazneen, the introduction of paid work into the home is not connected to a radical change in consciousness or position but is, instead, accompanied by a gradual shift in self-understanding. With the sewing machine and the paid homework, new 'patterns of active practices of potential' enter Nazneen's home space (Wetherell 2012: 22). Practice theory regards human beings as part of complex assemblages of body, mind, things as well as social structures and processes. It is interested in how humans make sense of themselves and the world through diverse routine activities. While these routine practices are seen as foundational to people's sense of self, subjects are not solely determined by them. Subjects are active agents, while, at the same time also, shaped by different practices and their entanglements with larger social, cultural, economic, political and affective configurations that may be outside their conscious grasp. In other words, people are part of complex 'object/subject/affect assemblages' (Knudsen and Stage 2015: 9). A practice then is a 'routinized type of behaviour which consists of several elements, interconnected to one other' (Reckwitz 2002: 249). A focus on practices makes it possible to explore the connections between 'bodily routines of behaviour, mental routines of understanding and knowing and the use of objects' in relation to micro- and macro-level social, cultural and political structures (Reckwitz 2002: 258).

Practice theory examines the points of intersection and divergence of object/subject/affect assemblages and follows their patterns across time and place: ways of cooking, consuming, sewing or embroidering. Performing such practices implies knowledge about the way in which certain elements are put together, what materials or objects are needed, and what movements need to be performed, for example, when sewing a button to a shirt. In addition, the performance of these practices may include certain emotional states and affective experiences that may be fleeting or recurring, may assist with the performance of the practice or even disrupt it (Martinussen and Wetherell 2019; Reckwitz 2002; Wetherell 2012). These feelings may include the pleasure of playing with colourful materials and creating objects like a new dress or a quilt that can be admired and used once completed. Likewise, the moment of making can be accompanied by states of frustration as a particular seam will not lie flat or it turns out that a piece of fabric has been cut too small and will not fit. In addition, as I outlined in my discussion of Black women's resistant quilting practices in the previous chapter, making can also be accompanied by feelings of anxiety, fear or anger as well as love and care as it is linked to beloved family members or social justice issues.

Synthesizing the work of practice theorists from the social sciences, psychology, neuroscience and philosophy, Margaret Wetherell (2012) has developed a theory of affective practices to highlight the crucial role of affect in routine activities and to explore the links between feelings and the unequal flows of power that make up everyday life. As a result of exploring these entanglements she encounters 'shifting, flexible and often over-determined figurations rather than simple lines of causation, character types and neat emotion categories' (Wetherell 2012: 4). In this sense, theories of affective practice reject - or rather find it impossible - to differentiate between emotion and affect in the way that some affect scholars like Brian Massumi (2002) and Patricia Clough (2007) suggest. Broadly speaking, for scholars following the critical trajectory of Massumi, affect and emotion are two separate entities, because emotion can technically be controlled and is actively felt and experienced. In contrast to that, affect supposedly exceeds discourse and is outside the conscious grasp of humans. However, affective practices are entanglements 'in which all the parts relationally constitute each other' (Wetherell 2012: 18). Meaning, then, is the result of the various constellations of the parts and, yet, is also subject to change in response to new configurations. The shift from being an unconscious sensation (i.e. affect) to a conscious emotion cannot be pinpointed either and, as other affect scholars have argued, one might actually imply the existence of the other (Ahmed 2004: 6).

According to Wetherell, theories of affective practice need to recognize that 'affect has conscious and non-conscious, bodily and cognitive, elements linked in highly complex ways' (2012: 61). Consequently, the study of affect needs to be concerned with the conscious and unconscious as much as with the social, the discursive and the material. It is only through an attention to all these elements, she argues, that processes of affective meaning making can be traced as the 'flow of affect is located in the body [and] in the flow of ordinary life' (Wetherell 2012: 77; see also Ahmed 2004; Stewart 2007). For Wetherell 'an affective practice is a figuration where body possibilities and routines become recruited or entangled together with meaning-making and with other social and material figurations' (2012: 18). Affective as well as social practices co-constitute each other and can be generatively perceived as object/subject/affect assemblages that are interconnected but also constantly in flux. For this reason, it is not always useful to try to single out particular elements of this assemblage as this could have a debilitating effect on the dynamic patterns and 'lines of flight' they create as well as make it impossible to trace them, and I refrain from doing so throughout this book.

Housework is one key affective practice that shapes Nazneen's sense of self and her everyday life. The term 'housework', since the early seventeenth century, has functioned as an umbrella term for all the practices associated with housekeeping and the armada of chores found in the domestic sphere (OED n.d.). While typically these chores include cleaning, cooking and childcare, the term is ultimately rather vague in that 'it can include all these elements (and more) and has no specific practices, set of objects or temporal boundary' (Highmore 2011: 91). It is unclear where it begins and ends, both with regards to the temporal structure of a day and with the practices it includes. Some of them will be the same on a daily basis or as part of a weekly or monthly routine such as doing the laundry, changing the sheets or thoroughly cleaning the bathroom. However, it may also include unexpected tasks that could not have been scheduled in advance, such as nurturing the sick or attending to various forms of spillage and breakage, for example, a child's spilt glass of orange juice, or, though more extreme, dealing with the excess of water flooding the home because of a burst pipe. It is a practice marked by repetition and ephemerality, 'essential to the life of a household, but so quickly needed again' (Highmore 2011: 91). For feminist theorist Rita Felski (1999), such forms of repetition are an essential part of the experience of everyday life: on the one hand, they provide a form of security and reassurance within the chaos of the contemporary world as a reliable habit that structures one's life; on the other hand, this repetition can be experienced in terms of endless drudgery and boredom. In sum, 'repetition can signal resistance as well as enslavement' (Felski 1999: 21). The same can be said of the home space as the epitome of everyday life. For Highmore, due to 'ordinary life [being] the arena of fear and threat as much as it is of reassurance and safety', the home is also a 'highly charged political arena' (2011: 20). Unequal flows of power can be reproduced in everyday life and the home space, but both can also form the realm in which people are slowly moved towards imagining and materializing different ways of being.

The figure of the housewife is tied to this complex perception of housework and the home space. As the traditional manager of the household, the home space falls within her domain. As a result, particularly in the 1940s and 1950s, the figure of the housewife became a dominant popular representation of women and also a specific target for advertising (Hardy 2012; Johnson and Lloyd 2004). This narrative suggested that the experience of physical drudgery that many housewives encountered could be alleviated through new technological gadgets that were intended to aid women with their daily chores (Johnson and Lloyd 2004: 157). The regained freedom of time, however, was soon reframed within discourses of boredom and in opposition to the popular myth of the 'happy housewife', especially as part of the second-wave feminist movement (Johnson and Lloyd 2004: 157). In addition, as techno-feminists have argued, the introduction of new technologies into the home did not actually reduce the workload for women but just shifted it along with expectations about what constitutes a clean home (Schwartz-Cowan 1997). Second-wave feminism paid particular attention to the ways in which housework functioned as a form of enslavement for women, because it was basically a form of unpaid labour in the home. As a result, many second-wave feminists placed housework at the root of wider social issues of sexism, gender inequality and patriarchy (Friedan [1963] 2010; Greer [1970] 2012; Oakley 1974; Malos 1980). According to these narratives, housework and the role of the housewife denied women the freedom of self-actualization. As a result, demands for wages for housework were voiced, particularly, in the 1970s, partly also as a means of demonstrating that women did not simply perform domestic labour because it was in their nature to do so (Weeks 2011: 113). However, as Leslie Johnson and Justine Lloyd show, second-wave feminism grounded its critique of housework within wider modern narratives about individual identity and choice and, ultimately, within a 'linear narrative of liberation' through paid work (2004: 13–14).

I am conscious of the danger of conflating Nazneen's experience as a South Asian immigrant in London between the 1980s and the mid-2000s with a narrative put forward primarily by white, middle-class, second-wave feminists in the United States and Britain. However, as will become clearer throughout the rest of this chapter, the novel does echo second-wave feminism's narrative of women's self-actualization through paid work, alongside perceptions of the oppressive home space. Second-wave feminism attempted to trace and explicate the patterns of women's everyday domestic experience and its attendant affective practices in consciousness-raising groups. These meetings were intended to provide women with a space in which to 'reach a feminist account, as an account for oneself with and through others, connecting [personal] experience with the experience of others' (Ahmed 2017: 30). The home space, with its attendant practices of housework, was the primary realm in which these accounts formed and, thus, the starting point for a politics in which the personal was always also political. Nazneen's cluttered apartment is the space in which she experiences oppression, boredom and unhappiness. Once in London, Nazneen's everyday practices of housekeeping and her daily rhythms align themselves with everyday British ways of being. Her life is marked by repetition as she spends her days cleaning the flat, doing laundry and preparing food for her husband and children, as well as tending to her husband's corns and facial hair.

When Nazneen is ill and unable to complete her regular chores for a number of days, Chanu stays home from work in order to assist his wife. Failing to properly perform any tasks, he tries to gloss over his shortcomings by 'philosophizing about the nature of housework' as Nazneen and the girls attempt to tidy up the flat (Ali 2003a: 251). Still shaky on her legs, Nazneen finds that:

> the sitting room crawled with toys, clothes, books and abandoned kitchen utensils. A pack of toilet rolls stood on the table; five tins of baked beans nested

on the sofa. Attempts had been made to unpack shopping bags, but at some stage between bag and cupboard each attempt had foundered. If a bag had been emptied it lay on the floor and gaped with the mess. Emergency rations of food marked the path from door to sofa to table.

Ali 2003a: 244

Chanu is described as 'helpless in the face of this natural disaster', while he tries to 'direct [the] operations' of the clean-up (Ali 2003a: 251–2). He explains to his daughters that housework is 'not easy' and reminds them that their mother does not 'have an easy job' – without recognizing how he contributes to the difficulty of this job as he 'ate slices of bread spread with ghur and saw no necessity for a plate' while 'Nazneen swept around him' (Ali 2003a: 252). Housework is described as being a 'little like God, without end or beginning. It simply *was*' (Ali 2003a: 251, original emphasis). It is not clear who is speaking at this point, whether it is the third-person narrator repeating Chanu's expostulations or free indirect discourse with Nazneen as the focalizer. Nonetheless, it highlights how the woman's presence in the home is taken for granted in the same way that her labour is. For Nazneen, however, the messy apartment also provides 'some satisfaction' because 'for years she had felt she must not relax. If she relaxed, things would fall apart. Solely, the constant vigilance and planning, the low-level, unremarked and unrewarded activity of a woman, kept the household from crumbling' (Ali 2003a: 244). Only once the household does start to crumble does this activity get dragged out of its invisibility.

Patterns of Everyday Making and Being

As Nazneen cooks, cleans, sleeps and keeps her husband company, her everyday life is, at least, in some aspects, familiar to many people. Surprisingly though, the most defining feature of the everyday as a shared experience is the fact that it is lacking any explicit characteristics. It is ubiquitous in that it refers simply to the ordinary elements of our daily existence, but in a manner that is also 'strangely elusive, resists our understanding and escapes our grasp' (Felski 1999: 15). At the same time, it is also the realm in which the extraordinary takes place and the backdrop against which we define the latter (Highmore 2002a: 16; see also Stewart 2007). As such, as Highmore puts it, everyday life 'signifies ambivalently' (2002a: 1). It can be the realm of reassuring routine as well as of oppressive boredom and these perceptions may alter depending on their context. As the realm in which Nazneen's homemaking and sewing practices are performed, the everyday is also where her personal change starts to take shape.

Although ubiquitous, the everyday 'is not abstract' (Highmore 2011: 2) and neither are affective practices. They are grounded in material structures that make up the physical environment of the everyday. With regard to the home space, the 'banal materiality of everyday life in the home' includes items of furniture, and utility objects as much as decorative ones (Pink, Mackley and Morosanu 2015: 210). On her arrival in England, Nazneen finds that her husband has already filled their home, a small flat in London's Tower Hamlets, with more furniture than she had ever seen in one room before. The living room houses:

> a low table with a glass centre and orange plastic legs, three little wooden tables that stacked together, the big table they used for the evening meal, a bookcase, a corner cupboard, a rack for newspapers, a trolley filled with files and folders, the sofa and armchairs, two footstools, six dining chairs and a showcase. . . . There were plates on the wall, attached by hooks and wires which were not for eating from but only for display.
>
> Ali 2003a: 14

The glass showcase is 'stuffed with pottery animals, china figures and plastic fruits' graced with a fine film of dust (Ali 2003a: 14). It is in this environment that Nazneen spends the majority of her life in England, particularly in the beginning as she barely leaves the house – passing her days cooking and cleaning, or aimlessly drifting around from room to room in between these activities.

For literary critic Sukhdev Sandhu, Ali's detailed attention to the apartment's interior and Nazneen's daily chores appears 'flatly compendious . . . or pointlessly accretive' (2003: para. 31). He fails to acknowledge the importance of the material structures that shape the quotidian as they themselves are subject to continuous change. They can shift place and shape, break, disappear or be replaced and as such are part of 'an ongoing process through which the textures of home are continually renegotiated and renewed' (Pink, Mackley and Morosanu 2015: 221). They provide the space 'for the exploration of Nazneen's sense of self' (Cuming 2013: 340) and, as such, are deeply connected to affective meaning-making practices. As Nazneen's situation becomes more unbearable, so does the flat become more cluttered and packed with books, stacks of papers and broken chairs that Chanu plans one day to repair and sell. The interior of the apartment forms part of what Cvetkovich in her analysis of the intersection of private life, public feeling cultures and life in contemporary neoliberal capitalist systems refers to as 'the texture of lived experience and its complex combinations of hope and despair' (2012: 158).

When Nazneen first arrives in London, she takes pride in the interior of her husband's apartment and in the sheer number of its contents since no one in her Bangladeshi home village had ever had such possessions (Ali 2003a: 14). However, her perception shifts over time and 'the flaws in the flat's décor' become representative of her own unfulfilled hopes and desires (Hiddleston 2005: 65). Nazneen feels 'trapped inside this body, inside this room, inside this flat, inside this concrete slab of entombed humanity. They had nothing to do with her' (Ali 2003a: 56). Her daily activities become perforated by what the novel refers to as 'domestic guerrilla actions' as Nazneen 'hated the socks as she rubbed them with soap, and dropped the pottery tiger and elephant as she dusted them and was disappointed when they did not break' (Ali 2003a: 75, 30). Yet, Nazneen eventually discards these actions because, ultimately 'they annoyed only her' and her husband appears immune to her unhappiness (Ali 2003a: 75).

The experience of everyday life, according to affect theorist Kathleen Stewart, is essentially a phenomenological one as it is 'a life lived on the level of surging affects, impacts suffered or barely avoided' (2007: 9). It cannot only be felt through the material which impresses on the body, including the clothes that we wear, but also through what Highmore calls 'the immaterial material, [that is] affect, emotion and the senses' (2011: 140). As Nazneen conducts her daily life within the confines of her council flat and the wider council estate, 'life made its pattern around and beneath and through her' (Ali 2003a: 30). Her body adjusts to these domestic rhythms as she cleans and prepares meals for her husband, but also rebels against them as she avoids sharing meals with him and eats while cooking in the afternoon or gets up in the middle of the night to raid the fridge for leftovers (Ali 2003a: 30). For Wetherell, the study of affect is ultimately the study of patterns, although these patterns are not necessarily fixed but:

> multiple, dynamic, intersecting, sometimes personal and sometimes impersonal. Patterns are sometimes imposed, sometimes a matter of actively 'seeing a way through' to what comes next, and sometimes, like a repertoire, simply what is to hand, relatively ready-made and 'thoughtless'.
>
> 2012: 46–8

The patterns are part of the texture of everyday life and Nazneen's sewing work becomes part of these patterns.

However, it takes time and, literally, practice for patterns to settle and this is not a straightforward process either. The motions required to operate the sewing machine, at first, are foreign to Nazneen and she has to learn how to use it. Nazneen has to practise for two weeks in order to learn how to sew on buttons, hem trousers and insert zippers, under the guidance of Chanu and her friend and neighbour, Razia. Once she has mastered all the features and techniques, Chanu claims that 'all you have to do is sit there' in front of the sewing machine and perform the motions (Ali 2003a: 154). Nazneen's piecework is placed in the same supposedly omnipresent space that her housework occupies. She sews while the other activities of the household are taking place around her – such as Chanu reading or watching the television, and her daughters doing their homework. Placing the fabric under the presser foot of the machine, inserting the bobbin and controlling the foot pedal become routine motions that in their specific pattern form a practice. Yet, the motions of a practice can be interrupted and one may be required to pause and realign. Thread might get tangled up in the sewing machine, bobbin thread might run out, and a glossy material may cause the piece to slip; stitches may need to be taken out and reworked. Changing emotional landscapes and sudden bursts of affect may also defer the seamless flow of a practice. For Nazneen, it is her lust and yearning for Karim that comes to interrupt the regular flow of her sewing.

Orienting Desire

Desire plays an important role in Nazneen's self-transformation and serves to orient her along different lines of being. With the paid homework comes not only the promise of a salary and ultimately financial independence, but also the young and attractive middleman Karim who delivers her sewing to her home and collects the finished pieces. He awakens a physical desire in Nazneen that she has never before experienced. With her husband, sexual intercourse is an act that is part of Nazneen's routine of married life, in the same way that cooking, cleaning and cutting her husband's corns are. It is an act she endures, but it does not give her pleasure. Her perceptions of her husband and their shared bed are tied up with his capacious physical presence and the way his large belly sticks out and his body comes to touch hers in the middle of the night, as he takes up most of the bed (Ali 2003a: 57, 96, 131, 246). Although Nazneen is the focalizer of these observations, they are mainly descriptive in nature and do not necessarily resemble expressions of repulsion. By contrast, when Nazneen takes note of Karim and his body, it is clearly linked to pleasure and desire as Nazneen takes in his broad shoulders and muscular forearms as well as his confident movements.

Chanu, on the other hand, is presented as insecure and ultimately unsettled, despite his large physical presence, as he struggles to find his place in British society and the wider Bangladeshi immigrant community. The discovery of her own desire is as new to Nazneen as actually embracing this desire. Following tradition, she had subordinated her own needs and wants to those of her husband, as well as to society's normative expectations, and had never directly voiced them. Instead, she had learned to ask for things by framing them as her husband's wishes or concerns for his well-being. Her lust for Karim is experienced as intensely embodied as she becomes acutely aware of her own body and presence 'as though just now she had come to inhabit it for the first time and it was both strange and wonderful to have this new and physical expression' (Ali 2003a: 255).

Though the first moment of intimacy between the two is not narrated, Nazneen is subsequently presented as an active participant in their sexual encounters as Karim moans 's-slow down. . . . But she could not' (Ali 2003a: 223). Desire for Nazneen comes to interrupt her daily routines as:

> in the mornings she said her prayers and did housework and began her sewing and there was nothing inside her that demanded more. By lunchtime when she looked for Karim out of the window, her stomach began to surge with excitement and dread and on the days when he did not come she had to leave the flat and walk around the streets for fear that she would wear out the remaining threads of carpet.
>
> Ali 2003a: 285

Her ordinary state of being is upset by the experience of these new and conflicting feelings that 'give everyday life the quality of a continual motion of relations, scenes, contingencies, and emergences' (Stewart 2007: 2). Nazneen's experience of her newly found desire is charged with tension as it makes her way into the rhythm of her everyday life. The meaning of this desire and its attendant affects of exhilaration, but also shame and remorse, is unclear to Nazneen. It is impossible to reduce to something that is simply good or bad. Nazneen's yearning for Karim, although new and exhilarating, is experienced within the same quotidian setting in which she feels sad, tired and bored; and it is precisely in these relational modes of experience – in which different practices and affects intersect – that alternative meanings and forms of being outside restrictive binary categories become a possibility (Stewart 2007: 3). Nazneen's desire leads to the development of its own routine grounded in her and Karim's daily schedules as they attempt to fit in meetings in her flat while the girls and Chanu are not at home under the pretence of Karim delivering or collecting Nazneen's sewing (Ali 2003a: 223). 'Notions like "routine" and its cognates', for scholar Don Slater, 'are labels that accord particular social status and value to particular forms of action and practices, and that strategically stabilize them in specific ways' (2009: 217). In this sense, a practice constituted by a mental and physical routine can 'be evaluated … in terms of [its] potential for expanding or contracting social agency, reflexivity and critical consciousness' (Slater 2009: 217–18), in the same manner that the everyday can be described as a realm of potential, but also oppression. A routine practice can resemble an attachment to certain structures that secure the status quo, but can also be a starting point for redefining it through a change in routine in the way that Nazneen's new relationship with Karim affects her daily habits and sense of self.

Feminist media studies and affect scholar Kristyn Gorton describes desire as a 'fluid, multiple and dynamic force that is transformative, destructive and life-changing' (2008: 1). Desire signifies ambivalently in a manner similar to the everyday and affective practices in its embodiment of potential as well as lack and restraint (see also Menon 2018). Phenomenologically speaking, desire can be conceptualized as movement, as it orients a person towards certain objects, people, places, affects or ideals in the past, present and future (Ahmed 2006a; Gorton 2008). As such, desire is 'always in progress and therefore difficult to pin down', in the same manner that affect is dynamic in its traversing different patterns of ordinary life (Gorton 2008: 4; Menon 2018: 21; Wetherell 2012: 77). While Nazneen, on the one hand, reproaches herself for her illegitimate relationship with Karim, she, nonetheless, does not bring it to a close as 'she drew him like a moth to the flame' and 'tenderness could not satisfy her, nor could she stand it' (Ali 2003a: 223). The affective surges of her own desire cannot be quietened and during their intimate encounters, Nazneen is moved by 'desire's pull towards an impossible transcendence [which] creates a lack and, at the same time, a draw' (Gorton 2008: 10). For Nazneen, 'in the bedroom everything changed. Things became more real and they became less real. Like a Sufi in a trance, a whirling dervish, [Nazneen] lost the thread of one existence and found another' (Ali 2003a: 223). It is in those moments that Nazneen gives in to her desire, as opposed to social norms or the passive submission to fate preached by her own mother. As her desire disrupts the monotony of her everyday life, she is reoriented in her sense of self as new affective patterns take shape that offer different forms of being.

Through much of the novel, Nazneen's relationship to her own desires is conflicted, especially with regard to her affair with Karim: it makes her both 'sick with shame [and] sick with desire' (Ali 2003a: 223). This experience is powerfully captured by a scene where Nazneen spontaneously tries on one of the sequined vests she has been working on for the sweatshop. The sparkling material of the sequins reminds her of the figure ice skaters she enjoys watching on television and she is intrigued by the potential that appears embedded in the fancy material. As she slips on the vest as opposed to her usual sari, her mind is transported to visions of herself elegantly floating across the ice with Karim by her side. Yet, she suddenly becomes acutely aware of the adulterous nature of her thoughts and quickly slips off the top. She notices that, in reality, 'the sequins were cheap' and, in a matter of seconds, the formerly beautiful garment had changed to what 'looked like fish scales' (Ali 2003a: 163). Nazneen is well aware that adultery is a crime within the Bangladeshi community, one that in her home country might be punished with the death penalty. Eventually, her guilt about her affair, in part, causes her nervous breakdown as Nazneen becomes overwhelmed with juggling her household chores, filial and cultural responsibilities, and her personal desire. '[I]n between the sheets, in between his arms, she took her pleasure desperately, as if the executioner waited behind the door. Beyond death was the eternal fire of hell and from every touch of flesh on flesh she wrought the strength to endure it' (Ali 2003a: 223). However, 'out of the bedroom, she was – in starts – afraid and defiant' (Ali 2003a: 223), as she is stricken with inner turmoil about her actions, her own desire and her knowledge about what is considered appropriate social conduct. In this scene, as in others, 'the cloth appears to express and absorb desire and pleasure without pressuring to resolve the difficulties it implies' (Millar and Kettle 2018: 14). It is a tangible material expression of Nazneen's most secret desires and dreams and at the same time a cruel reminder of her transgressive thoughts, feelings and actions.

Affective Sartorial Potential

Nazneen is worn down by the patterns of everyday life and 'had to concentrate hard to get through each day' (Ali 2003a: 152). The death of her infant son Raqib leaves her with trauma from which she never fully recovers. Although the period directly following Raqib's death is not actually narrated, it is insinuated that much of Nazneen's later mental health struggle is connected to this experience. The everyday rhythms and demands of life as a wife and mother of two girls take their toll on Nazneen's well-being as 'sometimes she felt she held her breath the entire evening. It was up to her to balance the competing needs, to soothe here and urge there, and push the day along to its close' (Ali 2003a: 152). Nazneen questions her ability as a mother as:

> on bad nights when her thoughts could not be submerged by rice or bread or crackers she began to wonder if she loved her daughters properly. Did she love them as she had loved her son? When she thought of them like this – when they grew distant – her stomach fell down through her legs and her lungs shot up against her heart. . . . And she squeezed Raqib from her mind. That way lay the abyss. So she swallowed hard and prayed hard, and she used prayer, in defiance of her vows, to dull her senses and to dull her pain.
>
> Ali 2003a: 152–3

Steady perseverance with her daily chores becomes Nazneen's coping mechanism to deal with personal loss and her unhappiness, though 'it took all her energy. It took away longing. Her wants were close at hand, real and within her control. If only she focused sufficiently' (Ali 2003a: 152). These patterns of perseverance, however, are also regularly interspersed with what Stewart calls moments of 'surging affects' (2007: 9), as, 'sometimes, when [Nazneen] put her head on the pillow and began to drift into sleep, she jerked herself awake in panic. How could she afford to relax?' (Ali 2003a: 152). The instances in which Nazneen 'failed' to sustain the household's equilibrium are described as 'eruptions' accompanied by 'a flogging or a tantrum or a tear-stained flat cheek' that make her feel 'dizzy with responsibility' (Ali 2003a: 152).

As a 'shifting assemblage of practices and practical knowledges', the ordinary and quotidian are closely linked with affects (Stewart 2007: 1). Yet, it is also this shifting nature that makes it almost impossible to capture the quotidian through cultural, sociological and empirical research. The ordinary and its attendant affects can only ever be approximated by zooming in on the object/subject/affect assemblages that are often fleeting and yet also recurring through their repetitive performance (Knudsen and Stage 2015: 9). In this context, the literary offers a medium through which to zoom in on these entanglements and explore the texture of everyday life without staging authoritative claims. It becomes a means to discovering and tracing various patterns as opposed to establishing one guiding plot line around which all stories must be arranged (Ingold 2016: 77). Narrative, or the telling of stories, is thus always also a 'form of world-making' (Nikoleris, Stripple and Tenngart 2017). It recognizes the value of individual women's lived experiences and the way these experiences 'do impact and are impacted by' what scholar Michelle M. Wright calls '"glocal" forces': the interconnection of the global and the local (2014: 335). It is through storytelling as a shared practice of meaning making that attention to 'the actual lines of potential that a something coming together calls to mind and sets in motion' becomes possible (Stewart 2007: 2). Tracing how these lines come together, how patterns are interwoven and form 'affective ruts' offers ways of exploring how people engage with the 'momentous and the global political' (Wetherell 2012: 14, 7). In the rest of this chapter, as I look at the ways in which Nazneen's sewing for the sweatshop and her daily homemaking routines orient and move her, I flesh out how these practices are implicated within the 'glocal forces' of the garment industry, gendered discourses about homework and neoliberal discourses about women's self-actualization.

The sewing comes to inhabit an ambiguous, but also flexible and generative, position in Nazneen's life. On the one hand, it resembles a mindless routine similar to housework as she stitches zip after zip, and hem after hem, trying to meet the deadlines amidst finishing her other household chores. On the other hand, the homework for the sweatshop and the sewing machine as a material object become tied intrinsically to Nazneen's sexual desire and her illegitimate relationship with Karim. In this relationship, Nazneen is driven by her wish to take her own pleasure above his or anyone else's and as such it also symbolizes potential, that is, 'a layer, or layering to the ordinary, [that] engenders attachments or systems of investment in the unfolding of things' (Stewart 2007: 21). Through her relationship with Karim, Nazneen 'sense[s] her own existence for the first time in her marriage' (Kuo 2014: 180). In the conversations with her friend, Razia, and the wider Bangladeshi community on the housing estate, the sewing homework becomes representative of the open rumour about Nazneen and Karim's affair. His frequent and prolonged visits to Nazneen's apartment have made the neighbours suspicious that their relationship might be more than simply professional. When her neighbour, Nazma, casually drops by Nazneen's flat to borrow some spices, Nazma suggestively slides her hands across Nazneen's sewing machine on the dining table as she inquires in a supposedly casual manner whether Nazneen is still being provided with sufficient work by her middleman (Ali 2003a: 272, 285).

As Nazneen and Razia canvas the various fabric shops in London's East End, Nazneen is acutely aware of her secret as she cradles and examines the different types of fabric on the bolts. Razia clearly has her own suspicions about Nazneen's relationship with Karim but, instead of addressing the subject, they 'discussed material. They spoke of weight and colour, texture and sturdiness, loveliness and ease of care. They pulled out roll after roll . . . [and] all the while Nazneen counted her secrets' (Ali 2003a: 232). Sewing is further linked with Nazneen's sexual desire, as she is unable to concentrate on her work with Karim in the room. She is aroused as Karim teasingly hides a handful of buttons that belong to Nazneen's work assignment in the pocket of his jeans and 'Nazneen felt an electric current run from her nipples to her big toes. . . . Nazneen tried not to think of the buttons. She could think of nothing else' (Ali 2003a: 194). Nazneen's descriptions of her own arousal are linked to sartorial imagery as 'her skin was attached to thousands of fine silk threads, all of them pulling, pricking at the point of tension' and she perceives 'a needle of excitement down her thigh' (Ali 2003a: 194, 255). Echoing long-standing links between cloth and the erotic (Kettle and Millar 2018), the fabric and sewing paraphernalia become imbued with Nazneen's sexual desire for Karim.

Sewing a New Sense of Self

While Nazneen sews, Karim often keeps her company. He works on texts for the Muslim activist group he recently founded on the estate and lectures her about Black and Muslim resistance. However, unlike the occasions in which Chanu lectures her about the world, Nazneen is actually expected to participate in these conversations by answering and she consciously soaks up the information and reflects on it. In fact, Karim criticizes her for 'always working' and demands that Nazneen 'talk to [him]. Leave it' (Ali 2003a: 194). Nazneen replies that '[she] will listen. You talk' but also remarks that 'buttons will not sew themselves', thus drawing attention to the fact that her homework, like housework, does not take place in the omnipresent manner that Chanu believes; it requires her active participation (Ali 2003a: 193). While Chanu appears to need an audience to which he can feel superior, Karim 'makes [Nazneen] feel as if she had said a weighty piece, as if she had stated a new truth' (Ali 2003a: 194).

Through Karim, Nazneen is introduced to another world outside the domestic and the marital unit, as she is encouraged by his political activism to attend the meetings of the local Muslim activist group which 'stimulates Nazneen's awareness of ethnic politics and how she might be able to reposition herself in the wider society' (Kuo 2014: 179). Yet, their relationship is not only marked by the exciting and exceptional, it also involves familiar practices that Nazneen usually performs as part of her married life. She serves and assists Karim in the way that she normally does Chanu, bringing him food or anything else that he requests while he lounges on the sofa in Nazneen's apartment. However, unlike with her husband, for Nazneen these chores are connected to her sexual desire to Karim and 'this playing house' provides her with a 'thrill' (Ali 2003a: 223). They are affective practices elevated above the routine of the everyday through new attachments and yet firmly grounded in it.

Due to its flexible and transformative nature, desire has been linked to processes of self-awakening. Gorton, in her discussion of desire in fiction and film, is particularly interested in 'the way in which desire does something to the characters and the narrative to move them along, to change the path they have been on, to transform the way they see the world' (2008: 4). In this vein, literary studies scholar Hsin-Ju Kuo argues that 'bodily transgressive acts generate, in Nazneen, a process of becoming, moving her from a fixed identity inscribed by conventional patriarchal society in her early years of marriage, to a more fluid and borderless one at the end of the story' (2014: 179). Towards the end of the novel, Nazneen decides to separate from Chanu. She will not accompany him back to Bangladesh, but remain in London with her two daughters. In addition, she rejects Karim's offer of marriage as she realizes that her sexual desire for him was coupled with a desire for personal self-transformation. She also comes to see that their relationship was driven by their mutual longing for a negotiation of the meaning of home and the self within the context of their migrant cultures. In his mind, Karim had framed Nazneen as 'the real thing. A Bengali wife. A Bengali mother. An idea of home. An idea of himself that he found in her' that was inherently tied to Nazneen's background as a supposedly 'unspoilt girl. From the village' (Ali 2003a: 337, 286). Nazneen, likewise, realizes that Karim had served as a mirror for her desire and the wish to negotiate her position as a woman in London's Brick Lane community. She acknowledges that she 'had patched him together, working in the dark. She had made a quilt out of pieces of silk, scraps of velvet, and now that she held it up to the light the stitches showed up large and crude, and they cut across everything' (Ali 2003a: 337). Her image of him had to be actively created and pieced together through acts of affective meaning making. The sartorial imagery, once again, highlights the deep connection between her sewing practice and the awakening of desire. Nazneen concludes that they both 'made each other up', because, throughout their relationship, 'I wasn't me, and you weren't you': they were both idealized materializations of each other's desires (Ali 2003a: 337). With this realization, Nazneen decides to remain in London as a single mother supporting her daughters and herself through her own labour.

On multiple levels, her relationship with Karim helps Nazneen 'to know what [she] could do' in terms of her economic, sexual and political agency (Ali 2003a: 361). As a result, her adultery is reframed in terms of women's autonomy and removed from the patriarchal and hierarchical discourse that paints it as immoral

(Kuo 2014: 179; Das 2016: 17). Her sexual relationship with Karim functions as a 'means of psychological development' and 'less as a moral transgression' (Kuo 2014: 171). Through new patterns of affective social practices that include, among others, the anticipation of their meetings, their arousal and actual physical intercourse, their joint time spent in the living room, as well as Nazneen's sewing work for the sweatshop, she discovers forms of consciousness that empower her to position herself differently within her diasporic environment. The home space and the everyday, in this context, provide a 'liminal space' in which Nazneen is restrained in her desire and choice of options while she struggles with familial conflict. Yet, it is also within these very confines that she comes upon a 'threshold of transformation created by the intertwined relationships among and continuous traversing of private/individual and public/ community spheres' (Kuo 2014: 178). As a symbol of this change within Nazneen's identity, the sewing machine remains on the dining table as the last item to be packed while the remaining household goods have already been placed into boxes or marked for auction and charity in anticipation of the family's proposed move to Bangladesh (Ali 2003a: 342). The sewing machine is representative of Nazneen's ongoing development as she decides to remain in London and join her friend Razia in the latter's newly founded fashion business.

New Affective Trajectories

At the close of *Brick Lane*, discontented with the subcontractor system that leaves homeworkers with a meagre income, Razia turns from homeworker to entrepreneur and opens her own fashion business, which produces garments inspired by South Asian fashion for Western customers. Homeworkers or machinists in sweatshops usually perform only individual steps of the garment process like inserting a zipper, but do so in large quantities. By contrast, Razia and her fellow seamstresses from the estate construct the garments from start to finish. Furthermore, they aim to expand their business model to include design work as well. As a result, the women's work is moved from the invisibility of the home space into a sewing and design studio and, as such, replicates more traditional liberal and capitalist work settings, as well as progressing from unskilled to skilled work. Literary scholar Naomi Pereira-Ares identifies this development as 'new practices which enable female empowerment without entailing exploitation' (2012: 1) because the business is founded on ideas of mutual support and female friendship that exclude exploitative sub-contracting methods. The novel appears to support this reading in the final scene when Razia and the girls take Nazneen ice skating. When the latter protests that she cannot ice skate in her sari, Razia replies: 'This is England. You can do whatever you like' (Ali 2003a: 365). This scene, and Razia's statement, which is the novel's final sentence, have been at the forefront of much of the popular and scholarly discussion of the novel. It is arguably problematic, and critics have used it to support either of the two opposed readings of the novel I pointed towards at the beginning of this chapter: a celebration of British multiculturalism versus a stereotypical and uncritical rendering of the immigrant experience based on a glorification of neoliberal narratives of individuality and economic success. Throughout this chapter, I have attempted to show that such an analytical attempt is not particularly useful as it locks the text within problematic binary categories rather than attending to its full narrative complexity. By focusing on processes of affective meaning making, grounded in everyday practices, my analysis has unpacked some of these entanglements with regard to the textual practices of the novel as well as the textile practices featured in the novel.

My analysis of *Brick Lane*, through a focus on affective practices of needlework in the context of housework and paid homework, has highlighted how the literary can allow for a narration of the complexity of lived experience and the way moments of friction and discord sit alongside those of cohesion. Through tracing the affective patterns that Nazneen's everyday sewing practice creates, I have shown how sewing moves her towards a new perception of self, grounded in her own desires. Nazneen is not only moved by desire, but also towards desire as she sews hem after hem, and zipper after zipper. As a result of this orientation, Nazneen becomes capable of taking actions that place the objects of her own desire within reach. She begins an affair with Karim and refuses to accompany her husband back to Bangladesh in order to create an autonomous life in Britain for herself and her daughters. In Nazneen's case, the sewing practice becomes the starting point for a politics of embodied (re)orientation. She transforms from passive figure to conscious actor within the transnational entangled context of the garment industry and the South East Asian diaspora to the United Kingdom.

The following chapter, though not focused on literary texts, continues with the idea of entangled transnational practices in the context of a cross-cultural needlework initiative between Afghan and European women. I explore how a focus on affective social practices of needlework can highlight similarities between women and thus provide a ground for empathy and solidarity, while at the same time emphasizing the unequal flow of power that is often enmeshed in such encounters.

3

Stitching Transnational Solidarity: Textile Crafts and Cross-Cultural Encounters

In 2004, the French-German textile artist and tutor Pascale Goldenberg travelled to Afghanistan to meet with women in Laghmani and the surrounding villages, in Parwan province on the Shomali Plain, about sixty kilometres outside the capital Kabul. Her suitcases were filled with colourful fabric and handmade accessories like tote and shoulder bags and book covers. The plan was to teach local women how to design and sew their own bags and covers and to incorporate traditional Afghan hand embroidery into the designs. Goldenberg was acting in collaboration with the charity Deutsch–Afghanische Initiative eV (German–Afghan Initiative, DAI for short). The organization aims to provide development aid focused on relieving poverty, especially in rural Afghanistan, through promoting women's and young people's education and employment opportunities. As a passionate textile aficionado, Goldenberg was also on a mission to preserve Afghanistan's rich embroidery heritage. Together with the DAI, she set up the cross-cultural, needlework initiative, Guldusi. The word *guldusi* is the colloquial Farsi term for embroidery; it is a composite noun made up of the term *gul*, which means flower and the word *dusi*, the more formal term for embroidery. Today, the initiative provides an income for about 230 women in Afghanistan by selling their embroidery across Europe.

I locate Guldusi as part of a broad landscape of women's transnational solidarity projects involving various forms of traditional handicrafts like needlework (Hemmings 2015; de Jong 2017; Jones 2019; Rhodes 2015). In this landscape, Guldusi inhabits a special position as it sells small embroideries intended for incorporation into new textile artefacts, such as quilts or clothing, as opposed to selling finished products. This is significant to the way Guldusi's customers engage with the embroideries because they are encouraged to enter into the process of creating something new in response to the Afghan embroidery. In this chapter, I analyse Guldusi's website, travel reports, newsletters and gallery books, interviews with Goldenberg as well as textile artefacts to examine critically the way in which meaning about practices of needlework is construed. As such, unlike the previous two chapters, this chapter focuses less on literary texts like novels or short stories. Nevertheless, it is concerned with the textures of narratives or, in other words, with the stories we tell to make sense of things. It explores the unequal flows of power in the construction of meanings related to needlework and women's solidarity that emerge in relation to Guldusi.

I show how supposedly universal representations of everyday practices of homemaking and of needlework are attributed with the power to connect women across different cultures because of their shared gendered identity as women and needlework practitioners. I contend that, while similarities can be found in material practices of embroidering, as well as in popular cultural customs similar in Britain and Afghanistan – for example, tea drinking – there are limits to the extent that these connections can foster generative acts of transnational feminist solidarity. Indeed, I expose how acts of feminist solidarity grounded in assumptions about a shared gendered identity as needlewomen risk reproducing contemporary Orientalist discourses that privilege the narratives and experiences of white women from the Global North. I want to be clear, however, that my aim is not to defame Guldusi and its participants or to accuse them of cultural insensitivity or negligence. Rather, I hope to draw attention to the way assumptions about the meaning of needlework practices and women's shared gendered identity can emulate unequal global power relations through craft-based solidarity initiatives. In this context, I am not only interested in how Orientalism circulates on the level of the discursive, but also in the affective attachments to these structures. In other words, I tease out the way in which European women's intimate investment in needlework practices influences perceptions about the political potential of cross-cultural needlework initiatives between women in the Global North and South.[1] As a result, I call for a more nuanced awareness in textile scholarship as well as craft-based women's solidarity initiatives about how narratives of difference and sameness are produced and by whom.

Guldusi: An Afghan–European Embroidery Initiative

During that first trip to Afghanistan, Goldenberg hired two local women who were skilled in traditional embroidery to teach the others. Afghanistan has always had a rich and varied embroidery heritage, but decades of war and displacement have threatened to make this knowledge extinct. Across the country, different ethnic groups specialized in distinct styles and techniques (Paine 2006). The Hazara, for example, are famous for their use of graphic patterns, whereas the Uzbek are known for their couched threadwork. A fine satin stitch, called *Kandaharidusi*, is popular across all regions and groups and traditionally embellishes the fronts of men's shirts or children's clothing. It often graces the *tshador* or burqa, the full body cover for women, in combination with some drawn threadwork to create tiny stars, rosettes and cross motifs.[2] Embroidery was a staple feature in everyday Afghan life. Besides clothing, it was common to embroider functional items for the home that protected a prized possession like a watch or the Koran. Imagery like birds, flowers or religious motifs, that often carry symbolic meaning, are common across these embroideries (Paine 2006).

The rise of the Taliban in the 1990s and the US-led invasion that started in 2001 have brought (and continue to bring) immense hardships and daily challenges for the people and nearly caused hand embroidery to disappear. Livelihoods were destroyed during the war and the Taliban's restrictions on women, and particularly women's freedom of movement, prevented them from engaging with life outside the private sphere (Heath 2011; Skaine 2002).[3] After the Taliban's return to power in the summer of 2021, many media outlets reported increased restrictions on women's freedom of movement and educational and professional opportunities (Kumar and Noori 2022). Displacement within and outside Afghanistan has affected many Afghans and continues to do so. For example, people who sought shelter in refugee camps near the Pakistani border have found their everyday trajectories and routines affected because of this change in the spaces and places that housed them. Thus, common practices associated with the everyday underwent major transformations within the timespan of one generation as the material and social environment in which such practices could flourish or be passed on and shared between multiple generations no longer exists (Heath 2011: 12). Skills like embroidery, but also crucial knowledge about farming the country's mainly arid land, have been lost as a result. In addition, an influx of cheap manufactured textiles from Pakistan reduced the need for handmade clothing (Paine 2006: 19).

Parallel to these developments, many young girls stopped showing an interest in hand embroidery. They believed it to be 'old-fashioned' and unsuitable to the 'modern' identity they were attempting to fashion for themselves (Goldenberg 2016b: n.p.). While embroidered clothing and textiles were and are still popular, according to Goldenberg, many Afghans now prefer to buy manufactured goods, which are regarded as 'better', instead of investing time and effort in making their own. This attitude to embroidery is reflective of, on the one hand, global narratives of capitalism and globalization. On the other hand, it provides insight into yet another iteration of the continuous struggle about the value of the handmade in comparison with the mass produced. In a number of industrialized countries in the Global North a renewed appreciation for the traditionally handmade can be observed as part of anti-capitalist movements and/or as a reflection of popular contemporary do-it-yourself aesthetics linked not to an economic need to make-do-and-mend, but to the financial and cultural capital of having the resources to dedicate time and money to the handmade (Campbell 2005; Dawkins 2011). By contrast, in the Global South, those aspiring to become active participants in capitalism, symbolized for them by a spending power that allows the purchase of the ready-made, may disregard the handmade as old-fashioned, backwards and a sign of economic deficit (Appadurai 1996). As a result, embroidery as a skilled practice, but also as a material object that would be saved and treasured as an heirloom, was under threat of disappearing from everyday Afghan life. Guldusi has made it its mission to preserve this craft knowledge and to support Afghan women.

Goldenberg had anticipated that the Afghan women would be excited by the prospect of making and selling their own textile goods and developing a business network. However, this was not the case. Given the reality of the women's living conditions, they had neither the time nor the energy to spare to design products and develop a business network. Their sole focus was on making ends meet. On top of that, there was a range of practical problems, including access to properly functioning sewing machines and flat irons and with regard to the logistics for growing a business network. Of the initial more than thirty participants, only two, a young unmarried woman and a widow, were allowed to travel by taxi to the nearest town to offer their goods to the local women's centre. In retrospect, Goldenberg describes her expectations as the rather 'naive' vision of a 'nice European woman' (2005: n.p.). Her vision was not feasible for the women's situation which was so very different to her own life in Germany.

As a result, the initiative's focus changed. Instead of supporting individual women in developing their own products for the Afghan market, Guldusi commissions Afghan women to provide small hand embroideries for the European market. This way, the Afghan women need only be concerned with the production of embroidery, while Guldusi takes care of the marketing and sales aspect as well as providing the women with a stable salary. The women in Laghmani embroider small squares or circles in cotton floss with common motifs including flowers and fruits or abstract patterns. Subsequently, a second

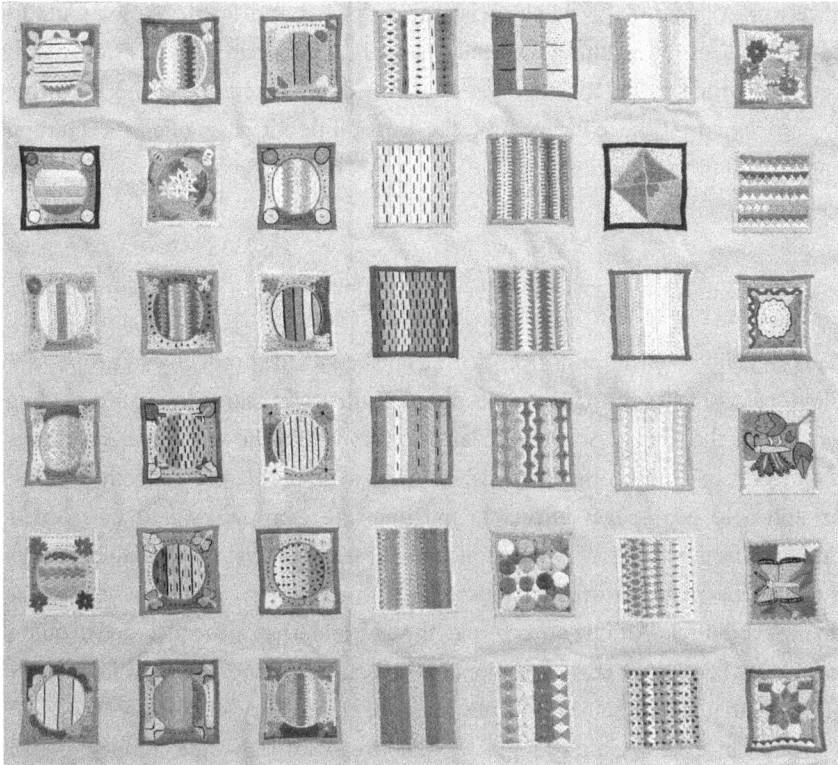

Figure 3.1 Embroidery for Guldusi by Shafiqa from Afghanistan. (© Pascale Goldenberg/Guldusi).

project was started in west Afghanistan in Herat with women from the ethnic group of the Hazara. They embroider in silk thread only and the particular geometric patterns for which the Hazara are known. Photographs of Hazara embroidery were compiled in Germany and then sent to the women to be used as templates and to (re)familiarize them with the patterns.

The women are provided with all the necessary materials for the embroideries. Completed embroidery work is collected quarterly and the women are paid for the previous delivery as they hand over the next one. Goldenberg usually travels to Afghanistan to perform this handover and meet the women in person, but Guldusi also employs a couple of local people as coordinators for the initiative. With each collection, about 3,500 to 4,000 pieces of embroidery are shipped to Germany. Volunteers in Germany cut the embroidered sheets into individual squares and sort, bag, price and label the pieces with the name of the embroiderer. The embroidery is then sold across Europe through the initiative's website, or by a network of national representatives at craft fairs and textile shows. Guldusi conceptualizes the resulting textile artefacts created by Europeans as 'four-hands projects' which bring together people from different cultures. The following section explores the concept and the possibilities it may offer for cultural encounter and transnational solidarity in more detail.

Four-Hands Projects

Guldusi deliberately refrains from selling finished textile products in Europe, as is often the case with transnational needlework initiatives geared towards providing women in the Global South with an income. While the embroidered squares themselves, in a sense, resemble finished pieces of embroidery, the way they are cut up and sold encourages buyers to integrate the embroidery into new textile projects. The possibilities for inclusion are endless and the website and Goldenberg's publications about the initiative offer only a small window into these options, as do the exhibitions. Among other things, the embroideries can be included in quilts, patchwork bags, book covers, fashionable belts and clothing, as well as in intricate art quilts that feature screen printing, machine embroidery and felting.

To advance sales, Guldusi regularly organizes European-wide competitions in cooperation with well-known sponsors from the textile sector. Often, special motifs like leaves, letters, hearts or a particular animal will be commissioned from the Afghan embroiderers for these purposes. European participants in the competition are required to purchase one or more pieces of embroidery and to include them in their own textile works. Exhibitions which include a selection of successful submissions are frequently shown across Europe and are often embedded in large textile shows such as the annual European Patchwork Meeting in France.

Guldusi defines the finished textile works that European makers create with the Afghan embroideries as 'four-hands projects'. In each of them, the handicraft of at least one Afghan and one European woman are combined. Goldenberg claims that, through this practice of including one woman's work in another's, two different needlework techniques get combined and 'symbolically speaking – two cultures meet' (Goldenberg 2009: 14). This connection between women from different cultures is supposedly established through the makers' shared practice of needlework as well as their shared gendered identity. In line with this, the very first European-wide competition organized by Guldusi in 2005 was named 'Threads Unite Women' and aimed to 'promote curiosity and interest for the other's culture, the act of meeting between two peoples and solidarity' (Guldusi n.d.). A subsequent publication featuring a brief history of the embroidery initiative as well as an array of images of embroidered squares and completed four-hands projects is, similarly, titled *Threads Unite* (Goldenberg 2009).

Testimonials from buyers of Guldusi embroidery indicate that European needlewomen are drawn to the Afghan embroidery not only because of its aesthetic qualities, but also by the context of its production. They are interested in the cultural encounter that Guldusi promotes. A quilter from Germany reports: 'I love the concept [of incorporating the Afghan embroideries into my own works]. It's doing good and having fun at the same time!' (Guldusi n.d.). A maker from Italy states: 'I was keen to learn more about Afghanistan, the initiative and the embroidery. I love to travel and getting to know different cultures and traditions' (Guldusi n.d.). Another from Germany reports that, due to her engagement with the embroidery, she became more attentive to news reports about Afghanistan. She claims that this is not due to an actual increase in reports about the country, but because she had developed a new sensitivity for news about Afghanistan because of a growing connection with its people: 'I feel that through the embroidery I am able to form a connection with an individual person; Afghanistan is no longer simply a country far away from me' (Guldusi n.d.). This maker, like many others, has become affectively oriented towards Afghanistan and its people through her own creative practices. When news of the resurgence of the Taliban broke and the media was flooded with images of Afghans desperately trying to flee their country, Goldenberg was inundated with messages from concerned crafters who feared for the life of the Afghan embroiderers and their families as well as the viability of the initiative.

For Guldusi, one of the key challenges for facilitating this envisaged cultural encounter is to ensure that the Afghan women produce embroidery of high quality and of a style that appeals to potential European buyers while at the same time preserving traditional Afghan embroidery techniques and motifs. The selection process for the embroiderers is therefore necessarily rigorous. Women interested in joining are invited to participate in a trial. The women may work on a trial piece from home but then will have to complete the embroidery in Goldenberg's presence to assure her that the woman present is indeed the embroiderer of the piece. With successful applicants, Guldusi agrees official employment contracts, which highlight the need for high-quality embroidery. The number of squares a woman is contracted to deliver per quarter varies. The work's quality and its popularity on the European market play an important role, but social factors are also considered. For example, women who have to support many children are allowed to deliver more squares than young unmarried girls.

Figure 3.2 Pillowcases with Guldusi embroidery by Bärbel Riedl. (© Pascale Goldenberg/Guldusi).

However, Goldenberg also makes sure always to employ a significant number of unmarried girls in an attempt to revive this dying craft among young people (Goldenberg 2006: n.p.). In order to ensure that the initiative remains financially viable, over the years, Goldenberg has found herself forced to fire some of the women because their embroidery was deemed to be lacking in quality and did not sell. However, in recent years, the DAI has been able to provide stipends to women in situations of extreme hardship. The work of the successful embroiderers also allows Guldusi to keep women whose work is not so popular employed.

Embroiderers are free to choose the design but they are required to use more than one colour of thread. They are also encouraged to take inspiration from their local surroundings and Afghan traditions. Even when special motifs or themes are commissioned for competitions, the women are at liberty to create their own designs. Most of the Afghan women's lives revolve around their compounds, their families and the everyday tasks of homemaking, such as cooking, gardening and farming – but all within the context of the aftermath of the US invasion and the country's more than forty-year-long legacy of occupation and continual warfare. The villages' plain brick constructions covered in sandy brown mortar and surrounded by trees stand out amid the flat landscape of the Shomali plains with large grey mountains in the background. This landscape forms the visible background in which these everyday practices take place and is often represented in the embroideries. The types of embroideries for sale, as well as those commissioned for competitions, suggest that the everyday, its practices and representations, emerged as a general theme that allows the charity to negotiate its vision of cultural encounter alongside market demands and cultural difference. Obviously, the cultural, social and geographical context that makes up the ordinary life of these Afghan women is certainly different to that of their European counterparts. However, in general, homemaking practices, such as washing and cooking, and – since their participation in the initiative – needlework, are similar across this cultural divide. They consist of 'forms of bodily activities, forms of mental activities, "things" and their use, a background knowledge in the form of understanding, know-how, states of emotion and motivational knowledge' that many can relate to (Reckwitz 2002: 249). They are routine everyday affective social practices in the lives of the women in the Global North, as well as the South, embedded within distinct social and emotional structures.

A series of embroideries by Meshgans from Laghmani details some of these practices in almost comic-strip fashion. Some show a woman and a man, most likely husband and wife, collecting firewood. Others portray a woman getting water from the village well, laundering the washing by hand in a basin and hanging it up to dry on a clothes line, before she is shown perching on the floor of her stone house ironing the clothes with a coal iron. Another series shows a woman lighting a fire indoors to prepare tea and food, which is then served to members of the household seated underneath a *sandal*, a common device for keeping warm in the winter whereby a bowl of hot coals is placed underneath a short table covered with a blanket. As everyone congregates on the floor around the table, feet and legs are slid under the cover for warmth.

These are all acts of everyday domesticity that in their modified form are familiar to Guldusi's European customer base. Other descriptive Afghan embroideries feature farm animals, common fruit and vegetables, ordinary items like cups and bowls as well as local plants and animals. Birds, for example, are popular embroidery motifs and feature prominently in Afghan culture – many people keep birds as pets in small cages. Flowers are also a favourite among the women embroiderers as many tend opulent flower gardens that form colourful oases in the brown, ochre, yellow and green of the Afghan landscape (Goldenberg 2009: 42, 46–7). In this sense, the women's gardening practices appear to echo Alice Walker's observations about her mother's flower garden, discussed in chapter one, which provided a colourful and creative outlet amidst the hardships of her everyday life and the limited material means available. The flower gardens along with the embroidery represent the women's refusal to be bogged down by the aftermath of war and conflict, as well as by the harsh condition of the land which has likewise suffered from years of war and destruction.

Many of the works created by European needlewomen that are shared with Guldusi or submitted as part of competitions appear to embrace the initiative's visions of the textile artefact as a dialogue between two cultures and as a connective medium between women. The works clearly show that the maker has put some thought into the cultural context of the embroidery. With pieces that respond to a particular competition's theme, this may be due to the competition's guidelines and requirements. Yet, this is surely not the case for every completed textile artefact. The engagement with Afghanistan and the socio-cultural context of the women embroiderers is fostered by Guldusi repeatedly bringing this to the foreground. The website, which can be accessed in English, German and French, provides detailed information about the initiative and the situation of the Afghan embroiderers. In regular travel reports available on the website, Goldenberg and her fellow volunteers recount their experiences of visiting the women in Afghanistan and, most recently, of the difficulties of contacting and visiting the embroiderers since the resurgence of the Taliban. Only by ensuring that the buyer and exhibition visitor know about the background of the small embroideries can the vision of creating a 'bridge' between two different cultures be realized. The resulting 'four-hands projects' may then form another such 'bridge' in their own right. They invite the viewer at an exhibition, in the home, or at a local quilt group's 'show and tell', likewise to engage with the cultural context in which the piece was conceived.

I contend, however, that these visions of encounters are enmeshed in Orientalist discourses and affective attachments that often remain unacknowledged in popular and scholarly discussions about cross-cultural needlework initiatives and cultural diversity in textile crafts, and this I shall unpack in more detail in the rest of this chapter.

Stitched Orientalisms and Women's Identity

I now turn to the concept of Orientalism to address how colonial legacies shape contemporary affective attachments and visions of transnational feminist solidarity. In his eponymous book, Edward Said (1978) defines Orientalism as a

'Western style for dominating, restructuring, and having authority over the Orient' ([1978] 2003: 3). As part of these century-old practices which he locates in everyday life, politics, art, history, literature as well as popular culture, the so-called West represents itself as the centre, while placing the so-called East and its inhabitants and culture on the periphery through practices of 'othering'. In setting up this binary, the East becomes a crucial marker through which the West conceives of itself.

Although still a foundational work for the field of postcolonial theory, Said's *Orientalism* has been variously expanded and critiqued since its publication. The most salient feminist critiques have questioned Said's relegation of gender and sexuality to mere sub-categories in the analysis of colonial discourses (Farris 2017; de Groot 2013; Yeğenoğlu 1998). Meyda Yeğenoğlu contends that 'representation of sexual difference ... is of fundamental importance in the formation of a colonial subject position' (1998: 2). Drawing on a vast archive of eighteenth- and nineteenth-century texts, Yeğenoğlu shows 'how the discursive constitution of Otherness is achieved simultaneously through sexual as well as cultural modes of differentiation' (1998: 2). In these discourses, the Orient is framed in relation to sensuous and feminized fantasies of 'the exotic' as well as 'gendered and sexualized depictions of dominance and subordination' (de Groot 2013: 193).

Arguably, the dualism that Said sets up between East and West is problematic and prone to essentializing Eastern as well as Western subjects and cultures. Yet, the legacy of Orientalism continues to inform the contemporary social, cultural and political imaginary of the Global North and South (Behdad 2010; Farris 2017; Hanifi 2018; Keskin 2018; Makdisi 2018). Indeed, these practices affect not only the way women in the Global South are represented in the Global North – for example, in the media or in political rhetoric – but also mediate people's affective attachments in relation to the self and others. The Orientalist framework of 'us vs them', that is 'civilized West vs backwards East' was heavily utilized by the US government under President George W. Bush in the context of the War on Terror and the US invasion of Afghanistan. In addition, Bush and his global allies, including the UK government, stressed women's rights, especially concerns about the Taliban's rules on veiling, as a further justification for military intervention (Ayotte and Husain 2005; Stabile and Kumar 2005). Feminist postcolonial theorist Gayatri Spivak, in the context of British colonial governance in India, famously referred to such acts of appropriation of women's rights in the interest of colonization as 'white men saving brown women from brown men' ([1988] 1994: 93). Sociologist Sara Farris (2017) and others

(Mulholland 2018) observe a similarly surprising and troubling interest in women's rights by contemporary European nationalist parties in order to foster anti-immigrant and anti-Islam agendas.

Women's veiling practices play a key role in these (ab)uses of women's rights and broader global political framework. In these discourses, little attention is often paid to the socio-cultural context of veiling practices and this particular item of clothing is caught in the complexity of 'larger confusion regarding the intersection between Afghan women, culture, and religion' (Abirafeh 2008: 98; see also Abu-Lughod 2002; Ayotte and Husain 2005; de Groot 2013; Kensinger 2003). This type of confusion can be traced in multiple instances in which Western feminists made the liberation and empowerment of their so-called Third-World sisters their primary objective (Cooke 2002; Roy 2016). Echoing Orientalist narratives of the civilized West as the saviour of a barbaric and backwards East, these discourses, in fact, deny the women in question the agency that they are supposedly to gain through the support of Western feminists. Like the Orient itself, its women are fashioned as a homogenous whole (Mohanty 1988: 51–3). This reduction to one singular group is already apparent in terms such as 'Muslim women', 'Arab women', 'Oriental women' or 'Middle Eastern women' which uniformly give these women an 'identity that may not be theirs' (Lazreg 2001: 283).[4] These practices of naming carry a 'reductive tendency to present women as an instance of a religion, ethnicity or race' and, thus, show the same kind of 'unwarranted generality' that Orientalist discourses do about the Orient as a whole (Lazreg 2001: 283). Middle Eastern women are regularly depicted as helpless victims of an archaic religious system that they are forced to obey; or, alternatively, as devout and submissive, but unreflective believers (Lazreg 2001: 289–90).

In her seminal postcolonial feminist text 'Under Western Eyes' (1988), Chandra Talpade Mohanty identifies in this the colonial move. She argues powerfully that this kind of representation 'ultimately robs [Middle Eastern women] of their historical and political agency' (Mohanty 1988: 72), while simultaneously managing to present Western women as liberated and active agents. Mohanty exposes the complicity of Western feminism and scholarship in a colonial project that claims representative knowledge of the 'Third World' woman, both as a category and, more specifically, about those women's situation and struggles. In these discursive constructions of 'Third World' women, Western feminist scholarship, however, conveniently ignores its own position within global capitalist structures of power. Images of veiled women as symbols of oppression confirm Western women in their self-perception as liberated and emancipated women and, thus, are important foils to their identity (Farris 2017; de Groot 2013; Lazreg 2001). Just as the concept of the 'barbaric East' is important for the self-construction of a 'civilized West', so is the veiled Muslim woman for that of Western non-Muslim women. Many postcolonial and decolonial feminist critics have thus pointed out the complicity of Western feminism with imperial and Orientalist endeavours (de Groot 2013; Lazreg 2001; Mohanty 1988, 2003, 2013; Roy 2016; Spivak [1988] 1994; Yegenoglu 1998).[5] In the following section, I examine 'four-hands projects' by British participants in the competition 'Afghanistan Inspiration' to illustrate how the Afghan embroideries are implicated in these problematic Orientalist legacies.

The Challenge of Everyday Representation

The EU-wide Guldusi competition, 'Afghanistan Inspiration', took place in 2007; fourteen European countries were each assigned a specific embroidered motif that participants should engage with in their submissions. The motifs were carefully chosen with the intention that they would have symbolic resonance for each respective European country as well as for Afghanistan. The Netherlands, for example, was assigned tulips in recognition of the popular tulip fields that every year draw thousands of visitors to the country. The plant is native to Afghanistan and enjoys large popularity in domestic flower gardens. Austria was assigned mountains which grace the landscape of this central European country as well as that of Afghanistan. Latvia in Eastern Europe shares with Afghanistan the experience of long and bitter cold winters. The UK was assigned teacups, teapots and other kinds of drinking vessels with a nod to shared British and Afghan traditions of tea drinking. In an extraordinary turnout compared to the other participating countries, Guldusi received seventy-seven submissions from the UK.[6]

Tea drinking as a form of encounter between two people and, more specifically, two cultures emerges as a strong theme across all the submissions. For example, Eva Cantin's submission shows a flower carpet with an embroidered square with a teapot in the upper centre of the piece. It is titled *Tea with Latifa* (2007) after the name of the Afghan embroiderer whose stitched teapot she included in the creation (Guldusi 2007). Liz Ashurst's piece similarly features an embroidered square of a colourful teapot on a table against a background of different sections of green fabric embroidered with the contours of leaves. The work is called *Tea in the Forest* (2007) and, while it does not feature any human figures, the idea of an encounter at the tea table resonates clearly with the viewer (Guldusi 2007). *Ways to Communicate – Voices on the Road* (2007, figure 3.3) by Molly Bullick expresses this idea of tea as a medium for cultural encounter more directly through its title. The work also features a teapot above a strip of fabric with Arabic or Persian lettering on it. Likewise, Janet Clark's *Hobeda and Me* (2007), a narrow rectangular wall hanging in dark red and blue with an embroidered drinking vessel as an eye-catcher, explicitly addresses an encounter between two different needlewomen that symbolically happens through joint creativity (Guldusi 2007). In the spirit of 'four-hands projects' the finished textile artefact is the work of Hobeda from Afghanistan and Clark from Britain.

It appears that, in both countries, the women can relate to the practice of tea drinking and can recognize a teapot, cup or other type of drinking vessel as representative of it. Yet, the representation is not an unbiased one of a neutral shared practice. Like any other affective social practice, tea drinking is implicated in global and local trajectories of meaning making. Tea drinking has a long cultural history in Afghanistan and is part of common hospitality practices that

Figure 3.3 *Ways to Communicate – Voices on the Road*, 2007, Molly Bullick, 'Afghanistan Inspiration'. (© Pascale Goldenberg/Guldusi).

are important in traditional Afghan customs (Coulson *et al.* 2014). These practices 'require' Afghans to serve tea to any guest whether known or unknown and day-to-day politics are also addressed and resolved over a cup of tea. Though tea does not grow in Afghanistan, it is a readily available commodity mainly sourced from neighbouring Pakistan. Similarly, tea is not a plant native to Britain and its consumption and status as a national beverage is deeply tied to the country's colonial legacy as it was sourced in the empire's South East Asian territories. As a popular nineteenth-century commodity in Britain, tea was consumed by all genders across all social classes and ascended to the status of British national beverage (Fromer 2008a, 2008b). In addition, it enabled a large number of Britons to participate in the imperial project literally by consuming it (Daly 2011; Fromer 2008a). Throughout the Empire, the British were united in the practice of tea drinking as it embodied 'idealized notions of English social practice such as social charm, personal grace, and lively but polite discourse' (Fromer 2008b: 533). As such, tea played a significant role in the self-fashioning of a unified British Empire by uniting its scattered citizens under this emblem of British domesticity.

However, while tea provided comfort in the home space, it also 'simultaneously jeopardized the ideological safety of those spaces by bringing the public world of the marketplace and the empire into the private space of the parlor' (Fromer 2008a: 27). Indeed, tea can be regarded as emblematic of the necessary negotiation with the exotic which confronted British subjects in the nineteenth century and beyond as a result of the formation of the Empire and its continuous expansion. The introduction of the practice of tea drinking to colonial subjects of colour even became a means to civilize the 'barbarous Other' through exposure to the 'socializing properties of the tea table [which] were understood to have a salutary effect' (Daly 2011: 92). This rhetoric, in the spirit of Orientalism, dismissed any already existing practices of tea consumption in the colonies as inferior. As such, while tea can be consumed as an individual activity, it also stages a figurative as well as a potentially real encounter with foreign others. Whether or not makers are aware of this, the type of cultural encounter that many of the 'four-hands' projects envisage is shaped these histories as is the extent to which such an encounter can have a transformative effect on visions of solidarity.

The challenge of accessible representations of the everyday is a key factor in this. As I have discussed in previous chapters, everyday life cannot be reduced to a common denominator 'given the radical diversity and contingency of daily life at a planetary level' (Procter 2006: 65). Nonetheless, for centuries, the everyday has been caught in processes of normativization. The civilizing mission of the was one of the cornerstones of the imperial project of the nineteenth century alongside the economic and hegemonic interests of the European powers. In this context, a white (and often middle-class) Western European everyday was framed as the norm, in opposition to the practices and representations of the everyday life the colonizers encountered abroad, and, as I have outlined, tea drinking played a key role in this.

The advent of postcolonial theory questioned the whiteness of these approaches that operated within an Orientalist framework geared towards penetrating the most private spaces of the Oriental other (Said [1978] 2003; Yegenoglu 1998). Rather than providing a space for cultural encounter that could lead to a dismantling of power structures, these encounters were 'underpinned by the [West's] reassuring fantasy of difference and distance that ritually reallocates the other to (or beyond) the margins' (Procter 2006: 76). The lure of exoticism enabled the inclusion of exotic objects in the (colonial) European home, consequently, 'remov[ing] the everyday object (a digging implement, a cooking vessel, a novel) from the daily concerns of both "native" and Western mainstream culture' and attributing to it the status of the exotic that deserves specific attention (Procter 2006: 76; see also Huggan 2001: 22; McClintock 1995).

I contend that the Guldusi embroideries, to some extent, operate within an Orientalist discursive and affective legacy marked by a fascination with 'the exotic' (May 2018). Through the purchase of the squares and the integration of them in a craft piece, the exotic other can be consumed from the safe space of one's home. This is evident through the recurring themes that can be found across completed four-hands projects. These themes include: cultural encounters, dialogue and travel; the Oriental in a range of different contexts, such as clothing, architecture or myths; women and practices of veiling; and women, identity, creativity and agency in relation to needlework. European needlewomen's use of the embroideries provides a space to fantasize about the life of the Afghan women and to muse about differences and commonalities.

Theorizing a Transnational Everyday

According to James Procter, the everyday, the local and the home interact to secure a 'national imaginary as a taken-for-granted site' that resists contamination by the other, even when the other enters the homeland (2006: 72). Offering a critical reading of postcolonial studies, he suggests that, often, postcolonial studies is less concerned with the mundane and the ordinary. Rather it attends to the heightened intensities of the extraordinary conditions of 'the colonial encounter, war, catastrophe, independence struggles, migration' (Procter 2006: 62). Such an approach, however, may serve to establish postcoloniality as that which is always 'other', always outside everyday routines and ordinary life, thus, replicating some of the very practices it critiques (Quayson 2000; Procter 2006). Such an approach is problematic, of course, as it attempts to define the everyday based on a binary between the ordinary and extraordinary. Ultimately, this is a futile move, because it disregards the fact that what becomes defined as exceptional is already grounded in the mundane and ordinary.

Attention to specific aspects of the ordinary – for example, a particular object in a living room – moves this object from the realm of the ordinary into that of the extraordinary by classifying it as worthy or as deserving of specific attention. As a result, the home space is a realm in which the struggle between the everyday and the exotic is regularly negotiated. For Paolo Boccagni, 'home as an experiential dimension of migrants' everyday life' (2017: xxiii) becomes the locus through which migrants – by means of various home-making practices – negotiate their identity in relation to everyday normativity in their country of origin and their new place of residence. I have shown in the previous chapter the way in which this process played out for the character of Nazneen in *Brick Lane*. In his study of the 'West Indian' front room, Michael McMillan argues that the interior of this room and the practices associated with it 'symbolised working-class respectability' for West Indian migrants in Britain, whereas, 'in the Caribbean, the front room reflected the performance of middle class values – that is, the colonial elite in the domestic interior' (2008: 44). As I explained in chapter one, the home space has also been identified as an important place of resistance for African Americans against white supremacy. In sum, the home space is a principal site in which norms and structures of power are reproduced, contested and actively subverted.

Postcolonial theory itself is implicated in this struggle, as there seems to exist 'a more general anxiety about the passage of the postcolonial into the realm of the mundane, the clichéd, the everyday' (Procter 2006: 62; see also Loomba 2005). This is also reflected in the standardization of postcolonial studies and decolonial theory within academia and the curriculum, to the extent that it may be performed formulaically rather than from a deep commitment to decolonizing exclusive and discriminatory structures of knowledge and representation. Eve Tuck and K. Wayne Yang note with concern that decolonizing discourses, especially in relation to Indigenous peoples, have become appropriated within the academy as forms of 'civil and human-rights based social justice projects' that are not committed to changing what is ultimately an education and knowledge system based on settler colonial power structures (2012: 2). Instead, decolonial theory and its commitment to decolonizing power structures have been appropriated as part of institutional box-ticking exercises that embrace challenges to 'racism, imperialist ideologies, and colonial violence' only in rhetoric and not as an attempt to fundamentally transform social, political, cultural and economic relations and, by extension, the quotidian as we know it (Dar, Dy and Rodriguez 2018: para. 6). Thus, 'a critical analysis of the everyday must be central' not only to ethical decolonizing practices, but also to transnational feminist solidarity initiatives (Quayson quoted in Procter 2006: 63). Only through such practices can it become possible to move away from the West and the Western subject as the central vantage point in relation to which everything else is constructed as the periphery.

Using the concept of transnationalism, anthropologist Aiwah Ong suggests attending to 'the condition of cultural interconnectedness and mobility across space' (1999: 4; see also Pedwell 2014: 22). Rather than looking at the world in terms of centre and periphery or through cardinal directions such as East/West or North/South, Ong uses 'flows of capital, information, and populations' to map the 'cultural specificities of global processes' (1999: 5). In other words, she deals with everyday entanglements of meaning and practices that resemble 'a form of cultural politics embedded in specific power contexts' (Ong 1999: 5). As such, practices of decolonization ultimately operate within a transnational context because they recognize how oppressive structures and practices like Orientalism circulate and take different forms. In this context, representations of everyday life are not 'stopping points or crystallizations that become fixed and internal meanings' (Pink 2012: 33). Instead, they are reflective of the global unequal flow of power, and conscious or unconscious affective investments in the structures it produces. Since representations have been actively constructed as part of these cultural politics, they are not permanent, but subject to change. For these reasons, as I demonstrate throughout this book, the everyday also offers such a generative lens for making sense of the relationship between the global unequal flow of power and the workings of social transformation in the minor key.

Texturing the Representation of Afghan Women

Guldusi, like many Western feminist and political discourses, appears to use the burqa, or rather its increasing absence, as a symbol of progress. In 2006, in one of her travel reports, Goldenberg takes positive notice that, at her Afghan hosts' home, there are no longer burqas hanging on a hook behind the front door. Women's embroidered self-portraits that show the subjects without any headcover are similarly interpreted as progress and highlighted on the website and across the initiative's publications. Certainly, these portraits may be representative of advancements in women's opportunities for creative self-expression outside the restrictions the Taliban placed on arts and culture. However, using the embroideries as an indicator of wider social progress seems a stretch, in particular, because this raises the question about what is considered progress and about who gets to define what counts as transformation.

Goldenberg's own artwork has developed as a result of her engagement with Afghanistan and its women and she recognizes a large 'discrepancy between her own situation as a Western European woman and that of the Afghan women' (Guldusi n.d.). She describes Afghan women as 'not free' (the inverted commas are hers) because the women have no right of freedom of movement: they do not own a passport, nor are they allowed to make their own decisions nor simply to leave their compound as they please. In addition, she laments that women have to be fully veiled in public and cannot decide whether or not they would like to send their children to school (Guldusi n.d.). By contrast, Goldenberg describes herself as 'free' (again using inverted commas) (Guldusi n.d.). As a symbol of these two different realities, Goldenberg's own artistic textile practice explores the veil as a central theme. She explains: 'As a symbolic carrier of this particular global issue, I have chosen the *tshaderi*, the full body cover of the Afghan country woman, as the theme for my artworks' (Guldusi n.d.). For her, the burqa appears to be a convenient shorthand for the multiplicity of everyday problems and forms of oppression to which Afghan women are exposed. In this sense, the resulting textile artefacts, like many others created in response to Guldusi embroideries, at least partly reflect the dominance of practices of veiling in discourses by the media and policymakers about Afghanistan and Middle Eastern women more broadly.

One of Goldenberg's art pieces is a textile book titled *Die Afghanin* ('The Afghan Woman') (n.d.), which includes a selection of articles about Afghan women that are primarily about the burqa. She has collected these articles over the years from different types of media, such as newspapers and books. The art book is fashioned as a concertina in which the front and back of a page are filled so that, due to this special folding technique, the viewer can endlessly flip back and forth between the various pages. According to Goldenberg, this design invokes the 'endless history of suffering caused by the *tshaderi*' (*Die Afghanin* n.d.). The garment is fashioned as the root cause of Afghan women's suffering even though, judging by her statement about her own art practice, Goldenberg appears to have some knowledge about the socio-cultural context of veiling practices in Afghanistan, since she defines the burqa as 'the full body cover of the Afghan country woman' (Guldusi n.d.). In addition, in the publication *Gardens Around the World* (2016a), Goldenberg notes that the *tshaderi* is commonly worn by elderly women and that many young girls no longer use it (n.p.). She implies that the burqa may have been worn prior to the Taliban regime thus breaking the discursive chain that repeatedly uses the burqa as a symbol of Taliban atrocities. Nonetheless, she also appears to contextualize the burqa as a symbol of a patriarchal Afghan society, whose general 'backwardness' is mirrored in the treatment of its women. As a result, the West is once more fashioned as superior in its general treatment of women based on its lack of veiling practices.

A series of textile installations by Goldenberg titled *Verstellte Blicke* ('Disguised Views') (n.d.) similarly deals with the topic of veiling. In one section of the installation called 'Three Women from Laghmani', three burqas from very light to bright blue are hung from the ceiling, suspending them as ghost-like figures directly above the floor. This installation is striking, given that one of Goldenberg's main reasons for her first trip to Afghanistan was to get to know the women and she has, after more than ten years as the initiative's manager, become very familiar with the embroiderers' individual stories. At sale stalls at quilt shows, she often makes casual comments about the embroiderer as part of the sales transaction, pointing out things like 'this woman has been with the initiative from the very beginning' or 'she really struggled at first, but her work has improved so much' (Goldenberg, Appendix 2017: telephone interview). In this process, the women are framed as individuals with their own talents and stories. The empty shapes of cloth at the installation, however, reduce the women's identities to the burqa in the manner common to Western discourses about Afghan women and practices of veiling.

As part of an installation at a gallery in Leipzig, Germany, these figures are surrounded by painted and photographed portraits of women in a hijab, a special type of veil that covers the hair, but leaves the woman's face fully exposed to the viewer. In the gallery space, the empty shapes of cloth form a stark contrast to the individual portraits that grace the walls. Given the current unstable political climate, the women are afraid of a potential backlash should they be publicly identified beyond their immediate community as women employed by a foreign organization (Guldusi n.d.). For this reason, the website features barely any pictures of the embroiderers that show the women's faces as the women have refused Guldusi permission to show their portraits online. They have, however, given permission for their portraits to be shown as part of exhibitions. In this sense, the exhibition functions as an exclusive act of unveiling during which the embroiderers' faces can be viewed for the length of the installation only. *Gardens Around the World* also includes an active act of unveiling. A photograph covering the full height of the page shows the embroiderer Shila with the burqa lifted and tossed over her head so that her face is visible (Goldenberg 2016a: n.p.).

Through media, government and aid discourses, as well as art pieces like the ones described above, the everyday life of Afghan women is inherently connected to a garment. The burqa, as a woven piece of material, is a tangible texture through which the encounter with the Afghan woman takes place. It is as if the Afghan's own perception of the quotidian, as well as others' perceptions of her are only possible through the fabric of this piece of cloth; it is an actual texture but also conceived as symbolic of the texture of the Afghan woman's everyday life. To this extent, the veil not only physically covers women's bodies, and, at least somewhat, restricts their movement and vision, but also figuratively constrains them in their development and their right to claim their own identity as Afghan women, while, at the same time, locating agency within this category. Western feminism's 'deficit model of agency' (Emejulu 2011: 383) categorizes Afghan women as lacking in this capacity. As a result, rather than making space for Afghan women to define their own experiences on their own terms, Western women configure themselves as the saviours of oppressed Afghan women (Sharoni *et al.* 2015).

Consequently, the act of solidarity, in fact, becomes one of protectionism (Russo 2006). In this sense, the European women's practices of needlework in response to the Guldusi embroidery become a means to negotiate their own positionality as well as their perceptions of the Middle Eastern woman. It can be a space for critically reflecting about one's own agency in contrast to the perceived lack of agency of the Afghan women – in the way that Goldenberg thinks of herself as 'free' and the Afghan women as 'not free'. However, it can also reproduce power dynamics that place European women's sense of agency and self at the heart of transnational feminist solidarity. Such forms of solidarity are obviously problematic because they take as their starting point the affective attachments of white women in the Global North to their particular sense of self and privileged position. This undercuts the possibility of developing new relationships and attachments grounded in the recognition of affective dissonance in women's experiences of their shared gendered identity.

British artist Gillian Travis' wall hanging, *Add this Square* (2015), echoes such problematic attempts at transnational feminist solidarity. The pattern of an embroidered Guldusi square is repeated across the whole background of the piece. In the foreground there are two brown women clothed in blue and white niqabs that cover their faces and torso but leave a slit for the eyes. They sit cross-legged next to each other, their heads bent over embroidery hoops, diligently stitching another square for Guldusi. Again, the veil as a symbol for the women's situation dominates the artwork, even though this piece once more decontextualizes the practice of veiling. As Goldenberg explained to me during our April 2017 interview, the women would not normally be covered while embroidering because they stitch in the privacy of their homes or compounds, sometimes alone, sometimes in the company of other embroiderers. Yet, the expressive power of the veil as a substitute for the women's lives and experiences seemingly overshadows, or literally veils, the political potential and agency immanent to the particular performance of practices of needlework and everyday practices more broadly.

Shared Practices of Meaning Making

The home, as well as the objects associated with it, supposedly speak to women's universal experience of domesticity. The embroidered Afghan motifs considered as representations of the quotidian and as objects produced within the realm in which these practices take place, 'invite viewers to imagine rhythms, sensations and experiences of other people's everyday lives' (Pink 2012: 44). In 2013, the Guldusi competition, 'Out of the Kitchen', for example, invited European needlewomen to work collaboratively on a textile piece with the Afghan embroiderers. For the first time, rather than producing embroidered squares for Europeans to buy, the Afghans were tasked with continuing a needlework project that had already been started by a European needlewoman. In a third step, the piece would then be returned to the original maker who would complete the work. According to Joëlle Jan-Gagneux, who initiated the collaborative project alongside Goldenberg, it was important to ground the exchange in a concrete theme that all women could relate to, as opposed to focusing on complex interpretations of a potentially abstract topic (Jan-Gagneux and Goldenberg 2014). As a result, kitchens and kitchen utensils were chosen because of their relevance to the daily life of both Afghan and European women. Jan-Gagneux hoped that this theme would 'allow each woman to express something personal or individual that was still universally accessible' (Jan-Gagneux and Goldenberg 2014: n.p.).

However, the execution of the project proved difficult. Some of the Afghan women struggled to recognize and interpret the objects outlined by the European needlewomen. Consequently, Goldenberg attempted to tutor the Afghans in the process through a guided analysis of the original piece. When visiting Afghanistan, she examined each submission together with the respective Afghan embroiderer exploring questions like: 'What do you see on the surface? What is it used for? How is that done in Afghanistan? What kind of complementary development might be possible? And so, what should you embroider, and where, on this space, for a surface equating to two classical embroidered squares?' (Jan-Gagneux and Goldenberg, 2014: n.p.) Looking at the different submissions, it can be noted that the Afghan women drew on their standard repertoire for embroideries, including some of the usual motifs and patterns like flowers, birds and ornamental filler designs. Others added female figures as well as some writing. In addition, many embroidered objects typically found in Afghan village kitchens, such as cups, bowls, jugs, spoons, spatulas and different kinds of fireplaces, including open wood fires or camping stoves, as well as a selection of different fruit and vegetables. However, the alignment of objects, at times, does not adhere to that of the initial layout suggested by the European needlewoman. Indeed, sometimes, it is exactly the opposite so that a teapot embroidered by an Afghan woman might be upside down compared to the one that had been originally placed on the cloth by the European maker. Barely any of the works appear to have considered depth and many of the objects in them appear to be floating in space.

Each step of the process was photographed, and the online art book that accompanies the final exhibition chronicles the three-step process. In 2015, the competition 'Gardens Around the World' repeated this three-step process on the theme of gardens. In the total of seventy-seven juried submissions, eleven European countries were represented. Goldenberg sums up: 'The diverse perception of gardens and aesthetic attitudes of the Afghan embroiderers are reflected in the works of art. Whilst several of the women aimed to reach a uniform composition, the remainder in many cases portrayed a contrast' (2016a: n.p.). The results of both competitions, according to Goldenberg, represent some new developments in the women's embroidery that were 'satisfying in some instances, sometimes surprising, not to say puzzling' and representative of an apparent 'gulf' between the two cultures which in itself is part of the special character of the finished pieces (Goldenberg 2016a: n.p.).

This so-called 'gulf' shows that, while there are certainly some universal characteristics to the everyday, and its attendant affective social practices, it is not generalisable; nor, as I show throughout this book, are practices of needlework. As social anthropologist Sarah Pink argues, 'there is undeniably a relationship between everyday life as lived and everyday life as represented' (2012: 44). However, these representations and their attendant theories are not neutral. Particularly in the context of cross-cultural encounters and collaborations, it is important to question who has the power to represent and to make representations 'true'. Whose everyday comes to signify the norm and why? Tracing the affective meaning-making trajectories of different representations allows for an attention to power structures at work in the making of a representation. Representations – of the meaning of practices of needlework or of what resembles feminist solidarity – are not inherently meaningful; rather they are actively invested with meaning (Hall 1999; Pink 2012).

Consequently, attention to the everyday is vital to transformative decolonizing projects because of the deep ties between the local and the global. Like postcolonial feminist theorist Chandra Talpade Mohanty, I see potential in

Figure 3.4 *Pause – Café – Coffee Break*, Christiane Sechet and Soraya, 'Out of the Kitchen'. (© Pascale Goldenberg/Guldusi).

'grounded, particularized analyses linked with larger, even global, economic and political frameworks' (2003: 501).[7] In the context of Afghanistan and its women, this means recognizing how their particular situation is implicated in wider global power structures deeply linked to capitalism and globalization. As we have seen, Western feminist discourses about feminist solidarity and empowerment are similarly caught within these larger trajectories of capitalism. Likewise, development aid often functions within this framework, which influences the kind of aid provided and the values and discourses attached to its distribution. For example, projects focusing on financially empowering individuals and, as a result, making them active participants in the market economy, are grounded in the assumption that participation in capitalism can solve existing problems as opposed to recognizing this particular economic system and its unequal distribution of wealth as responsible for the problems in the first place (Abirafeh 2008). Feminist cross-cultural work needs to be based on an awareness of these trajectories and how power travels along them in order to commit fully to transnational practices of feminist solidarity that 'move through the specific context to construct a real notion of the universal and of democratization rather than colonization' (Mohanty, 2003: 518; see also Mankekar 2015).

In contrast to that, a relational approach to difference is not supportive of such projects of solidarity because through such discourse 'questions of power, agency, justice, and common criteria for critique and evaluation are silenced' (Mohanty 2003: 520). Such an approach focuses on framing distinct practices as different only to the extent to which they appear particular to a specific cultural context, as opposed to attending to the embodied and affective entanglements of these practices. So instead of emphasizing difference over commonality or the other way around, feminist solidarity should, according to Mohanty, be envisaged as 'relations of mutuality, co-responsibility, and common interests' that allow for 'differences and commonalities [to] exist in relation and tension with each other in all contexts' and at all times (2003: 521). With regard to practices of needlework, this implies a recognition of the ways that embroidery, sewing or quilting are intertwined in particular entanglements between the local and global.

In the context of cross-cultural, collaborative needlework initiatives like Guldusi, then, it is important to consider the meaning of practices of needlework and making in relation to discourses about women, identity, agency and empowerment. As such, it is also crucial to pay attention to the power dynamics at play in the creation of these discourses. Who tells the stories that serve to 'authenticate' theories about the meaning of practices of needlework for women

(Hemmings 2006: 117)? What and whose stories get marginalized and how is this marginalization representative of wider power struggles, particularly within the context of transnational feminist solidarity?

Stitching the Self and the Other

In a wall-hanging for the competition 'Message' organized by Guldusi in 2016, UK textile artist Gillian Travis included the following quote in French: 'Each stitch is a reaffirmation of identity, a setting down of the past. Embroidery gives us a sense of belonging, connects us to our land and gives us an identity.' The wall hanging is titled *Letter to my Friends* (Travis 2016) and, while the quote originated in a Palestinian context, Travis explained to me during during an interview that she believes that a similar argument can be made for the Afghan embroiderers or indeed for needlewomen across the world (Appendix 2017: telephone interview). She notes: 'I have worked with different textile initiatives around the world, for example in India, Palestine and Guatemala. The statement [on this wall hanging] shows how important the work is to the women' (quoted in May 2018: 38). In this discourse, practices of needlework are closely linked to women's identity, agency and sense of empowerment. A connection between the women and their respective cultures is established through the women's shared practice of embroidering and sewing as well as, perhaps, through their shared gendered identity as women. Consequently, these discourses risk echoing the kind of problematic solidarity narratives produced by Western feminists which spotlight a supposed unity based on 'shared womanhood' (Salem 2018: 245), but often disregard the ways in which Western feminists reproduce the colonial power structures that marginalize women in the Global South.

Embroidery is strongly connected to identity as it provides a medium for women to engage with their personal past as well as the wider geographical and cultural histories in which they are located. Fiona Hackney suggests that many contemporary activist makers are 'historically savvy' and 'possess an awareness of an alternative history of domestic crafting' beyond stereotypical ideals of traditional femininity that enables them to be 'quietly active as they open up new channels of value and exchange by engaging in alternative craft economies and harnessing assets in often surprising, productive ways' (2013: 171). In addition, Hackney argues that the 'spaces of the amateur' form the realm in which the 'masculine system of capitalist culture' can be resisted because they allow for a different affective investment in practices of making (2013: 175). She locates potential in affect precisely because affect has historically been sidelined and dismissed as unimportant or ineffective in the context of overarching patriarchal and capitalist structures of governance. Physically and affectively removed from traditional capitalist spaces of production, the amateur hobbyist is conceptualized as existing in a space of potential in which she can be affectively moved to imagine different ways of being.

In one of her travel reports, Goldenberg writes that she hopes that the regular practice of embroidering might serve the women as a 'kind of therapy' or 'meditation'. The time spent embroidering would give participants the opportunity to pass a couple of hours in creative engagement with different colours and designs as well as time to focus on themselves. While the women embroider, they might be able to forget, at least for a little while, their daily challenges and hardships. The feedback Guldusi receives from participants appears to support this idea. The embroiderers claim that they enjoy the activity very much. In addition, the Afghan women's works show a high 'potential of individuality' in the design and execution of their embroidery which is indicative of the creativity involved in the process of embroidery. In this context, women's self-portraits were explicitly encouraged by Guldusi (Goldenberg 2016b). According to Rozsika Parker:

> the finding of form for thought ha[s] transformative impact on the sense of self ... the experience of embroidering and the embroidery affirms the self as a being with agency, acceptability and potency. ... The embroiderer sees a positive reflection of herself in her work and, importantly, in the reception of her work by others.
>
> 2010: xx

Guldusi has always placed high importance on supporting participants in developing their own individual embroidery styles. This includes going over the women's work and providing them with feedback on composition, stitch quality and colour choice during Goldenberg's regular visits to the villages. Thus, emphasis was put on 'individualism and the assertion of creative authorship', which are important markers for art in the Global North (Dawkins 2011: 269). In addition, it may have been seen as a generative way for boosting Afghan women's self-confidence in their ability to create, not only with needle and thread, but also in other areas of their lives.

Likewise, Guldusi attempts to foster a sense of achievement and accomplishment in the women by asking them to develop a personal signature with which to sign their embroidery, as well as by paying them wages for the completed squares. To the mainly illiterate women, this initially appeared to be a strange request since, for many, the concept of a signature, as an 'unmistakable way to be individually identifiable', was quite foreign (Goldenberg 2016b: n.p.). This may also be due to traditional kinship structures, which define the individual primarily in relation to his or her wider relationship to the family, tribe and ethnic group (Monsutti 2004; Emadi 2005). Goldenberg observes that the majority of the women from Laghmani all seem to be related in some way or other and that it is common to marry within the extended family. Women from the same compound may embroider in each other's company but many also work in solitude. Guldusi offered literacy classes to the women and girls of the village alongside the request to develop an individual signature and, over time, many embroiderers have started to incorporate the written word into their works. For Goldenberg, the production of self-portraits as well as the inclusion of writing in the embroidery have been developments of 'revolutionary' character: 'It was as if a rift had been vaulted, as if the shadow of the Taliban had been forced back by a degree' (2009: 101). It appeared to her as if the women were no longer afraid to embroider anything they wanted to, after the abolition of the Taliban's policies which had, for many years, placed restrictions on the women in almost every area of daily life. Similarly, in an update about the initiative since the return of Taliban government, Goldenberg expresses fears over the end of stitched portraits as the Taliban's restrictive policies on women's visibility are becoming widespread again (2022). It is possible that for the Afghan women the practice of embroidering, to a certain extent, has a similar effect on personal well-being as has been recorded in the case of women in so-called developed countries in the Global North (Burt and Atkinson 2012; Pöllänen 2013, 2015).

Nonetheless, there is one essential difference between the meaning of practices of needlework for the Afghan women and the European supporters of Guldusi. For the Afghan women it is 'not a hobby', but a job (Goldenberg 2006: n.p.). The women of Laghmani and Shahrak embroider because, considered by rural Afghan standards, they will be paid a substantial wage for their work. By Western standards, the communities of Laghmani and Shahrak are both affected by extreme poverty. In the aftermath of the Taliban occupation and the ensuing war, the embroiderers' wages are a welcome and necessary addition to the subsistence farming of the village. Widows, especially, often have no other form of income or support, and outside Kabul, employment opportunities for women are generally rare (Billaud 2015). The women report that they have used the money to buy groceries and firewood or to pay for medical treatment. Some of the younger girls have spent it on new 'modern' clothing like a jeans jacket (Goldenberg 2006: n.p.). While the women's wages are clearly used to supplement any additional, meagre family income, Goldenberg feels that it is generally the women who decide on how the money is spent. At the start of the initiative, there was a concern that men would not allow women to participate in the programme, would seize women's wages or would be upset about the fact that their wives were earning more money than them. These fears, however, have not been confirmed and many men appear happy about the additional income. Some have even pressed Goldenberg to hire their wives after they had been rejected during trials. Indeed, Goldenberg feels that the income gives the women greater negotiating power in the household (2006: n. p).

The embroidery is an activity the women can practise from the confines of their home and compound and it is, therefore, a convenient form of work that is not very physically demanding.[8] In addition, it can be worked around their numerous other daily duties that include food preparation, garden and farm work and looking after the home and children. Goldenberg has noticed that over the summer months the quality of the embroidery often deteriorates and the work seems rushed. The women are so busy looking after their fields and gardens at this time, and preparing for the cold winter months, that they do not have sufficient free time to dedicate to the embroidery. Homemaking practices literally find their way into the embroidery squares in the form of uneven and large stitches or sloppily executed designs. As such, the textile comes to physically encapsulate the texture of the women's everyday life.

While, generally, the Afghan women claim to enjoy embroidering, Goldenberg reported during our interview (Appendix 2017) that the women freely admit that they would not embroider if there were no financial gain involved. For the average Western needlewoman, on the other hand, needlework is often defined by its non-economic character. In this context, Marybeth Stalp argues that needlework functions not only as a form of care work for the self, but also for the larger family, which is often the beneficiary of the finished textile artefacts (2007: 129). However, in recent decades and with the rise of online sales platforms such as Etsy, many Western hobby sewers have, in fact, transformed their hobby into small business ventures (Luckman 2013; Walker 2007). Some of the participants in the Guldusi competitions are such entrepreneurs; they sell patterns or finished products and work as professional textile artists as well as tutors. Consequently, the needlework practices of these women are, to a certain extent, influenced by external factors such as competition deadlines, a perceived responsibility to online followers and, in some cases, certainly also financial needs. In addition, they may struggle to make time for their personal hobby alongside demands on their presence as carers and/or professionals (Luckman 2013; Stalp 2007).

The Afghans are required to deliver their completed squares in time for the quarterly collection. For each embroiderer, the number of squares she is commissioned to produce can vary from ten to 100 squares. The pressure of time, or lack thereof, naturally also affects not only the execution of the embroidery, but also the initial design process. This became very obvious in the two projects described earlier in which the Afghans had to engage with an initial design that was provided to them. As I mentioned, despite detailed guidelines to align their embroidery with the work provided to them, many did not do so. Some did not even consider the orientation of the already embroidered motifs. 'It was only then that I realized the sharp contrast to the amount of time the European women had to engage with the project, to design and to become acquainted with the concept', explains Goldenberg, 'To the Afghans this must appear as a complete luxury' (2013: n.p.). After all, each European needlewoman participated in the scheme because she chose to do so, whereas for the Afghans it was a work assignment, which they had only six days to complete. Nonetheless, Goldenberg feels that the resulting textile artefacts form interesting examples of cross-cultural, collaborative textile works in their own right. For her, they resemble the 'different realities and expectations that collide as two very distinct cultures meet' (Goldenberg 2013: n.p.).

These expectations also clash in the reception of the completed four-hands projects – at least in Europe. Testimonials from Guldusi's website, as I have indicated, suggest a high degree of awareness of the cultural background of the embroideries and interest in the Afghan women on the part of the Europeans. For example, a needlewoman from Germany states: 'The project made me want to find out more about the country, its history and culture and the lives of its people, especially the women in Laghmani. By now I have an invested interested in them – they have become a part of my world and of our shared world' (Guldusi n.d.). Concerns by customers about the situation of the embroiderers during the Taliban siege in summer 2021 further supports this. By contrast, as Goldenberg explained during our interview, the reaction of the Afghan women appears to be very different:

> The Europeans are often disappointed when I say this, but experience shows that the Afghan women are neither very interested in what happens with their embroideries nor do they show much appreciation for the finished works. Their homes do not feature any wall decorations from an artistic angle. But even if there are practical aspects to a piece, for example, a bag, they do not understand why someone would invest time and money into making something when its manufactured equivalent could be easily purchased.
>
> Appendix 2017

In other words, the envisaged act of cultural encounter and exchange appears to be primarily one-sided and to take place through the expressive narrative power of the European needlewomen. Both Afghan and European women speak of the enjoyable and meditative effect of practices of needlework. Yet, these embodied experiences take place within very different contexts and thus do not reflect similar investments in the meaning of the practices, or indeed in the feelings attached to them. However, as I argue in the next section, drawing on David Gauntlett's concept of 'making is connecting' (2011, 2018), practices of needlework provide both the Afghan and the European needlewomen (albeit in diverse ways) with the opportunity to become oriented towards different ways of feeling and being.

Conclusion: The Power to Connect

This chapter has highlighted the complexity of transnational feminist solidarity initiatives between women in the Global North and South. I have shown how needlework practices and representations of everyday, shared cultural practices, like tea drinking, cooking or gardening, are not a neutral foundation through which to mediate cultural encounters. Women's affective relations to these practices differ with regard to their personal positions and reflect larger unequal power structures that privilege the experiences of women in the Global North. Thus, the extent to which shared practices and a shared gendered identity as needlewomen can function as a building block for transnational feminist solidarity is limited. Indeed, as I have shown, the encounter between the different women and their cultures, as well as the resulting textile artefacts regularly frames the Afghan women and their embroideries within contemporary Orientalist discourses. The cultural encounter is shaped within a discursive and affective framework that constructs the Afghan women (to some extent) as the Oriental other, fixed within dominant cultural narratives about a backwards and oppressive Islam and its disenfranchised women, in contrast to the supposedly empowered and autonomous women of the Global North.

For cultural studies scholar David Gauntlett, however, any act of making is always also an act of connecting. Not only are disparate pieces put together, but 'acts of creativity usually [also] involve, at some point, a social dimension and connect us with each other' (2011: 2). Such connections take place, for instance, when Goldenberg advises the Afghan women on their embroidery, or when European women purchase Guldusi embroidery from a national representative at a quilt show, or as hundreds of people view a selection of four-hands projects in a local gallery somewhere in Europe. On another level, Gauntlett proposes that making is connecting because 'through making things and sharing them in the world, we increase our engagement and connection with our social and physical environments' (2011: 2). As such, making generates encounters with materials, people, ideas and also affects. Through needlework, the Afghan and European needlewomen are moved affectively and socially. The European women are gestured towards the experience of women from a different cultural context and, in many cases, become invested in a country, culture and a group of women to which they previously did not pay much attention. Guldusi invites and encourages European needlewomen to engage creatively with the history of the Afghan embroideries and the textured life of their makers. As such, the purchase of an embroidered square is not necessarily an act of mindless consumption but can also resemble an act of participation based on beliefs about 'the social, communal, reciprocal, and identity-forming aspects of amateur making' (Hackney 2013: 182).

The Afghan embroiderers develop new relations with themselves and others in their immediate community as a result of their new creative routine. As Gauntlett suggests, 'making and sharing is already a political act', because individual and collective creative practices provide a space for the negotiation and expression of the self in relation to others (2011: 233). As I have explained, this negotiation does not necessarily result in a shift in people's intimate attachments to unequal structures of power that privilege their experience over that of others. It does, however, put the possibility of this shift within reach. In this sense, cross-cultural needlework initiatives like Guldusi may orient people towards a transformative transnational feminist solidarity: one not grounded in the presumed shared gendered experience of (needle)women, but rather in the recognition of the affective dissonance of this experience. Through the making and sharing of the embroidered squares and the four-hands projects, different individuals and cultures become connected within existing structures of knowledge and power. In this sense, Guldusi provides a space for political acts to take shape and place. A received awareness of power structures and their workings, however, is indispensable. Only then can needlework practitioners and scholars engage productively with cross-cultural collaborative needlework projects as spaces for cultural encounter and as a means to foster solidarity and support between needlewomen from different backgrounds. As a result, the status quo, which places certain narratives over others, can be questioned and redefined.

4

Knitting Feminist Politics: Craftivism and Affective Tension

On a cold day in January 2017, the National Mall in Washington, DC, was filled with well over four hundred thousand marchers. The majority were women and each wore a two-pointed, fluffy pink hat known as a Pussyhat. With this 'sea of pink', Krista Suh's vision of a visibly united front of marchers had been realized. Not only in Washington, DC, but also in many other cities across the United States and the world, this 'sea of pink' became one of the defining features of the Women's Marches that took place the day after the inauguration of Donald Trump as president of the US. Together with Jayna Zweiman, Suh had come up with the idea of the Pussyhat in order to facilitate those unable physically to attend a march to contribute and have a material presence. The Pussyhat immediately gained iconic status; it was featured on the cover of *Time Magazine* and a Pussyhat worn at the Women's March on Washington was admitted into the collection of the V&A Museum in London just shortly after the march took place. The V&A catalogue identifies the hat as 'a global symbol of female solidarity and the power of collective action' (n.d.). Yet, from the outset, the Pussyhat project and the Women's March had also been subject to much criticism from all sides of the political spectrum.

This chapter considers the Pussyhat project as a texture in the transnational feminist struggle for liberation. The initiative along with the Women's March, of which it was part, has received ample scholarly scrutiny, including in textiles and material culture studies, feminist theory, geography, sociology, media and communications studies, as well as worldwide media attention. Many of these analyses variously examine the Pussyhat project and the Women's March in the context of histories of textile craft and feminist activism and appear overly concerned with determining whether both can be classified as good or bad activism/feminism (Banet-Weiser 2018; Boothroyd *et al.* 2017; Derr 2017; Dvorak 2017). Others are more concerned with highlighting the complexity of both initiatives and the concept of craftivism more broadly (Black 2017; Bruder

2019; Mandell 2019). Extending the analysis in the previous chapters, I use texture as a methodological lens through which to trace some of the different threads that have shaped the Pussyhat project, its reception and legacy, including a craftivist initiative called the Kudzu project, while, at the same time, also paying attention to the entangled nature of these threads. Texture here encompasses the materialities of woollen or acrylic yarn, completed hats, and the needles and bodies involved in the making process, but also the moods, sensations and affective intimacies created through networked forms of making and activism. By conceptualizing the Pussyhat project as texture, I point to the role of affect, embodied orientation and making for ontologies of social transformation and becoming activist. My focus on affect and texture allows for looking at the way in which people become moved and oriented differently towards the potential of liberation and changing the status quo. Such an approach also makes it possible to consider and stay with the affective tension that characterizes much of transnational feminist solidarity, yet, as I have argued, is also pertinent to a transformative feminist politics that does not privilege the experiences of white middle-class women from the Global North (May 2023).

In addition to the Pussyhat project, this chapter examines the Kudzu project, a guerrilla knitting initiative which began in the southern United States. Although directly inspired by the grassroots organizing of the Pussyhat project, the Kudzu project has received little scholarly attention so far (Beetham 2020). This is particularly surprising given the latter's explicit engagement with questions of white supremacy, white privilege, activism and solidarity – topics which, as I shall outline in more detail below, were at the heart of critiques of the Pussyhat project and the Women's March. Founded in Charlottesville, Virginia, the Kudzu project campaigns for the removal of Confederate monuments across the southern US and especially those positioned outside courthouses. It uses knitting and crochet installations to draw public attention to the relationship between certain monuments, white supremacy and racism at a time when this topic has become of public interest not only in the US but also in other countries such as Britain, Germany and South Africa (Nasar 2020). By exploring these two craftivist initiatives in relation to each other, this chapter contributes to and expands burgeoning debates about craftivism, white supremacy and social change (Ivey 2019; Hewett 2021; Walker 2020).

I explore how craftivism, which is often referred to as a gentle form of activism, is combined with traditional forms of direct political action, such as protest marches, as well as online and offline forms of social organizing, to flesh out the resistant potential of 'fabriculture', a term which captures the connection between textile crafts and the digital (Bratich and Brush 2011). By bringing these topics in conversation with prefigurative politics, I flesh out how practices of needlework can be part of resistant practices through which a more egalitarian and democratic society may evolve as part of the very process of taking action and 'doing politics' (Dixon 2014: 7).

The Pussyhat Project: Knitting Anger, Discontent and Solidarity

Suh and Zweiman's vision of a 'sea of pink' was very much steeped in an awareness of the power of images and the speed at which they spread thanks to digital technologies (Suh 2018: 71). They wanted to empower marchers through 'a unique collective visual statement ... which will help activists be better heard' (Pussyhat Project n.d.). Devastated by Trump's election win, Suh and Zweiman, like many others, embraced the Women's March and subsequently the Pussyhat project as a powerful outlet for their feelings of fear, frustration and the need somehow to react and do something. For many liberals and leftists in the US and across the world, the election result came as a surprise and shock (Singh 2016). Feminists feared especially the devastating effects Trump's administration might have on reproductive rights, LGBTQ+ rights and immigration legislation; fears which turned out to be entirely warranted because the Trump administration would rescind the rights of trans people and pave the way for the 2022 Supreme Court decision which overturned American women's right to abortion (Litvan 2022). Zweiman and Suh launched the Pussyhat project to 'provide people who cannot physically march on the National Mall a way to represent themselves and support women's rights' (Pussyhat Project n.d.). They conceived the now-iconic pink hat with the two cat-like ears as a means of demonstrating solidarity with the marchers, by the making of such a hat and gifting it to a marcher. The hat would be symbolic of a person's support for women's rights even if that person was not physically present at a march.

The fact that Suh and Zweiman, although novice knitters, had managed to produce this basic hat in a short amount of time under the guidance of an experienced knitting store owner, convinced them that others would be able to do so as well (Suh 2018: 72). They set up a partnership with a local knitting store owner in Los Angeles and with an artist to create accessible knitting, crochet and sewing instructions for the hat. Next, they began harnessing the internet and social media to publicize their initiative (Suh 2018: 124). The project ties in with the wider spirit of craftivism, which regards the time and effort invested in making something as a sign of one's dedication to a particular cause. Suh explains: 'If it was too easy, people wouldn't feel that they were really doing something meaningful. . . . Challenge will add meaning and purpose, which will inevitably draw people in, and those will ask others to be involved, and so on and so forth. And in this way, movements are born' (2018: 125). Indeed, the initiative soon became so popular that knitting stores had trouble restocking the bright pink colour that the pattern called for (Fielding 2017).

The hat design itself addresses in various ways the concerns of the marchers and the reasons for the organization of the protest. The project's website states: 'The name Pussyhat™ was chosen in part as a protest against vulgar comments Donald Trump made about the freedom he felt to grab women's genitals, to de-stigmatize the word "pussy" and transform it into one of empowerment, and to highlight the design of the hat's "pussycat ears"' (Pussyhat Project n.d.). By calling the hat a Pussyhat in a humorous gesture, Suh and Zweiman also aimed to reclaim the term 'pussy' from its derogatory usage not only in relation to female genitalia, but also with regard to 'the feminine' (Pussyhat Project n.d.), a term that is still regularly associated with weakness, inadequacy and irrationality. Similarly, according to Suh, the colour pink was chosen precisely because of its connotations with femininity and how by extension it becomes 'a code for women' and, as such, 'is considered a little bit frivolous, girly, weak, soft, [and] effeminate' (quoted in Compton 2017: n.p.). Wearing this hat as part of a women's protest, for Suh and Zweiman resembles an act of reclamation in which 'the symbolism is all about "pussy power"' (quoted in Compton 2017: n.p.).

Although the project quickly gained in popularity and Pussyhat collection points were arranged all over the country, along with meeting points ahead of the start of the march, the initiative also received criticism from all sides of the political spectrum with regards to the design and name of the hat, as well as its general vision. The name and its association with female genitalia came under attack on social media and in the mainstream press for being transphobic by reducing women's identity to female genitalia (Boothroyd *et al.* 2017; Compton 2017; Derr 2017; Gentile 2018; Richardson 2018; Shamus 2018). Conservatives, on the other hand, expressed outrage at the perceived vulgarity of the hat (Andrews 2017; Levenson 2017). The pink colour of the hat has also come under attack for being white-centric and racist as it has been interpreted to suggest that female genitalia are naturally pink thus excluding women of colour (Brewer and Dundes 2018; Bunyasi and Smith 2018).

This critique in particular resonates with more general criticisms of the Women's March and its agenda as primarily white and mainstream feminist – and thus lacking inclusivity and intersectionality (Banet-Weiser 2018; Boothroyd *et al.* 2017; Brewer and Dundes 2018; Bunyasi and Smith 2018; Moss and Maddrell 2017). These points, voiced by organizers from Black Lives Matter, among others, 'suggest concerns that white feminists lack motivation to prioritize issues that disproportionately affect Black communities' (Brewer and Dundes 2018: 50). In this vein, the work of Sierra Brewer and Lauren Dundes shows that a number of women of colour believe that 'the march provided white women with a means to protest the election rather than a way to address social injustice disproportionately affecting lower social classes and people of color' (2018: 49). Further, drawing on Lauren Berlant's work, one could say that the election of Trump – and the Women's March as a response to it – are examples of how 'the genre of crisis can distort something structural and ongoing into something that seems shocking and exceptional' when, indeed, it is part of everyday life for many (2011: 7). Misogyny and racism are certainly not new problems for the US, nor indeed for any of the other places where satellite marches took place. Yet, the election of Trump – and the public social acceptability of hate speech that arguably accompanied it (in a manner similar to Brexit in the UK and right-wing populism across Europe) – were perceived as a shocking surprise by many white liberals in the West (Singh 2016). However, the ongoing and often unprosecuted police killings of Black people in the US, the acquittal of white vigilantes like Kyle Rittenhouse, and the violent storming of the US Capitol just weeks before the Biden/Harris presidential inauguration are evidence that, even with a Democratic president and the first woman of colour as vice president, these issues have not lost their relevance post-Trump presidency.

For many people of colour, the election of Trump was no surprise, nor indeed a sign of crisis, but rather confirmed the structural racism that they experienced to various degrees throughout their lives (Singh 2016; Pedwell 2021). The peaceful atmosphere of the Women's Marches with no arrests nor any direct clashes with police recorded can be viewed as a further manifestation of white privilege because for many white women the march appeared to be a 'fun' experience of protest and direct action. Their whiteness, and in many cases heteronormativity, enabled them to 'march freely', whereas Black Lives Matter protests which are primarily attended by Black people invariably encounter police in riot gear (Ramanathan 2017). Thus, the marches also echo ongoing debates about participatory citizenship and who has access to the public sphere and, consequently, about who is heard politically (Ratto and Boler 2014: 14). Yet, some critics also suggest that the Pussyhat project and the 'fun' atmosphere of the marches diminish the radical political potential of the protest as its playfulness and connotations of cuteness, craft and homemade comfort supposedly 'undercut the message that the march is trying to send' (Dvorak 2017:

n.p.). Although *Washington Post* columnist Petula Dvorak remained strangely vague about identifying this central message, she called for 'grit, not gimmick' at the Women's March (2017: n.p.). She appeared to be convinced that having anything playful or fun at a women's protest would be detrimental to its effectiveness, thus echoing larger debates about strategic direct action and different activist tactics.

I contend that the Pussyhat project and the Women's March, like other feminist craft initiatives (Foster 2019), faced particular scrutiny in this respect because they were women-led and made use of a stereotypically feminine practice, namely knitting. As such, critiques of the protest and the Pussyhat project as too playful and, consequently, too feminine resonate with the long cultural history, that I outlined in more detail in the Introduction to this book, in which femininity, women's work and activism repeatedly have been dismissed as irrelevant within a society in which patriarchy is the overarching structure. In addition, some of the critiques echo positivist approaches to measuring the effectiveness of a protest or social movement in terms of, for example, quantifiable changes within existing governmental structures which may include new laws and federal budgets (Dean 2016; Kauffman 2017). Such approaches are limited because they can lead to restricting social movements to a framework where success is measured according to standards put in place by the very system the movement is trying to change. In other words, if policy change is the ultimate measure of success, radical visions for a society founded on alternative forms of governance are side-lined from the outset. Within this framework, it is also difficult to conceptualize change outside a linear narrative, which moves inexorably from action or protest to policy change, when, in fact, it is more often a non-linear and iterative process (Pedwell 2021). Claims about the necessity for movements to be united around a single issue are similarly part of such a positivist approach to understanding social transformation (Petrick 2017). In the following sections, using texture not just as a metaphor, but as a method through which to conceptualize the entangled nature of personal and social transformation, I offer a different framework for making sense of the complexity of craftivist initiatives like the Pussyhat and the Kudzu projects within the context of a transnational feminist struggle for solidarity and an end to oppression.

Textures of Activism

From the very beginning, the Women's March was not a single-issue protest, but was marked by a multiplicity of concerns that made protesters take to the streets:

ranging from reproductive rights, healthcare and police brutality, to outrage about Trump's sexist comments, and a disappointment about Hilary Clinton's election loss (Brewer and Dundes 2018; Bunyasi and Smith 2018; Moss and Maddrell 2017). The organizers of the Pussyhat project appear to have been aware of this diversity and indeed embraced it as a means to start conversation across different issues and to develop intersections between them. Knitters were given the opportunity to print a simple paper tag on which they could write about what inspired them to support the protest and the issues that were deeply important to them. This form could then be attached to the finished hat to be shared with others.

As the critiques of the Pussyhat project and the Women's March show, and as I have highlighted throughout this book, solidarity between women, based on women's shared gendered identity, cannot be taken for granted. Instead, as Black feminist Akwugo Emejulu argues, feminist solidarity must be actively developed and practised 'through individual and collective action'. In addition, it 'requires tough conversations' about white women's complicity with racist and sexist structures that disproportionately marginalize women of colour, when white women themselves also experience oppression because of their gender (Emejulu 2018: 272). Critically assessing one's complicity with patriarchy and white supremacy, and how these structures are often (though perhaps unintentionally) reproduced in liberation movements and initiatives like the Pussyhat project, can be an uncomfortable experience for activists who consider themselves as anti-racists and ethical individuals. It requires personal reflection, as well as an active commitment to unpicking the fundamental weave of North American and Western European societies with the intention of assembling it anew, while being conscious of personal position and privilege (Hunter and van der Westhuizen 2022; Phipps 2020). The kinds of 'tough conversations' to which Emejulu (2018) refers can push people towards an awareness of their personal privilege and the intricate ways their actions are embedded within larger social structures. This process of recognition, however, is rarely a pleasant one and will invariably require white people to challenge their own behaviour. Being confronted with personal privilege and complicity can be an unsettling experience as it not only asks people to confront social structures, but also intimate attachments to institutions, feelings, relations and systems that, at the very least, have provided a degree of comfort and stability to them (Sullivan 2014, 2019; Yancy 2014, 2018). So rather than dismissing the Pussyhat project as 'bad activism', it seems valuable to consider how it may have acted as a catalyst to have these 'tough conversations' on social media as well as through the mainstream press (May 2020) and how its commitment to long-term grassroots organizing has sparked new craftivist initiatives, like the Kudzu project, which are explicitly committed to dismantling white supremacy.

I suggest that participation in the Pussyhat project, particularly as the knitter of a hat, can provide an initial entryway into exploring one's own affective ties with structures that oppress others and oneself. While this participation may not result in measurable social change, it may provide an opening for an engagement with the nature of these attachments. It is precisely because of our affective attachments to structures of power that reflection about our intimate connections may lead to a questioning of the status quo (Manning 2016; Pedwell 2021). In this context, scholars and craftivists Tal Fitzpatrick and Katve-Kaisa Konturri speak of a 'micropolitics' that encompasses 'focus and belief in the transformative power of brief political moments, slow repetitive processes, and subtle yet sensible relations' (2015: section 4). Following Deleuze and Guattari's work on micropolitics (1987), they locate the political in fleeting intimacies and momentary desires as well as lasting affective investments (see also Pedwell 2021). Crafting can initiate such a micropolitics, as in the case of the Pussyhat project; it can point people towards these brief political intimacies and towards the creation of new relationships without insisting on absolute unity (see also Fitzpatrick 2019). It can serve to create 'a greater extent of communality' because people who would not necessarily be sharing a space are brought together (Fitzpatrick and Konturri 2015: section 4).

In addition, initiatives like the Pussyhat project (and, as I shall outline in the next section, the Kudzu project) can make people more aware of their own position in relation to other bodies and, more importantly, make them open up towards these bodies 'and to feel how their relation to other bodies is both constitutive and indispensable' (Fitzpatrick and Konturri 2015: section 3). As a result, the focus can be moved from one that aims to eradicate differences to one that explores how it becomes possible to exist in a state of affective tension and dissonance and to collectively organize for a more just future (Hemmings 2012; May 2023). In the spirit of a prefigurative politics, collective visions for a future free from domination thus become part of the tactics of the present moment (Swain 2019; Yates 2015). These tactics are grounded in affective relations, and the making with hands and fibre contributes to the short- and long-term forging of such relations. The Pussyhat project defines itself not as a context-specific initiative that exists only in relation to the Women's March, but as 'an ongoing movement that uses design to create social change' (Zweiman 2018: n.p.). Like the Women's March itself, the project is invested in fostering grassroots community activism through facilitating activist networks and encouraging more women to become community leaders and to run for political office (Pussyhat Project: n.d.). The Kudzu project, with its knitting installations on Confederate statues, is one such grassroots initiative which claims to 'follow the powerful example of the Pussyhat Project' to use knitters' 'awesome talent and energy to change the world' (Kudzu Project n.d.).

The Kudzu Project

The Kudzu project is a guerrilla knitting initiative based in Charlottesville, Virginia. Charlottesville is the town in which a group of neo-nazis and alt-right Trump supporters marched on 11 and 12 August 2017. The marches were violent and one opposition protester was killed when an alt-right extremist purposefully drove his car into the crowd of protesters. Like many other towns in the American South, Charlottesville has a number of Confederate monuments that were erected during the era of the Jim Crow laws, which enforced racial segregation, between the end of the American Civil War and 1968. For example, there are statues of General 'Stonewall' Jackson and an anonymous Confederate soldier outside Albemarle County Courthouse.

Margo Smith, the creator of the Kudzu project, is a middle-aged white woman and a long-term knitter. She was an active participant in the Pussyhat project and knitted multiple hats for people who requested one through her Instagram account. As a resident of Charlottesville, she witnessed first-hand the violent white supremacist marches in 2017 in response to the city council's decision to remove a statue of Confederate general Robert E. Lee and rename the park of the same name in which the statue stood. In the aftermath of these white supremacist marches, Smith came across an image of a drawing by artist David Loewenstein on social media. Titled *Defunct Monument I – Racism*, the drawing in green, grey and yellow shows a statue: a large stone pedestal on which a male bronze figure stands with his right arm stretched out, palm facing upwards. All but the right hand of the statue is covered in bright green kudzu vines, including the stone pedestal. For Smith, seeing the image was the ultimate spark of inspiration: 'I was driving to work one day and it just all of a sudden hit me.... I thought we could realize the vision that this artist had of vine-covered statues ... get people to knit the leaves and put all this kudzu together in a way that we could blanket a statue' (quoted in Goldbard and Smith 2017: n.p.).

The choice of kudzu is deliberate. As a non-native invasive plant, kudzu has become a prominent plant throughout the South as it grows extremely fast, drowns out other types of vegetation and spreads across open spaces, buildings, discarded vehicles and, of course, also monuments if not managed and cut back regularly. According to Smith, 'kudzu covered ruins elicit romantic notions about the past' and this points to the ways in which the Confederate cause and the Civil War have been romanticized as individuals' commitment 'to protect states' rights rather than the institution of slavery' (Smith 2019: 33). The myth of the 'Lost Cause of the Confederacy', which is regularly evoked by those who insist on the relevance of Confederate statues, 'whitewashes and recasts the Confederacy [and] the reality of the Civil War' as the story of heroic white individuals in the South trying to protect their way of life without acknowledging that this way of life was based on the dehumanization of Black people (McNutt 2017: 142). For Smith, 'this rewriting of the Civil War narrative has concealed ugly historical truths in much the same way that kudzu hides whatever lies beneath it' (2019: 33) and thus makes the plant such a powerful symbol for activism.

Guerrilla knitting, alternatively called yarn graffiti or yarn bombing, started as a popular phenomenon in the early 2000s and refers to the covering of objects in public space with knitted items, ideally during the night to create a surprise effect in the morning. Often, the installations, which include covering tree trunks or lamp posts or decorating mailboxes in frilly covers, particularly engage with urban spaces and are seen as subversive acts of bringing colour and warmth into bleak cityscapes and their metal and cement facades (Goggin 2014; Hahner and Varda 2014). As such, they can also be seen as a form of political protest against the contemporary moment and its culture of high performance as they invite passers-by to pay attention to and appreciate the mundane (Mann 2015). Unlike practitioners of traditional spray-paint street graffiti, yarn bombers, many of whom are white middle-class women, barely face repercussions from officials even though the activity of covering up and, by extension, defacing public property is illegal in most settings. Moreover, while yarn graffiti does not usually do long-term damage to buildings and other objects in the way that spray paint does, the remnants of a yarn bomb installation once destroyed, either by vandalism or from prolonged exposure to the weather, can clog up sewage systems and storm drains. Yet, yarn bombing installations are rarely removed by officials and indeed often get appropriated by local councils for publicity and marketing stunts as evidence of a city's peculiar charm as well as official support for locals' creative projects (Farinosi and Fortunati 2018; Hahner and Varda 2014; McGovern 2022).

The installations are seen as a fun and cute but non-threatening activity performed by women (Close 2018). Spray-paint graffiti, although also a medium for subversive (as well as direct) expression of political critique and resistance, in contrast, is perceived as vandalism and subject to stringent prosecution (Hahner and Varda 2014). In addition, spray-paint graffiti has become the expressive cultural marker of unruly youth street culture, which is often conceptually linked to wayward male youths of colour (Hahner and Varda 2014). According to scholars Leslie Hahner and Scott Varda (2014), the celebration of yarn bombing as respectable acts of protest only serves to further vilify spray-paint graffiti. They claim that 'yarn bombing's emancipatory potential is warranted through the aesthetic sensibilities of privileged classes', namely, white middle-class (and often middle-aged) women as the primary practitioners of yarn bombing (Hahner and Varda 2014: 302). Yarn bombing installations are perceived as subversive but, because of the association between knitting/crochet and (white) femininity, also as non-threatening to the status quo. At the same time, a number of yarn bombers are appropriating the supposed connection between their own practice and that of Black graffiti and hip hop art by choosing aliases 'to tag their work' that echo this cultural tradition, for example, Knitta, Knitty Graffity, Knotorious N.I.T., or P-Knitty (Hahner and Varda 2014: 314; Close 2018).

Participant research suggests that yarn bombers embrace the 'juxtaposition between yarn bombing as something sneaky and deviant yet amusing and enjoyable' (McGovern 2022: 6). According to cultural criminologist Alice McGovern, 'while interviewees were cognizant of the risks involved in the act, it was clear that many felt these risks were not significant ones' (2022: 6). McGovern explores the question of yarn bombing and deviancy in the context of subcultural taste and broader understandings of aesthetic orders that apparently remain unchallenged by yarn graffiti, unlike with street graffiti. Although McGovern (2022) draws on the work of Hahner and Varda (2014), the issue of white privilege, which makes it unlikely that encounters between makers and the police would be life-threatening for the former, is eschewed in the discussion.[1] As I have argued in chapter one in my discussion of the reception of the quilts by Chawne Kimber and the Social Justice Sewing Academy, it is, however, crucial that analyses of the political potential of needlework and specific practices like yarn bombing, tackle this issue head-on. Avoiding it not only bypasses the issue at hand, but, as a result, also misses out on important opportunities for theoretical and practical social justice work.

The Kudzu project inhabits a unique position within the guerrilla knitting landscape because it actively taps into such transformative work. It uses guerrilla

Figure 4.1 The Kudzu project flash installation, Nelson County Courthouse, Lovingston, Virginia, 2018. (Photo by Tom Cogill; © Margo Smith)

knitting as a way to highlight white supremacy as an overarching issue that manifests itself in the presence of Confederate monuments across the American South. The knitting installations by which members of the Kudzu project cover a statue with a blanket of knitted and crocheted Kudzu leaves and vines is intended to draw attention to this issue. It states on the project's website: 'Confederate memorials play [a role] in perpetuating false narratives about the Civil War and white supremacy' (Kudzu Project n.d.). In particular, those monuments outside or within courthouses 'indicate that this civic space is aligned with the values of the Confederacy' thus 'proclaim[ing] a legal system that intends to disadvantage people of color' (Kudzu Project 2018: n.p.).

As such, the initiative plays on the connotations of craftivism and yarn bombing as the less threatening or more gentle form of activism to address issues such as white supremacy and racism that, often, white people do not want to engage with because they do not want to face their own complicity with racist structures. The white women installing the knitted kudzu, however, usefully utilize their white privilege in the interests of social justice as they are less likely to face police arrests or possibly violent attacks by passers-by than are people of colour. Since all participants act mainly anonymously and the initiative 'maintains a high level of secrecy to maximize the impact of the installation and to protect participants from backlash from white supremacists', it is also not possible for participants to participate as part of a public performance of anti-racism and 'good politics'. Nevertheless, many Pussyhat makers and wearers have been criticized for performing popular visibility feminism, which lacks sustained commitment to social justice for all (Banet-Weiser 2018; Phipps 2020). According to feminist scholar Sarah Banet-Weiser, 'the visibility of popular feminism, where examples appear on television, in film, on social media, and on bodies, is important, but it often stops there, as if *seeing* or purchasing feminism is the same thing as changing patriarchal structures' (2018: pos. 303–6, original emphasis). Smith, the creator of the Kudzu project, argues that, in the case of her initiative, 'the anonymity makes [participants'] efforts even more remarkable' (2019: 37). Anonymity and secrecy guarantee the project's viability, but they may also nurture more meaningful engagement on the side of the makers involved.

Their first installation was removed by a passer-by at dawn just minutes after it had been put up and, subsequently, the police were called to stop participants from putting it up again. So now the initiative practises 'flash installations'. During the early morning hours approximately thirty local Virginia members of the group will quickly cover a Confederate monument or name sign of a building or public space, take some pictures and then take the kudzu blanket down again for reuse in future installations. However, they leave behind one knitted strand of kudzu to greet passers-by and 'to symbolize the power and promise of small acts of resistance' (Smith 2019: 36). The idea for this was actually inspired by the act of destruction by the passer-by of the very first installation. When the blanket had been pulled off the monument, one lone strand of kudzu clung on to the figure's rifle. This lone strand of kudzu left behind at the installation site alters the public appearance of the statue but not irreversibly. Yet, for the time being it may affect the people passing by as well as the general atmosphere of the place. People may stop in their tracks taken by surprise on their way to a courthouse or school. Some might stop and wonder what's going on and bring it up in conversations with co-workers, family and friends. Others might shake their heads in disagreement and quickly walk on. Others yet may become irate and think about ways of taking down the lone strand, while some might not even notice as they walk past with their head down deep in thought or scrolling on their phone.

To make sure their flash installations reach a wide audience, the initiative posts pictures of the installation and the lone kudzu strand that is left behind on their Instagram and Facebook account as well as on their website. All the posts provide useful contexts about the relevant monument and the connection between Confederate monuments and white supremacy more generally. They also provide practical information in terms of what citizens can do to lobby the government officially to have the statues removed. Clearly, the initiative regards the knitting installations not as a means to an end but as part of a wider multi-pronged approach, which also includes petitions, lobbying local and state politicians and encouraging citizens to use their right to vote. The digital then is a key element for the Kudzu project, as it is for Chawne Kimber and the SJSA, to raise awareness, publicize their efforts and to encourage others. Similarly, the Pussyhat project, like so many contemporary activist movements, relied heavily on digital organising to realize its vision. Indeed, the combination of the handmade and the digital has been a defining factor of the contemporary craftivism movement, that both the Pussyhat and the Kudzu projects endorse as transformative models of activism and social change.

Digital Textures and Platforms for Creativity

The digital has come to play a vital role in contemporary activism and social organizing as well as for practices of needlework. From the Arab Spring to Occupy and Black Lives Matter, digital technology has helped to bring people together, arrange protests or spread the word about a particular cause. In addition, through hashtags like too or #FergusonFriday, it has enabled participatory digital archives that highlight the pervasiveness of sexism and racism in society (Gerbaudo 2012; Mendes, Ringrose and Keller 2019; Pedwell 2019).[2] Craftivist and scholar Tal Fitzpatrick explicitly includes the digital in her detailed definition of craftivism as a 'uniquely 21st century practice [that] involves the combination of craft techniques with elements of social and/or digital engagement' (2018: 3). In this sense, her definition reflects the way in which the digital is not only part of the texture of activism and craftivism, but of craft practices as a whole. Jack Bratich and Heidi Brush (2011) conceptualize contemporary textile crafts' deep intersection with the digital under the term 'fabriculture'. The term acknowledges the multiple ways in which the digital is used to share patterns and inspiration, purchase materials, network with other makers and display one's own creations. Fabriculture is also attuned to the ways the digital shapes the gendered spaces in which needlework is usually produced, including women's groups as well as the domestic environment, and how these spheres, in turn, are shaped by the capitalist craft industry. Thus, fabriculture is concerned with the entanglements of practices of needlework in relation to broader 'meaning-making, communicative, [and] community-building' activities (Bratich and Brush 2011: 234).

Networked technologies have not only enabled new forms of connection and sociality among makers, but, as sociologist Kate Orton-Johnson shows, 'have given users new ways to think about and engage with their creativity that, in turn, have become an embedded part of their construction and enjoyment of leisure practice' (2014: 305). The nature of the material practice of making something with your hands also changes in this context as 'the material, tactile processes of knitting are integrated with digital practices of livestreaming', for example, through recorded tutorials and work-in progress shots that are shared on platforms like Instagram, Flickr and Facebook (Orton-Johnson 2014: 305). During the pandemic these digital practices have increased hugely, connecting more crafters than before (Sullivan 2020). These digital practices, in turn, have an effect on the kind of meaning making that results from the performance of needlework as the process of making comes to accumulate meaning beyond individual notions of dwelling and relaxation. As research by Iona Literat and Sandra Markus (2020) shows, interest-based online spaces like the textile craft platform Ravelry's Pussyhat group were significant, in particular, also for the participation of older women in the initiative. Capturing and sharing the process of knitting a Pussyhat, sewing a dress or stitching a quilt across different types of digital media raises the possibility for new entanglements and orientations for the self and others.

Chawne Kimber's blogging, Instagramming and tweeting practices, outlined in chapter one, illustrate this. The work-in-progress shots that she shares are intended as ways to nudge, or 'poke', others towards dwelling in states of blockage or potential as part of everyday performances of the practice. Kimber hopes that her followers will take these work-in-progress shots and her comments about the project as a starting point for reflection about their own position and privilege in relation to race, gender, class and sexuality. Margo Smith was part of multiple craft and activism groups on Facebook that shaped her vision for the Kudzu project. Social media and other digital practices are not merely a supplementary element to the performance of needlework. They are a significant part of doing needlework and contribute to the experience and meaning of the practice. Many Stitch'nBitch or other types of needlework groups started out as leisure activity gatherings without a clear political agenda, but a significant number of groups transitioned into activism through the Pussyhat project (Literat and Markus 2020). As the initiative spread on social media and through the press, more and more knitting circles participated in making Pussyhats, and for many knitters their involvement culminated in their attendance at a Women's March. Likewise, the Kudzu project provides extensive instructions not only for knitting or crocheting leaves and vines, but also about how to organize installations. The digital, then, is as much an enabler for activism as the actual knitting or crochet itself.

According to media and cultural studies scholar David Gauntlett, the internet has enabled knitters and other crafters 'to collectively develop a firm and positive sense of shared meaning, and mission, which was probably more difficult to establish when craft activity was more fragmented and isolated' (2011: 6). The supportive feedback that the online community provides to the maker is extremely important, particularly since the internet and social media, in other areas, are marked by trolling and a reduced inhibition to give rude or offensive commentary (Gauntlett 2011). Jessica Bain's (2016) research into home dressmaking communities on Instagram, for example, shows that these spaces developed with the clear goal of practising kindness and body positivity, forms of communal conduct that the women felt were lacking in other spaces. Likewise, for many taking up knitting as a new hobby, '"becoming" a knitter occurs through and with the digital', as written and visual tutorials from blogs, YouTube channels and personal and commercial websites are used as resources for learning (Orton-Johnson 2014: 312). Meaning is therefore also created through the shared experience of practising the same hobby (Court 2020). However, it is important to note that engagement between practitioners in online and offline knitting circles regularly moves beyond the topic of knitting as they share personal stories and discuss day-to-day world happenings – and often, ultimately, also politics (Bratich and Brush 2011; Myzelev 2015; Stalp 2007). Though, as I noted in chapter one in relation to reactions to quilts by Chawne Kimber and the SJSA, bringing politics, and especially the issue of white supremacy and related injustices, into the textile crafts community, is often met with backlash. White privilege and white defensiveness, as I have outlined, are at the heart of such reactions which fail to acknowledge how systemic and structural inequalities disproportionately impact the everyday life of women of colour.[3]

For Gauntlett (2011, 2018), combining one's individual crafting practice with social media activity of all kinds is in itself decisively political because it allows for new personal connections to be made and networks to be forged. In this sense, sharing information about the Pussyhat or Kudzu projects and one's participation online is not only about spreading the word in order to secure a large turnout at a march, for instance, but also about entering into new relationships with others. In this context, sociologist Paolo Gerbaudo speaks of the important 'choreographing' function of digital technologies – and, in particular, social media – to social movements as it provides a 'means not simply to convey abstract opinions, but also to give a shape to the way in which people come together and act together' (2012: 4). Choreographing collective action is about more than simply getting a large number of people to show up at a specific place at a certain time. While social media surely played an important role in moving protest from the virtual to the town squares of Cairo, Egypt during the Arab Spring and to the streets of Ferguson, Missouri after the shooting of Michael Brown, it alone does not hold the power to create social movements. Instead, social media needs to be used in collaboration with face-to-face communication and interaction between participants (Gerbaudo 2012: 75).

The popularity of the Pussyhat project certainly grew through social media especially because the pattern and tutorials were available online. However, direct contact between women as part of knitting groups was probably equally as important. Participants came together in face-to-face knitting groups to knit alongside those who knitted alone from home but also connected online; they formed various affective relations with each other. More so, it was through the combination of the online and the physical community of knitters and marchers that a space could take shape in which not only to organize the logistics of the Pussyhat project and the Women's Marches, but to consider the very politics of these initiatives and their longevity. Fabriculture, in this context, involves the stories knitters share online and offline about personal experiences of sexism and discrimination, their concerns about the Trump presidency, but also their visions for mundane and extraordinary acts of resistance. As such, fabriculture not only choreographs collective action, but also resistant attitudes that can move people towards joining a march or knitting a hat for a protester. Because of the ephemerality of the Kudzu project's flash installations, digital photo galleries, like that of their website or Instagram account, are essential for gaining momentum and more visibility for their actions and the cause.

The Pussyhat project further capitalized on this virtual community through its Pussyhat Global Virtual March initiative to mark International Women's Day on 8 March 2017. The initiative asked people to 'Put on your pussyhat, make a sign about where you are and what you are for and take a picture. Upload to social media using #pussyhatglobal' (Pussyhat Project n.d.). People without social media were provided with an email address to which to send their images, which would then be shared on social media by the Pussyhat project team. On the website, the project also offers links to translations of the original hat pattern in multiple languages, while encouraging site visitors to provide translations in languages not yet included. In addition, the website provides a list of yarn stores across the world, which are allied to the project. As allies, these stores are committed to supporting those interested in making a hat as well as hosting Pussyhat-making sessions for groups and serving as a drop-off point for those keen on donating hats to marchers. In addition, allies allow customers who want to support the project but do not want to knit hats themselves to purchase yarn from them and to have it made into a hat by volunteers. Further, the Pussyhat project's website shares information about any Pussyhat-making gatherings that individuals around the world are organizing, thus serving as a virtual as well as a real-life community-building platform. These aspects of community building in relation to all kinds of making (physical or digital) are rewarding to participants, who typically value the recognition and support from a community of like-minded creators (Court 2020; Orton-Johnson 2014). In this context, online-to-offline functions as a continuum 'connecting the digital realm and the physical everyday world' (Gauntlett 2018: 307). Relationships and affective attachments developed in one arena carry over to the others and vice versa.

Craftivism: Practice and Potential

The craftivist manifesto on the website run by Betsy Greer, who is widely credited with popularizing the term in 2002, claims that 'craftivism is about raising consciousness, creating a better world stitch by stitch, and things made by hand, by a person', recognizing that 'activism, whether through crafts or any other means is done by individuals, not machines' (Greer n.d.). The manifesto, however, also asks that craftivists use their skill to 'share ideas with others in a way that is welcoming, not dividing', so that 'craftivism is a tool to instantly create a small part of the warmer, friendlier, and more colorful world we hope to see in the future' (Greer n.d.). According to this perspective, craftivism as a practice resembles a prefigurative politics in which the means used for activism in the present moment mirror the desired social relations of the future (Fitzpatrick and Kontturi 2015). It is about creating a welcoming and supportive environment for all.

This vision echoes popular discourses about needlework and the links between the handmade, femininity and comfort. Yet, as I have suggested throughout this book, it is vital to consider whose comfort is regarded as the baseline in this context. In chapter one, in relation to Chawne Kimber's work and the SJSA quilts, I showed how, when the comfort of those benefiting from white privilege and white supremacy is disrupted, they regularly take offence and are unwilling to engage meaningfully with the experiences of people of colour. Critiques of the Pussyhat project, as I have outlined, engage with questions of comfort and division from two main directions. The project has been dubbed inappropriate for political activism because of its playful nature and its associations with domestic craft and women's care work. At the same time, it has had a divisive effect in terms of alienating women of colour and trans women.

Greer, while advocating for the welcoming and restorative nature of craftivism also claims that 'the very essence of craftivism lies in creating something that gets people to ask questions; we invite others to join a conversation about the social and political intent of our creations' (2014: 8). In this sense, I argue that it is partly due to the heightened international visibility and popularity of the Pussyhat project that the concerns of women of colour and trans women, along with the wider histories of domination in which these concerns are embedded, have attracted widespread and unprecedented attention in mainstream media and on social media (May 2020). These conversations keep being revisited, along with a discussion of the perceived success and/or failure of the Pussyhat project, the Women's March and grassroot organizing initiatives like the Kudzu project that have followed in their wake. Without the Pussyhats as a possible visual marker for white- and cis-centrism within feminist movements, these oppressive legacies and the ways they affect contemporary feminist activism and solidarity could perhaps not have been addressed and discussed so widely. Prior to this, there seems to have been a lack of a tangible widely popularized marker in which to ground critiques, which relate not only to the Pussyhats but also to wider systemic and structural issues within feminism.

For Sarah Corbett, founder of the Craftivist Collective and, along with Greer, one of the most well-known craftivists, craftivism provides a form of gentle protest through which one can 'alone or in a group – effectively protest against harmful structures, attract people to protest, and reflect on the way we want our world to be, challenging injustice and harm through values of love, kindness and humility' (2017: 30). She claims that 'approaching injustice with aggressive anger is unhelpful for our protest' (Corbett 2017: 27). For this reason, Corbett suggests that 'compassion and empathy for all involved' including victims and perpetrators is the first step to a type of activism that recognizes everybody's humanity (2017: 27). The time invested in making a craft is a crucial aspect of this form of protest. It symbolizes compassion and introduces an element of mindfulness into protest because of the calming and restorative effects associated with craft practices. Further, the time investment should be seen as an important reminder to the often slow pace of change, which requires a long-term commitment as opposed to quick and rash, but showy, actions. According to an article in *The New Yorker*, Greer regretted the lack of recognition of the time commitment involved in the press coverage of the Pussyhat project. For her, this was, in fact, a vital aspect of the initiative as it 'may signify that we are ready to take action in a way we haven't seen before' (quoted in Walker 2017: n.p.). Given a tweet by Trump's lawyer Michael Cohen, which questioned whether the Pussyhats had been made in America, this point appears especially poignant (Walker 2017: n.p.). Trumpists seemed quick to dismiss protesters' efforts and credibility by drawing attention to the presumed ethical shortcomings of their actions, which were framed as evidence of the initiative's inability to live up to the same moral standards they demand from government and society.

Fitzpatrick argues that craftivism as a method for protest is also about turning anger into something sustainable for personal well-being, which can effectively promote social transformation (2018, 2019). Yet, she also acknowledges the legitimacy of anger in the face of social injustice and its importance for 'galvanizing and mobilizing large groups quickly' (2018: 2). In addition, she demonstrates an awareness of different forms of 'tone policing', which are historically directed specifically towards women of colour. The Black Lives Matter movement, for example, has been criticized for its 'refusal to contain Black rage', because this may lead to the alienation of white supporters as well as being counterproductive to eliciting white empathy (Hooker 2017: 484). However, as Black writer and activist Audre Lorde ([1984] 2007) argued almost four decades ago, anger is crucial to conversations about racism because to recognize Black women's anger is also to acknowledge the structural racism at the bottom of it. Indeed, for Lorde, this anger is generative because it can be transformed creatively into practices that foster social change ([1984] 2007: 128). Fitzpatrick suggests that this creative element can be provided through the process of crafting as well as the finished object (2018: 2). In this context, irony and humour and the incongruities they create are perceived as useful tools for highlighting different viewpoints so that craftivism can effectively be 'deployed to reveal dissensus instead of focusing on conviviality and consensus' (Fitzpatrick 2019: 185).

Not only do craft-based initiatives provide an opportunity to offer practical solutions to local problems, but they can also orient people differently as they may 'inspire that kind of love and generosity that gets people to open their hearts and change their minds' (Fitzpatrick 2018: 2). As such, craft can potentially also be a useful method to highlight the difference between hatred and anger: both emotions that dominated during the run-up to the presidential election of 2016 and continued to do so under the Trump administration and beyond (Bell 2019). For Lorde, hatred has only one objective: to be divisive and to cause death and destruction ([1984] 2007: 129). Unlike anger it cannot serve any generative purpose. Indeed, hatred has been identified at the heart of much of Trump's immigration legislation, including the forceful separation of children from their parents as well as the white-supremacist rally in Charlottesville that catalysed the inception of the Kudzu project or the storming of the US Capitol at the end of Trump's presidency (Bell 2019). Anger, in contrast to that, Lorde argues, 'is a grief of distortions between peers and its object is change' ([1984] 2007: 129). It resembles women of colour's sadness and frustration about white women's ignorance and refusal to recognize the links between racism and patriarchy, and the multiple forms of oppression that women of colour face because of this connection. Yet, grief, like anger, is linked to an investment in the possibility of change. In this sense, Black women's critiques of the Pussyhat project and the Women's March should be understood as a commitment to liberation and not as an attempt to derail the movement (Ivey 2019). They are also what can inspire new initiatives like the Kudzu project that actively place white supremacy at the heart of social injustice.

Craftivist initiatives like the Pussyhat project may create a texture on which this anger and grief can leave an imprint and function as a tool through which eventually to transform the fibres of individual and collective politics (May 2020). Indeed, the repeated process of making and the circulation of the finished object can become an instance of sticking with this anger and grief. It provides an opportunity to dwell in emotions that have generally been framed as negative and in need of being overcome or mastered (Cvetkovich 2012). Rather than simply supplying the opportunity to work through an issue, or to move beyond an impasse, the performance of practices of needlework makes it possible to be with discomfort. The material properties of the wool and needles, along with the bodily movement and accompanying affective atmospheres, provide a texture that facilitates being with the affective tensions that are characteristic of transnational feminist relations (May 2023). As such, practices of needlework can be productive for a transformative politics that questions linear narratives of progress and change rooted within the structures at the heart of oppression and social injustice, namely patriarchy and white supremacy.

Politics, according to Fitzpatrick, is 'a process of opening-out issues to conflict, disagreement, and alternative framing of socio-political relations' (2018: 16). While much of craftivism may be overly concerned with consensus and conviviality (Fitzpatrick and Kontturi 2015), craftivism can also be a powerful tool to open discussion and provide space for dissent within an anti-racist feminist politics that recognizes personal privilege and values the lived experience of others, as is the case with the Kudzu project. For art critic and historian Julia Bryan-Wilson, 'to textile politics is to give texture to politics, to refuse easy binaries, to acknowledge complications: textured as in uneven, but also ... as in tangibly worked and retaining some of the grain of that labor, whether smooth or snagged' (2017: 7). Practices of needlework then become a powerful way of staying with the difficulties and intricacies of social justice work.

Platforms for Creativity

For Gauntlett, 'any and all kind of events, spaces, environments, tools, or toys' that encourage and foster people's engagement with creativity and creative practices in any way can be conceptualized as platforms for creativity (2018: 231). I suggest that both the Pussyhat and Kudzu projects can be understood as such platforms for creativity, and by extension for social transformation – for creatively imagining a different kind of world. Platforms for creativity can connect people and provide ways for shared meaning making and fostering understanding of others. Consequently, over the course of time they may also be conducive to fostering 'social change, community resilience, and sustainability' as a result of sparking new affective investments (Gauntlett 2018: 318). Moreover, as Pedwell (2021) powerfully argues, these slow, barely noticeable changes in affective attachments and habits in the minor key are equally as constitutive of social change as major and seemingly significant events. Inviting people to knit or crochet a pink hat with two cat ears or a kudzu leaf is in itself a rather banal idea, yet it becomes elevated through the existence of a purposefully built platform for creativity to support the creation of a hat or kudzu vine and chronicle the afterlife of the finished object.

Both the Pussyhat and the Kudzu projects actively contribute to practices of social transformation in the minor key. In the case of the Pussyhat projects, people are encouraged to participate in the politics of this transformation by sharing their concerns and ideas on the personalized labels that get attached to the hats. The makers become engaged with both 'minds and bodies', which may 'help people to recognize that they can make and shape their own worlds' (Gauntlett 2018: 233). In addition, platforms for creativity ideally include the opportunity to exchange creative gifts among participants (Gauntlett 2018: 307). The Pussyhat project supports such an economy of gift-giving, as it was initially founded around the idea of offering those unable to march with a way to demonstrate solidarity with the movement precisely through the act of gifting a Pussyhat to a marcher. As a result, the Pussyhat project also refigures problematic twentieth-century models of leisure time as forms of passive consumption into an opportunity for creative connections and exchange between people. By extension, the possibility for people to become more attuned to those around them and their needs is put within reach.

Makers and viewers of Kudzu knitting installations are, perhaps for the first time, invited to reflect on white supremacy, its connection with Confederate monuments and its effect on the lives of all people living in the US. Waiving her anonymity for a local magazine article about craftivism, an eighty-year-old Kudzu knitter, identified as Ms Gibbs, reflects on coming to learn to reconcile her respect for her ancestors who violently defended the Confederacy and her newfound knowledge about the workings of white supremacy. Gibbs describes her initially negative reactions to her daughter's involvement in the Kudzu project using words like 'offended', 'hurt', 'distressed' and 'angry' and perceiving the call for removal of the monuments as a direct attack on her ancestors and, by extension, her own character (quoted in O'Hare 2018: n.p.). However, as her daughter persisted knitting Kudzu leaves, Ms Gibbs also started to take in the information her daughter and the Kudzu project provided about the context of the statues and their erection during the Jim Crow era as part of a concerted effort by individuals and public authorities to intimidate Black people in the American South. For her, this has led to a more nuanced understanding of the actions of her Confederate ancestors and new awareness about the role Confederate monuments play in perpetuating white supremacy (O'Hare 2018: n.p.).

In the same way that crafters use the internet to connect with like-minded spirits, feminists have come to embrace it as a useful tool for advocacy and consciousness-raising. Carrie Rentschler and Samantha Thrift speak of 'feminist activist techné' when referring to 'the technical practices and practical knowledge feminists come to embody as they do feminism with media' (2015: 240). This 'doing' of feminism is also an embodied practice. It makes use of the internet as a platform for creativity, and equally utilizes the medium's capacity to connect feminists to each other (Mendes, Ringrose and Keller 2019; Rentschler and Thrift 2015). 'Doing' feminism then also implies the 'making and sharing [of] feminism' as well as, I suggest, active participation in the shaping and reshaping of the meaning of the term; doing feminism is an active form of meaning making

(Rentschler and Thrift 2015: 331). In these processes of meaning making and doing feminism or politics, craft can then be a very useful tool because it 'fastens the concrete and the abstract into a material symbol' (Bratich and Brush 2011: 246). Moreover, it allows for an embodied outlet to work through 'the concrete and the abstract' as part of the process of making a craft item like a Pussyhat or knitting leaves and vines from green yarn for the Kudzu project, an activity Ms Gibbs has since joined in with her daughter.

Making, whether physical, digital or digitally mediated, encompasses not only the transformation of the material but also of 'the sense of self' (Gauntlett 2011: 244; Ratto and Boler: 2014: 1). The various opportunities for exchange of material gifts, but also of moods and knowledge, as people discuss their reasons for participating and make plans for future actions like voter canvassing or petitioning local councils for the removal of a Confederate statue, can sharpen people's perception of themselves and in relation to others. The individual experience of being a young, old, Black, white or trans woman in the contemporary United States is textured as a result of the participation in networked creative projects of resistance like the Pussyhat or Kudzu project. Instead of smoothing over these experiences and those of other identities, they become part of resistant fabricultures committed to redefining the status quo. The Pussyhat and Kudzu projects, as well as the Social Justice Sewing Academy, provide such an environment for critical making. In this case, these interactions with the material world apply to the act of using needle and yarn to make a hat, Kudzu leaf or quilt block either in the privacy of the home, or in a public setting like a café or a yarn shop, but also to the act of using digital technologies as part of the process. Consideration of the maker's, wearer's as well as viewer's positioning invites the maker to reflect on their relationship with the object they are creating through multiple avenues. What symbolism does a Pussyhat hold for the maker? Is it a symbol of empowerment or indeed of sadness and political depression? Is it reflective of how little meaningful progress has been achieved with regard to a particular issue for which an individual may have been actively campaigning for the last fifty years? The wearer might simply appreciate being provided with warming headwear for a protest march in cold weather or be deeply affected by the personal story of sexual abuse that the maker has shared on the hat's tag. In addition, the act of making as well as the handling or seeing of a knitted or crocheted Pussyhat or a lone strand of Kudzu vine dangling from a Confederate statue outside a US courthouse might invite people to think about how needlework and craft more generally are deeply entangled with contested histories of women's work, gender, race, class and activism.

The making and wearing of a Pussyhat or the making and displaying of a Kudzu leaf invites 'individuals and communities [to] participate in shaping, changing, and reconstructing selves, worlds, and environments in creative ways' (Ratto and Boler 2014: 5). Affect plays an important role in these processes of individual and communal reshaping and structuring because attention to affect enables the tracing of 'mediated and direct experiences of interacting with the material world' that take place as a result of critical making (Ratto and Boler 2014: 3). The material world, in this context, refers not only to tangible physical objects, but also to the textured structures that continuously affect our everyday being in the world, as we respond to the impressions they leave on us and that cause our 'bodily surfaces [to] take shape' while, at the same time, creating affective ruts on these textured surfaces (Ahmed 2004: 25; see also Wetherell 2012; Zouggari 2018). As such, 'affect theory is not only a theory of encounters between subjects' or 'of encounters with texts' (Grattan 2017: 26) but, I suggest, is also a theory of textures. These textures are already a tangled meshwork of the material and immaterial, both of which make up the affective practices of everyday life. The Pussyhat, in particular, as I have argued, makes visible a variety of these textures: histories of exclusion and discrimination as expressed by the critiques of women of colour and trans women, but also histories of empowerment, consciousness-raising and reclamation of women's voices. The Pussyhat project and the Kudzu project that followed in its footsteps allow for a consideration of 'making as a "critical" activity' because it provides people with the opportunity to take part in a questioning and restructuring of the status quo. However, it also provides a means to reflect on the unequal flows of power that make up this status quo and on how these inequalities are manifested and reproduced by 'infrastructures, institutions, communities and practices' precisely because of the critiques it has raised (Ratto and Boler 2014: 1; see also Phipps 2020). As a result, the potential for feminist solidarity based on the recognition of difference (upon which I touched in my discussion of the Guldusi embroidery initiative in chapter three) rather than on the insistence of reconciling this difference becomes part of a concrete political imaginary.

In her craftivist manifesto and methodology handbook, Fitzpatrick links craftivism to citizen participation because it enables individuals and communities to, at the very least, slightly alter the texture of the status quo through hands-on affective practices of meaning making that serve to reorient the individual (2018: 6). I have conceptualized this initial moment of reorientation throughout this book using Erin Manning's (2016) notion of the 'minor gesture'. She argues that 'the minor gesture is the force that makes the lines tremble that compose the everyday, the lines, both structural and fragmentary, that articulate how else experience can come to expression' (2016: 7; see also Pedwell 2021). While this little 'tremble' is certainly a long way from the revolution and a total makeover of society, I contend that it points towards it: it prefigures the vigorous rocking and shaking that is yet to come. More so, as a platform for creativity that connects people, the Pussyhat project, through its long-term commitment to the development of grassroots organizing communities like the Kudzu project, also provides a space in which the revolution can be imagined. Making something with the hands moves people physically and affectively because 'they break new ground materially and internally' (Gauntlett 2018: 24). As such, it can orient individual and collectives towards modes of being that actively engage in creative practices to reshape the world in which they live (Fitzpatrick 2018: 6).

The repetition intrinsic to practices of needlework – in the case of knitting, the repetition of knit and purl – is key in that it not only moves the maker once but over the duration of the whole project, thus allowing for the formation of affective ruts in Wetherell's (2012) sense or, to use Ahmed's (2004) terminology, for the formation of a sticky relationship between physical and affective gestures. This is not necessarily a smooth process, as (drawing on knitting imagery) stitches can be dropped, knots can form and knitting can unravel. As such, affective social practices of meaning making like knitting or crochet can provide 'a mode of social engagement attuned to inhabiting the present in all its ambivalence and complexity' (Pedwell 2016: 3). They become a way of being with the ambiguity and multiplicity of the status quo in order to become able to develop strategies for resistance in the midst of uncertainty and anxiety about a global rise in right-wing governments, climate change or widening inequality. In this sense, creative practices of making like knitting are generative because they make dwelling in potentiality possible, as well as gesturing towards the texture of these new worlds.

Following feminist theorist Clare Hemmings, it is in these modes of dwelling that I also locate the potential in initiatives like the Pussyhat project and Kudzu project for forms of 'affective solidarity' to emerge as a baseline for a 'sustainable feminist politics of transformation' committed to the dismantling of white supremacy and patriarchy (2012: 147). This type of feminist solidarity differs from other notions in that it does not assume solidarity on the basis of commonality of shared experiences and affects of gendered oppression. Instead, it looks to affective dissonance and tension as the starting point. While dissent may be openly experienced and expressed, Hemmings' affective dissonance appears to operate more on the level of gesture and in the minor key. It is often fleeting and its impact can be neither managed nor predicted. Like practices of needlework, or indeed everyday practices more broadly, it is not subversive or rebellious by default, yet it can gesture towards feminist politicization or more resistant modes of being.

This ties in with Fitzpatrick's (2018, 2019) call for using craftivism as a way to make space for respectful dissent as opposed to an oppressive focus on consensus and conviviality that often further manifests the comfort of the privileged. Participants in the Women's March as well as the Pussyhat project can be perceived to have acted – marched, knitted or both – 'from experiences of discomfort' about the incoming Trump administration, police brutality, pervasive sexism or reproductive rights (Hemmings 2012: 158). This shared experience of discomfort does not imply that all marchers shared similar concerns and certainly not in the same order of importance. Further, it does not lay the foundation based on which the differences between the individuals involved can be overcome nor does it aim to do so. It is about acknowledging how the unequal flow of power disproportionately affects the lives of people of colour in a myriad of subtle ways, for example, through the placement of Confederate statues outside US courthouses.

As such, we may consider how practices of needlework might open up generative ways for critically reconsidering white people's discomfort as an affective opening for entering into the 'tough conversations' that Emejulu (2018) calls for rather than a means for shutting them down. George Yancy (2018) and other anti-racist scholars speak of the need for white people to become 'vulnerable' and to refigure the legacy of Eurocentric Enlightenment's idea of the liberal subject and self-mastery (see also Hunter and van der Westhuizen 2022: 20). Vulnerability, then, is about being open to being affected and unsettled without intending to overcome perceived negative feeling.[4] Rather, it is important to 'fashion a new relationship to such feelings' (Applebaum 2014: 16) – very much like in the case of Ms Gibbs and her encounter with knitted Kudzu installations – which recognizes how perceptions of the liberal (white) self are 'constituted by history, white power, white epistemic regimes, repetitions of white norms, implicit white alliances, white axiological frames of reference, white communities of intelligibility, white modes of being-in-the-world, and so on' aimed towards dehumanizing people of colour (Yancy 2014: xxiii).

When used to shut down marginalized voices, white people's discomfort is just another manifestation of white privilege (Phipps 2020; Sullivan 2014, 2019; Yancy 2014, 2018). Craftivist initiatives like the Pussyhat and Kudzu projects can provide a texture through which it becomes possible to engage with the affective forces of injustice and the current political moment in relation to the rhythms of everyday life. Essentialist understandings of activism assume that recognisable activist actions, such as participating in a demonstration or starting a petition, are the consequence of an individual's prior self-identification as an activist and as a conscious opponent to the current systems (Springgay, Hatza and O'Donald 2011: 407). Yet, such an approach ignores the possibility of being turned into an activist through cultural production – that is, critical making – as well as through the experience of affective tension. While neither participation in critical making nor the experience of affective dissonance are a guarantee for turning people into activists (Hemmings 2012; Springgay, Hatza and O'Donald 2011), they operate as part of a micropolitics that leads people towards another politics.

This politics is not defined by traditional categories such as party lines or religious beliefs. Instead, people are united in a 'political tendency', committed to ending 'all forms of domination, exploitation and oppression', while acknowledging that the means to do so are varied and need to be actively created as part of the ongoing struggle to adapt to the changing political and social landscape in which we live (Dixon 2014: 6; Pedwell 2019: 132). This allows for an understanding of social transformation not as a project of conversion of the subject, but as an ongoing process of adjusting complex object/subject/affect assemblages that have formed in response to the unequal flow of power (Pedwell 2016, 2019, 2021). In other words, it is not about leaving difference behind or indeed about overcoming difference, but about acknowledging the existence of difference – and by extension that of affective tension and discomfort – as the starting point for a shared feminist politics of solidarity that does not centre the affects of people racialized as white.

A micropolitics, for Fitzpatrick and Kontturi, is concerned with the potential of fleeting moments of resistance, slow repetitive processes and profound affective relationships (2015: section 4). Thus, they locate the 'political efficacy' of craftivist projects like the Pussyhats and the Kudzu projects in their ability to bring together diverse people and groups around practices of making that allow them to become oriented differently and to engage in acts of direct action together. The possibility of the experience of affective tension, I argue, is part of this efficacy, as it may allow for an orientation towards diverse modes of resistance based on different experiences of discomfort. As such, gestures of feminist solidarity can move away from problematic expressions of solidarity 'based in a shared identity or on a presumption about how the other feels' that may ultimately reinforce existing power structures (Hemmings 2012: 158). The micropolitical on the level of everyday affects, practices, orientations and minor gestures may prefigure larger systemic structural changes. Yet, it offers no guarantee to bring about such changes, nor is it prescriptive with regard to what they may look like; rather, it is a way of becoming acquainted with and dwelling in the possibility of change.

Coda: Un-making Whiteness

'I want to be like her, [Faith Ringgold]. With dolls instead of quilts' (Jones 2018: 141). This is the vision of aspiring Atlanta artist Celestial, the female protagonist in Tayari Jones' award-winning novel *An American Marriage* (2018); and like Ringgold, Celestial manages to turn an everyday home-sewing practice into a flourishing art business that produces celebrated art commissions alongside high-end children's and collectors' dolls catering to the well-to-do Black community in Atlanta as well as to the white community. Like Ringgold's quilts, Celestial's 'poupées', as the handmade textile dolls are called, are a testament not only to the cruel legacy of slavery that Black people experience in the US, but also to everyday creative practices of resistance. *An American Marriage* chronicles the love story of Celestial and Roy, from the first jolt of new love and the cultivation of their everyday life as a young married couple, to that horrid night when both are brutally dragged from their hotel beds by police, to Roy's wrongful conviction as a rapist and his early release from prison five years later. Many of the poupées are likenesses of a baby Roy, 'adorably symmetrical, chubby-cheeked and shiny-eyed' dolls adorned with beaded crystal head caps and swaddled in small luxurious cashmere blankets (Jones 2018: 226). Celestial finds pleasure and solace not only in making them, but also in giving 'a pretty brown doll to a pretty brown girl and watch[ing] her squeeze and kiss it' (Jones 2018: 57).

Yet, the pretty dolls are also 'baby prisoners' (Jones 2018: 63): they are symbolic of the American criminal justice system's constant threat to Black boys' and men's lives through wrongful arrests and convictions, unusually long sentences and police brutality. When Celestial enters a beautiful poupée, dressed in a diminutive pair of prison blues made from waxed cotton, in an art contest at the National Portrait Gallery, the doll is chosen as the winner. She is struck by the way the quotidian structures of systemic racism and oppression in the United States are made visible, but also removed from everyday experience through the choice of material, the doll's outfit and the placement of the handsewn object in a public art gallery. Celestial comments: 'In the baby clothes it was only a toy. In the new way, it was art' (Jones 2018: 64). At the awards ceremony, Celestial does not share her husband's story with the audience, but instead names the prison abolition movement and the work of anti-incarceration activist Angela Y. Davis as inspiration for the doll. She explains to Roy: 'What is happening with you is so personal that I didn't want to see it in the newspaper' (Jones 2018: 64).

Roy, however, takes offence at Celestial's omission of his story and, indeed, of his existence as an innocent Black man in a prison cell. He questions the usefulness of her advocacy against mass incarceration: 'Please explain to me what a baby doll is going to do to help anybody in here. Yesterday, a dude died because nobody would give him his insulin. I hate to break it to you, but no amount of poupées is going to bring him back' (Jones 2018: 65). Roy's criticism echoes many discourses and critiques about the political efficacy of practices of needlework – critiques I have discussed and probed throughout *Needlework, Affect and Social Transformation*. He questions how individual craft-based acts of resistance can effect large-scale social change. Further, Roy's disappointment about Celestial's choice to keep their situation private echoes discussions about the relationship between the personal and the political, as well as the ways practices of needlework expose these links as part of a zone of entanglements that includes, but is not limited to, affect, (bodily) materiality and the social world. The poupée in the prison jumpsuit provides Celestial with the opportunity to raise awareness about an important social justice concern that affects herself and the Black community as a whole, without having to reveal publicly her personal experience. Indeed, in her experience, whenever she tells her personal story, 'the truth doesn't get delivered' (Jones 2018: 66). White audiences appear unwilling to consider the couple's personal story in relation to wider social and political structures, and focus only on Celestial and Roy's blackness and the negative stereotypes associated with it. As Roy's cellmate puts it: 'She is a Black woman and everybody already thinks she got fifty-eleven babies with fifty-eleven daddies; that she got welfare checks coming in fifty-eleven people's names' (Jones 2018: 67). Mentioning her incarcerated husband in the context of the public exhibition and the award, Roy eventually concedes, would be detrimental to her status as an up-and-coming artist and businesswoman, nor would anyone be likely to take her critique of the American policing system seriously.

Celestial's sewing practice, which developed from a personal need to deal with the trauma of an abortion into a flourishing, creative resistant practice and sustainable business model, also resonates with my analysis of the shifting meaning of practices of needlework in relation to the position of the makers. The poupées are not only political as 'baby prisoners', but their beautifully crafted black and brown soft bodies are positive affirmations for children of colour living in a world where, as Sara Ahmed (2014) argues, their bodies are constantly under threat. They are a form of self-care not only for Celestial and her small team, who appreciate the making process even in a capital-driven retail environment, but also for the children (and adult women) who receive or purchase a doll. Indeed, some of the poupées in the shop are 'flawed on purpose', with 'eyebrows too thick' or a 'long torso with short stubby legs' (Jones 2018: 226). To Celestial, these dolls are as lovable and 'crooked as real children' (Jones 2018: 226) and the same care has gone into making them as into perfectly symmetrical and polished dolls.

Through a careful selection of diverse case studies, *Needlework, Affect and Social Transformation* has zoomed in on a variety of entanglements around the political potential and meaning of practices of needlework in a transnational context. The variety of these case studies reflects the ways textiles, texts and narratives travel as part of global cultural, political and capitalist economies. In addition, my selection recognizes the extent to which many social justice and feminist solidarity movements are firmly committed to networked forms of organizing across national boundaries and beyond localized identity politics. Chapter one explored how African American women employ quiltmaking as a resistant practice in honour of a womanist legacy of opposition to patriarchy and white supremacy. The textile practices of African American quilters like Faith Ringgold, Chawne Kimber and young participants from the Social Justice Sewing Academy, alongside the narrative representations of quilting by Toni Morrison and Alice Walker, are a testament to their communities' commitment to social justice work and self-care as a radical strategy for survival. Further, as I have argued, these examples also demonstrate how practices of needlework can offer a space for dwelling in a state of potential in which it becomes possible to imagine a different and more just future that values Black lives. Chapter two scrutinized the relationship between paid home-sewing activities, emotion work, housework, immigrant experiences, representation and women's desires. Through a close reading of Monica Ali's *Brick Lane* (2003a), I showed how regular sewing orients the protagonist Nazneen towards an embodied mode of being, in which she becomes able to explore her own desires, especially in relation to her sexuality and her situation as a married Bangladeshi immigrant and mother on a London council estate.

Focusing on the Afghan–European embroidery initiative Guldusi, chapter three explored to what extent transnational feminist solidarity can be possible, based on a shared gendered identity as needlewomen. I contended that narratives about the power of practices of needlework to foster solidarity between women from the Global North and the Global South often privilege the stories of white Western women. I traced how these narratives and the textile artefacts created by women from the Global North, in response to the Afghan embroideries, reproduce contemporary Orientalist discourses that have regained new prominence through the political and media rhetoric accompanying the War on Terror. However, by placing these discourses in relation to the affect and materiality of practices of needlework, my analysis has also identified openings for the reconfiguration of the unequal power structures between needlewomen. Through attention to the transnational affective entanglements of everyday practices, like tea drinking, cooking and gardening, I have shown how making is a way of connecting not only materials, but also bodies and affects, in ways that generate new openings for feminist solidarity. Chapter four examined the Pussyhat project as a texture that is representative of the feminist struggle for transnational solidarity. I argued that the Pussyhats themselves, as well as the making of a hat, can point people towards different social imaginaries and provide a space for a prefigurative politics to emerge, one grounded in affective dissonance. The Kudzu project, which developed as a result of makers' involvement with the Pussyhat project, I suggested, is such an initiative through which white makers can affectively grapple with white privilege and the multiple ways in which white supremacy shapes society.

I have not given attention to zones of entanglement in an attempt to unpick their different strands or to assign them fixed meanings. Instead, I have trailed some of the strands and paths they create in order to explore the relationship between cultural narratives, individual accounts and literary representations about practices of needlework and feminist politics. As a result, I have shown how practices of needlework and their narrative renderings make possible multiple politics of embodied orientation that move makers, viewers and readers towards modes of dwelling in the potential of creating new social imaginaries that also reconfigure relationships between the self, humans and the more-than-human. In addition, I have argued that practices of needlework and their narrative representations provide a mode for being with or dwelling in the discomfort and negative affects that may arise as a result of experiencing these reconfigurations of relationships, especially when they involve the acknowledgement of white privilege and personal complicity. Indeed, my analysis of the Pussyhat and Kudzu projects shows how the practice and the finished object both function as a texture against which the discomforting affects and struggles that are part of transnational anti-racist and feminist organizing become visible.

In *Needlework, Affect and Social Transformation*, I have also attempted to give texture to the workings of whiteness and white privilege that, so far, often remain unaddressed in the scholarship on practices of needlework. This book is by no means a definitive guide on the topic but, rather, an initial attempt to sketch out some points of entry for bringing together critical race theory, affect studies and the scholarship on textile crafts. As such, this book is an important contribution to the scholarship of textile practices and gender as it complicates existing narratives about the meaning of practices of needlework in relation to feminist politics and exposes how whiteness shapes dominant narratives. Placing text and textile alongside each other, I have drawn on the etymological history of the two terms to explore some of the textures that emerge from everyday practices of needlework so as to show how they influence people's sense of self and their relationships with the world. I have highlighted how narrative, affect and bodily movement shape the meaning of practices of needlework and the types of resistant acts they make possible. *Needlework, Affect and Social Transformation* demonstrates the usefulness of interdisciplinary and innovative methods – of texture as a dynamic concept, materiality and interpretive framework which includes interviews and close reading in combination with different media for analysis, like literary texts, textile artefacts and the digital. The complexity of everyday life, affect and the meanings of practices of needlework require a diverse approach that looks at their various entanglements and textures, without attempting to fix meaning indelibly, and that recognizes the ways whiteness is embedded in structures of everyday normativity (Heinz 2022).

One of my key claims is that practices of needlework and their narrative renderings make new orientations possible. In the same spirit, I hope that this research helps to (re)orient the scholarship on textile practices and feminist activism. I advocate a more rigorous engagement with the role of whiteness and its affective entanglements in relation to the meaning of practices of needlework and, more importantly, with regard to how knowledge about needlework is created. The affective dimension of practices of needlework – the hope, pain, love, anxiety and potential connected with them – needs to be considered in claims about the meaning of needlework to account for how a privileging of some emotions (for example, love and comfort) marginalizes the lived experience of makers of colour. I therefore view *Needlework, Affect and Social Transformation* as an opening towards an 'un-suturing' of the white hegemonic structures that are reproduced even in many intersectional accounts about the meaning of practices of needlework. At the same time, however, I also want to acknowledge how these very structures are reflected in this book, in myself and, in particular, in the way my analysis takes the Global North as the vantage point from which to trail the transnational entanglements of practices of needlework and concepts like the everyday, the home space and domesticity. As such, this research also calls for heightened awareness about the different ways in which individual, cultural and scholarly narratives about the meaning of needlework and the representations of these narratives reproduce not only patriarchal structures, but also white hegemony.

Un-suturing Whiteness

American philosopher George Yancy speaks of the 'sutured' white self in order to describe a type of self-conceptualization that is protected and secured in place, similar to the way that the stitches of a seam hold together two separate pieces (2018: 105). Yet, these stitches are also reflective of the labour of maintaining the narrative authority of whiteness as an exclusive construct protected from outside influences and infestation from otherness (Yancy 2018: 105). They expose white hegemony as a social construct in need of constant reproduction in order to maintain itself: the stitches literally need to hold the construct together. To be sutured, then, is to be oriented towards whiteness as the default mode for conceiving of the self and the world in ways that influence how people take up space, act and envisage social change (Yancy 2014, 2018; see also Ahmed 2007). It means taking access to certain spaces and services for granted, being able to find 'nude'- or 'flesh'-coloured products that match one's skin tone in stores as well as walking down a street in a dark hoodie without being labelled as suspicious. Also, to return to Jones' powerful account of the dolls, it means not being a 'baby prisoner' simply by virtue of one's gender and colour of skin.

Yancy conceptualizes the process of becoming aware of whiteness and white privilege in terms of becoming 'un-sutured'. To be un-sutured is to have the seams of everyday white normativity ripped open and to be exposed to one's own conscious and unconscious complicity in structures and whole ways of life that discriminate and oppress people of colour not only in the United States, but across the world. It is a process during which people confront their own whiteness and recognize it as implicated within 'whiteness as a systemic hegemonic feature of American social, political, economic, cultural, and epistemic life' (Yancy 2018: 14). As a result, whiteness is disclosed as a social construct that, by the very nature of its own constructedness, is susceptible to change. Thus, un-suturing agitates the very foundations of the white hegemonic status quo as white people realize 'how [they] are always already exposed, vulnerable, and open to be wounded' (Yancy 2018: 112). Being subject to change and new impressions can open up the possibility of a shift in power relations that challenges white privilege. Consequently, un-suturing may be perceived as threatening by people racialized as white and is often accompanied by intense experiences of discomfort, fear and rage. Un-suturing, for Yancy, is not simply a metaphor for the realization of personal positioning, but a deeply phenomenological experience 'where your white body trembles in its contingency, openness and responsibility; where it stands in awe, where the perceptual and sensorial are shaken, unhinged' (2018: 112). To be un-sutured is to be moved into a state of heightened affects, brimming with potential, similar to the way practices of needlework can point people towards new forms of orientation.

While marked by discomfort, un-suturing also signifies a state of possibility. In fact, Yancy (2018) and others (Phipps 2020; Sullivan 2014) suggest that experiences of deep distress and vulnerability are a precondition for white people to embody and advocate for an anti-racist feminist politics. As I have argued throughout this book, while disorientation may imply irritation and uneasiness, it also includes the prospect of being oriented differently. According to Yancy, to exist in a state of disorientation is a 'radical way of being-in-the-world' (2018: 112) that *affectively* opens people up to new ways of encountering the self and others. Disorientation, as I have shown, can move people towards displays of solidarity with other women not simply on account of shared gendered experiences, but because of a recognition of the affective dissonance between the experiences of women based, for example, on race, class, sexuality and nationality. Indeed, it is in the dwelling in a mode of disorientation that does not focus on an immediate overcoming of this vulnerable state where I have located the potential of new creative imaginaries for social transformation to emerge. In *Brick Lane*, Nazneen struggles to identify and formulate her own needs and desires, but her sewing practice eventually moves her towards recognizing them. Similarly, African American quilter Chawne Kimber finds in her quilting practice the opportunity to address the various forms of discrimination and oppression that she experiences as a Black woman in the contemporary United States. Thus, building on Yancy's argument, I want to use this coda to suggest that practices of needlework can be a catalyst for processes of un-suturing and to stress the importance of further research in this area.

A recent piece by British embroidery artist Hannah Hill, *Healing Hands* (2019), captures the process of un-suturing that I have outlined above in all its rich affective dimensions (figure 5.1). The embroidery features two hands in

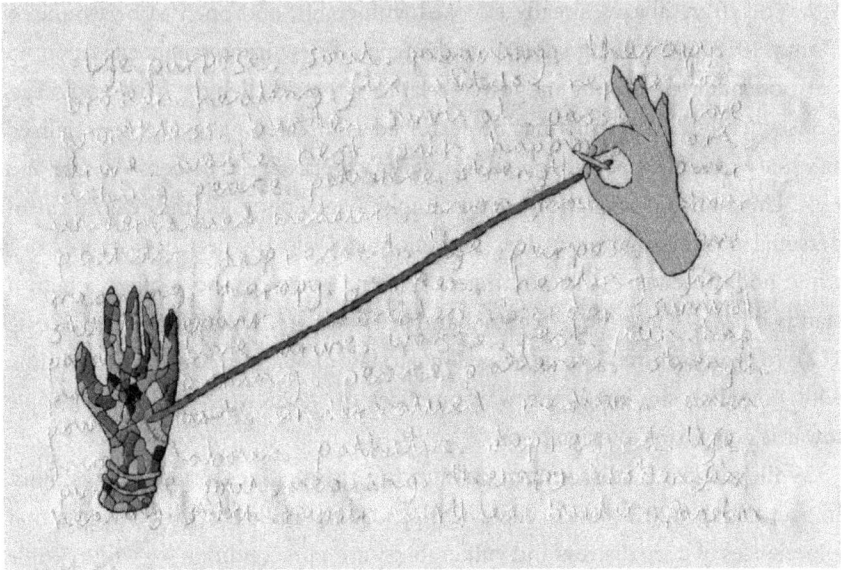

Figure 5.1 *Healing Hands*, 2019, Hannah 'Hanecdote' Hill. (© Hannah Hill)

front of a cream-coloured background on which words are stitched in an almost translucent thread. The hand on the left is filled with a mosaic of different patches of 'skin colour', from dark brown and caramel to a pale tan and the soft pink commonly referred to as the colour of 'flesh'. The hand on the right is completely embroidered in 'flesh' only, holding a needle between the thumb and index finger. The needle is threaded with a thick red thread pulled taught. The thread is attached to the middle of a large bright red suture across the palm of the hand in different shades of brown and pink. The suture appears unfinished, as if a first row of stitches has already been completed, but the second one, to be placed on top of the first for strength and durability, is only half finished. The words in the background include terms like 'burden', 'pathetic', 'broken' and 'therapy', but also 'meaning', 'soul', 'healing' and 'peace'. Although Hill explains that the piece is primarily a response to an ongoing hand injury which has made it difficult and painful for her to embroider, it also resonates with other themes she regularly addresses in her embroidery. She engages with topics like sex positivity, race, feminism, activism, social media and the history of needlework, as well as grime music and culture (Gipson 2022: 202–7). Hill is of white-European and Indo-Guyanese heritage and her ancestors were transported as indentured labourers to the Caribbean to work on plantations after the slave trade was abolished in the British Empire. For her, this positionality as 'half coloniser and half colonised' informs her point of view towards everything in life and art' (Hill 2022).

Although, to Hill, the suture in the embroidery described above is reminiscent of a physical injury, I argue that it also evokes another kind of wound inflicted by white hegemonic structures on the bodies and psyche of people of colour. According to Yancy, this type of wound is intended to harm, to debilitate and to violate (Yancy 2018: 100) or, to use some of the terms from the background of Hill's embroidery, to 'depress', to cause 'pain' and to be made to feel like a 'burden'. Unlike the wounding involved in the process of un-suturing, the hatred of racism and white supremacy cannot provide a generative space for becoming oriented in new ways (see also Lorde [1984] 2007). Nor will the suturing, or sewing up of this wound, provide relief and protection to people of colour in the way that whiteness offers a 'site of closure and control' to white people (Yancy 2018: 104). Nevertheless, in its seemingly unfinished state, the suture in the palm also represents a state of possibility for new orientations. More stitches could be added to tighten the existing seam and to close off any opportunities for openings. However, the suture may also be easily opened as stitches could be unpicked and taken out, consequently, putting the possibility of being un-sutured within reach. As such, the embroidery is not only symbolic of a wound but, as a creative and resistant practice, also offers a way of feeling it and staying with it, without being destroyed by it.

Hill's embroidery powerfully captures some of the struggles at the core of anti-racist feminist practices committed to a decentring of whiteness in all ways of life. In addition, like Celestial's poupées, it illustrates how the links between personal experience and social structures are mirrored in the difficulties Hill faces as a British woman of mixed heritage and aspiring embroidery artist in a competitive art world setting that has historically marginalized women and needlework. Yet, since Hill worked on this particular embroidery over the course of two years, the piece is also a testament to the ways practices of needlework enable one to stay with discomfort and pain for a prolonged period of time. Practices of needlework and their narrative renderings, as I have demonstrated throughout this book, are essentially political because of needlework's strong connection with contested understandings of femininity, women's work, protest and the political. Hence, my focus has been to identify the kinds of political acts practices of needlework and their narrative representations make possible in the context of craft-based, feminist transnational activism. This study, though, is certainly not exhaustive. By conceptualizing practices of needlework and their representations as modes of potential for affective orientation towards new social imaginaries and ways of being, I have uncovered a multiplicity of orientations and entanglements. Based on my diverse set of case studies, I have focused on some of these orientations and identified them as part of an embodied politics within transnational feminist struggles for liberation. I remain curious about the 'lines of flight' that are to emerge from these orientations and the potential that reverberates from and through them and I hope that others will do the same.

Notes

Introduction: The Affective Politics of Needlework

1   See Amos and Binkley (2020) for discussion of makers' agency and intention 'to fashion the self as an artist, educator, individual, activist, or a work of art; to forge new social ties, whether familial, professional, or political; or to recall identities lost or left dormant through processes of traumatic personal change or displacement' (3).

2   Though Parker's study is primarily focused on embroidery as a particular type of needlework, scholars in art, history, sociology and literary and cultural studies have applied her findings to other practices of needlework from lace making, knitting, crochet, patchwork and quilting to dressmaking and the sewing of household items such as sheets and tablecloths (Elsley 1996; Hedges 1991; Pristash, Schaechterle and Wood 2009; Tamboukou 2015).

3   The focus throughout my case studies is on women and their gendered intersectional identities across transnational feminist politics. This does not, however, imply that the affective potential I identify in relation to practices of needlework (drawing on work of queer theorists like Ahmed 2006b, Cvetkovich 2003, 2012 and Muñoz 2009) is exclusive to women and not open to other genders.

4   For more than ten years, I have been involved with various women's quilt groups in Germany and the UK. In these spaces, I had the privilege to be inspired, mentored and cared for by a variety of women, many of whom were my seniors by some decades. It is also through my experiences with these women, and the quilting and textile crafts community more widely, that I started to dig deeper into the meaning of practices of needlework for women and their relation to femininity and feminism. This research developed from the wish to provide an intersectional and interdisciplinary analysis of practices of needlework that is attuned to the background of the maker. As such, this research is also grounded in the recognition of a white, Western, patriarchal context as the starting point for many analyses of practices of needlework even in cases where these are using a feminist and transnational perspective.

5   See also Lindström and Ståhl (2016) for discussion on how the material may move bodies.

6   See Ahmed (2004, 2006b), Blackman (2012) and Khanna (2020) for illuminating analyses on the relationship between body and affect.

1 Quilting Black Resistance: Slavery's Afterlives, Creativity and Social Justice

1 I use the term 'African American' explicitly to reference the legacy of the forced
   African diaspora to North America and to refer to individuals who identify as part
   of this group. I use 'Black' or 'people of colour' more broadly to include also
   individuals who are not direct descendants of slaves but experience similar forms of
   oppression and discrimination in the United States. While experiences of
   discrimination and structural racism are certainly similar for both groups, I want to
   highlight the different cultural legacies that shaped their identities and through
   which they may have become acquainted with practices of needlework, specifically
   quilting. For an excellent literary engagement with these differences, see Adichie
   (2013). For a scholarly discussion of Black diaspora and identity, see Hartman
   (2007), Segal (1995), as well as Yenika-Agbaw and Mhando (2014).

2 It was common practice in the South for Black women slaves to assist their
   mistresses in the making of quilts, following traditional patterns popular at the time
   (Klassen 2009; Mazloomi 2015). After the abolition of slavery, Black quilters
   continued to have access to these patterns and kits in so far as they could afford to
   purchase them or received them as hand-me-downs from their employers (Klassen
   2009). As part of the Freedom Quilting Bee in Alabama from 1965 to 1975, members
   of the Gee's Bend quilters and other Black women produced handmade quilts in a
   'Eurocentric aesthetic' for US department stores like Bloomingdales and Sears
   (Scheper-Hughes 2004: 21). MacDowell's (1997) work on African American quilters
   in Michigan and her extensive registry of quilts made by African Americans also
   shows that in the second half of the twentieth century many African Americans
   made quilts according to patterns and kits available on the general market.

3 See Mitchell (2020) for a reworking of the idea of an aesthetics of existence in the
   context of a more deliberate commitment to critical analysis focused on Black
   achievement and success.

4 Nevertheless, it is worth noting that for Celie in *The Colour Purple*, the home, at
   times, was also a place of violence and abuse against women and girls. As hooks
   ([1981] 1987) argues, through these acts of patriarchal violence and displays of toxic
   masculinity the legacy of slavery also found its way into the Black home through the
   reproduction of gendered forms of oppression.

5 According to Walker, a womanist is a 'Black feminist or feminist of color' ([1983]
   2004). The concept acknowledges the link between gendered oppression and race
   and takes the particular lived experience of Black women as a generative starting
   point for inclusive transnational feminist practices of resistance (Layli 2006).

6 See Love (2007) for a discussion of such modes of dwelling in relation to queer
   trauma.

7 This, of course, is not to say that white people, especially poor white women, do not experience discrimination or oppression. Nonetheless, poor and working-class people may benefit from whiteness in ways that may not even be obvious to them or others. Shannon Sullivan (2014, 2017, 2019) offers a comprehensive analysis of the links between whiteness, white privilege, race and class (see also Phipps 2020).

8 See Tate and Page (2018) on how 'asserting that racism stems from "unconscious bias" diminishes white supremacy and maintains white innocence as a "will to forget" institutional racism' (141).

9 Nonetheless, in the context of climate change or environmental pollution, small changes in everyday behaviour and practices are often credited with a significant, but not directly tangible, impact (Shove, Pantzar and Watson 2012).

10 For a discussion of contemporary 'nudge' theory and policy as a means to control or guide humans in the interest of social stability, as opposed to more democratic ways of affectively (re)orienting people towards sustainable social change, see Pedwell (2017, 2021).

3 Stitching Transnational Solidarity: Textile Crafts and Cross-Cultural Encounters

1 I would like to acknowledge that I do not operate outside these power relations and am, at times, complicit with them. However, I hope that a reflexive approach can help to disrupt such hierarchies rather than reify them (see also Pedwell 2010: 7–8).

2 *Tshador* is the Farsi/Persian term for women's full body cover and primarily used in Afghanistan. Burqa is the Arab/Middle Eastern term, although a number of academic papers about veiling practices in Afghanistan also use this term (de Groot 2013). I use the term interchangeably because a number of the materials I look at, for example, the textile artefacts and testimonials by Guldusi customers, do not distinguish between the two, nor does it necessarily make a difference with regard to the wider meaning attached to this particular piece of clothing.

3 It should be noted that men's lives, under the Taliban, likewise became subject to severe restrictions and strict norms. Failure to adhere to these norms would also result in punishment (Abirafeh 2008).

4 Certainly, terms like 'Western feminists' are similarly reductive. However, I shall continue to use terms like 'Western feminists', 'European needlewomen' and 'Middle Eastern' or 'Third World' women to highlight how these identities have been constructed and shaped within Orientalist and imperial practices emanating from the hegemonic centres of the Global North. I shall use the term 'Afghan women/needlewomen' when referring to the female citizens of Afghanistan. Mohanty (2003) provides an in-depth discussion of these types of naming practices and their

reflection of global power structures. Like her, I am not opposed to the use of generalizing categories for analytic purposes as long as they are used with a critical awareness of the trajectories of the terms involved. Thus, 'Western' or 'Third World' feminist refers not to 'embodied, geographically or spatially defined categories [but] to political and analytic sites and methodologies used' (Mohanty 2003: 502).

5 By equating veiling practices with oppression and backwardness, a thoroughly Western and non-Islamic interpretation of the practice is applied, and Western forms of liberalism and agency are used as the benchmark against which the situation of Afghan women is evaluated (Russo 2006: 564). Indeed, Western complicity in the situation of Afghan women is further increased as questions of dress style are deemed more injurious to women than the effects of the US war with its myriad of civilian casualties and refugees, and its destruction of living quarters and agricultural resources (Russo 2006: 569). Rather than creating spaces in which Afghan women's voices can be heard, Western feminists present themselves as qualified spokeswomen for their Afghan sisters, and this has real consequences for the type of international aid that is provided to Afghanistan. As Saeed (2015) and Abirafeh (2008) note, development initiatives that presented themselves as geared towards women's empowerment were much more likely to be approved for funding by, for example, USAID, than projects focused on men. This is not to say that the initiatives for women did not deserve to be funded, but this observation exposes an interesting association that appears to assume that within a deeply patriarchal culture it is the women that must act as arbiters of change. Sharoni *et al.* (2015) identify this fixation on women as vanguards of change as a general problem across transnational feminism that is heightened at points of crisis.

6 The UK submissions were showcased in Greenstede Gallery in Sussex in 2007. Twenty-six of these pieces were selected for the European tour of the competition results which were displayed in multiple countries across the EU.

7 See also Cvetkovich (2003), (2012), Ong (2006), Stewart (2007) and Wimpelmann (2017).

8 Just as I was finalizing the edits for the book in late 2022, I received word from Guldusi that the new provincial Taliban government has granted the initiative permission to continue. Guldusi used the fact that women embroidered from home and that needlework is a traditional women's activity to convince the authorities that it be allowed to continue.

4 Knitting Feminist Politics: Craftivism and Affective Tension

1   See Sullivan (2019) on the role of white privilege in police encounters.
2   Of course, particularly in social media, but other digital and networked media may also drive division and backlash (Mendes, Ringrose and Keller 2019).
3   See Yancy (2018) for a discussion of racist backlash and Banet-Weiser (2018) for an analysis of misogynist backlash in response to feminist activism.
4   See Butler, Gambetti and Sabsay (2016) for a detailed discussion of vulnerability.

References

Abirafeh, L. (2008), 'Afghanistan "Gozargah": Discourses on Gender-Focused Aid in the Aftermath of Conflict', PhD thesis, London School of Economics, London.

Abu-Lughod, L. (2002), 'Do Muslim Women Really Need Saving? Anthropological Reflections on Cultural Relativism and Its Others', *American Anthropologist*, 104 (3): 783–90.

Adichie, C.N. (2013), *Americanah*, London: Fourth Estate.

Ahmed, S. (2004), *The Cultural Politics of Emotion*, Edinburgh: Edinburgh University Press.

Ahmed, S. (2006a), 'Orientations: Towards a Queer Phenomenology', *GLQ: A Journal of Lesbian and Gay Studies*, 12 (4): 543–74.

Ahmed, S. (2006b), *Queer Phenomenology: Orientations, Objects, Others*, Durham, NC, and London: Duke University Press.

Ahmed, S. (2013), 'Making Feminist Points', *Feminist Killjoys*, 11 September. Available online: https://feministkilljoys.com/2013/09/11/making-feminist-points/ (accessed 5 July 2017).

Ahmed, S. (2014), 'Selfcare as Warfare', *Feminist Killjoys*, 25 August. Available online: https://feministkilljoys.com/2014/08/25/selfcare-as-warfare/ (accessed 5 July 2017).

Ahmed, S. (2017), *Living a Feminist Life*, Durham, NC: Duke University Press.

Alcoff, L., and E. Potter, eds (1993), *Feminist Epistemologies*, New York, NY: Routledge.

Ali, M. (2003a), *Brick Lane*, London: Transworld Books.

Ali, M. (2003b), 'Where I'm Coming from', *The Guardian*, 17 June. Available online: https://www.theguardian.com/books/2003/jun/17/artsfeatures.fiction (accessed 3 December 2017).

Ali, M., and D. Adebayo (2004), 'Monica Ali with Diran Adebayo', in S. Nasta (ed.), *Writing across Worlds: Contemporary Writers Talk*, 340–51, Abingdon: Routledge.

Allen, A. (2017), 'The Beautiful Mind of Chawne Kimber', Modern Quilt Guild, 17 January. Available online: https://www.themodernquiltguild.com/resource/the-beautiful-mind-of-chawne-kimber/ (accessed 7 April 2023).

Amos, J., and L. Binkley (2020), 'Introduction: Stitching the Self . . .', in J. Amos and L. Binkley (eds), *Stitching the Self: Identity and the Needle Arts*, 1–18, London: Bloomsbury.

Andrews, T.M. (2017), '"Shop for Yarn Elsewhere": Tenn. Shop Owner to "Vile" Women's March Supporters', *The Washington Post*, 26 January. Available online: https://www.washingtonpost.com/news/morning-mix/wp/2017/01/26/shop-for-yarn-elsewhere-tenn-shop-owner-to-vile-womens-march-supporters/ (accessed 16 April 2023).

Anguelov, N. (2016), *The Dirty Side of the Garment Industry: Fast Fashion and Its Negative Impact on Environment and Society*, Boca Raton, FL: CRC Press.

Appadurai, A. (1996), *Modernity at Large: Cultural Dimensions of Globalization*, Minneapolis and London: University of Minnesota Press.

Applebaum, B. (2014), 'Flipping the Script . . . and Still a Problem: Staying in the Anxiety of Being a Problem', in G. Yancy (ed.), *White Self-Criticality beyond Anti-racism: How Does It Feel to Be a White Problem?*, 1–19, Lanham, MD: Lexington Books.

Arnett, W., ed. (2002), *The Quilts of Gee's Bend*, Atlanta, GA: Tinwood Books.

Ayotte, K.J., and M.E. Husain (2005), 'Securing Afghan Women: Neocolonialism, Epistemic Violence, and the Rhetoric of the Veil', *NWSA Journal*, 17 (3):112–33.

Bacchetta, P., S. Maira and H. Winant (2019), 'Introduction Global Raciality: Empire, Postcoloniality, Decoloniality', in P. Bacchetta, S. Maira and H. Winant (eds), *Global Raciality: Empire, Postcoloniality, Decoloniality*, 1–20, New York, NY: Routledge.

Bain, J. (2016), '"Darn Right I'm a Feminist. . . . Sew What?" The Politics of Contemporary Home Dressmaking: Sewing, Slow Fashion and Feminism', *Women's Studies International Forum*, 54 (2): 57–66.

Banet-Weiser, S. (2018), *Empowered: Popular Feminism and Popular Misogyny*, Durham, NC, and London: Duke University Press.

Bast, F. (2011), 'Reading Red: The Troping of Trauma in Toni Morrison's *Beloved*', *Callaloo: A Journal of African Diaspora Arts and Letters*, 34 (4): 1069–87.

Beauvoir, S. de ([1949] 1997), *The Second Sex*, trans. H.M. Parshley, London, Vintage.

Beetham, S. (2020), 'Confederate Monuments: Southern Heritage or Southern Art?', *Panorama: Journal of the Association of Historians of American Art*, 6 (1), doi: 10.24926/24716839.9844.

Behdad, A. (2010), 'Orientalism Matters', *MFS Modern Fiction Studies*, 56 (4): 709–28.

Bell, J. (2019), 'The Resistance and the Stubborn but Unsurprising Persistence of Hate and Extremism in the United States', *Indiana Journal of Global Legal Studies*, 26 (1): 305–15.

Benberry, C. (1980), 'Afro-American Women and Quilts: Introductory Essay', *Uncoverings*, 1: 64–7.

Benberry, C. (1992), *Always There: The African-American Presence in American Quilts*, Louisville, KY: The Kentucky Quilt Project Inc.

Berlant, L. (2011), *Cruel Optimism*, Durham, NC, and London: Duke University Press.

Billaud, J. (2015), *Kabul Carnival: Gender Politics in Postwar Afghanistan*, Philadelphia: University of Pennsylvania Press.

Black, A., and N. Burisch (2020), 'Introduction', in A. Black and N. Burisch (eds), *The New Politics of the Handmade: Craft, Art and Design*, 1–12, London: Bloomsbury Visual Arts.

Black Lives Matter (n.d.), *Black Lives Matter*. Available online: https://blacklivesmatter.com/ (accessed 9 August 2017).

Black, S. (2017), 'Knit and Resist: Placing the Pussyhat Project in the Context of Craft Activism', *Gender, Place and Culture*, 24 (5): 696–71.

Blackman, L. (2012), *Immaterial Bodies: Affect, Embodiment, Mediation*, London: SAGE Publications.

Boccagni, P. (2017), *Migration and the Search for Home: Mapping Domestic Space in Migrants' Everyday Lives*, New York, NY: Palgrave Macmillan.

Boler, M. (1999), *Feeling Power: Emotions and Education*, New York, NY, and London: Routledge.

Boothroyd, S., R. Bowen, A. Cattermole, K. Chang-Swanson, H. Daltrop, S. Dwyer, A. Gunn, B. Kramer, D.M. McCarten, J. Nagra, S. Samimi and Q. Yoon-Potkins (2017), '(Re)producing Feminine Bodies: Emergent Spaces through Contestation in the Women's March on Washington', *Gender, Place and Culture*, 24 (5): 711–21.

Boudreau, K. (1995), 'Pain and the Unmaking of Self in Toni Morrison's *Beloved*', *Contemporary Literature*, 36 (3): 447–65.

Boyer, A. (2015), *Garments against Women*, Boise, ID: Ahsahta Press.

Brackman, B. (2006), *Fact & Fabrications: Unraveling the History of Quilts & Slavery*, Lafayette, CA: C&T Publishing.

Bratich, J.Z., and H.M. Brush (2011), 'Fabricating Activism: Craft-Work, Popular Culture, Gender', *Utopian Studies*, 22 (2): 233–60.

Brennan, T. (2004), *The Transmission of Affect*, Ithaca, NY: Cornell University Press.

Brewer, S., and L. Dundes (2018), 'Concerned, Meet Terrified: Intersectional Feminism and the Women's March', *Women's Studies International Forum*, 69: 49–55.

Britex Fabrics (2016), 'Social Justice Sewing Academy (SJSA) Quilts Made with Fabric from Britex', *Britex Fabrics Blog*, 18 July. Available online: https://www.britexfabrics.com/blog/post/social-justice-sewing-academy-sjsa-quilts-with-fabric-from-britex (accessed 8 April 2023).

Brochin, C., and C.L. Medina (2017), 'Critical Fictions of the Global: Transnationalism in Latinx Children's Literature', *Bookbird: A Journal of International Children's Literature*, 55 (3): 4–11.

Brown, M. (2019), 'American Quilts Hailed as Miraculous Works of Modern Art Come to UK', *The Guardian*, 2 December. Available online: https://www.theguardian.com/artanddesign/2019/dec/02/american-quilts-gees-bend-miraculous-art-turner-contemporary-margate (accessed 8 April 2023).

Bruder, A. (2019), 'Stitching Dissent: From the Suffragists to Pussyhat Politics', in H. Mandell (ed.), *Crafting Dissent: Handicraft as Protest from the American Revolution to the Pussyhats*, 111–21, Lanham, MD, and London: Rowman & Littlefield.

Bryan-Wilson, J. (2017), *Fray: Art and Textile Politics*, Chicago, IL, and London: University of Chicago Press.

Bunyasi, T.L., and C.W. Smith (2018), 'Get in Formation: Black Women's Participation in the Women's March on Washington as an Act of Pragmatic Utopianism', *Black Scholar*, 48 (3): 4–16.

Burt, E.L., and J. Atkinson (2012), 'The Relationship between Quilting and Wellbeing', *Journal of Public Health*, 34 (1): 54–9.

Buszek, M.E., ed. (2011), *Extra/Ordinary: Craft and Contemporary Art*, Durham, NC: Duke University Press

Butler, J., Z. Gambetti and L. Sabsay, eds (2016), V*ulnerability in Resistance*, Durham, NC: Duke University Press.

Byerman, K. (1991), 'Remembering History in Contemporary Black Literature and Criticism', *American Literary History*, 3 (4): 809–16.

Campbell, C. (2005), 'The Craft Consumer: Culture, Craft and Consumption in a Postmodern Society', *Journal of Consumer Culture*, 5 (1): 23–42.

Certeau, M. de (1984), *The Practice of Everyday Life*, trans. S. Rendall, Berkeley: University of California Press.

Chang, A. (2016), *Disposable Domestics: Immigrant Women Workers in the Global Economy*, 2nd edn, Chicago, IL: Haymarket.

Chansky, R. (2010), 'A Stitch in Time: Third-Wave Feminist Reclamation of Needled Imagery', *Journal of Popular Culture*, 43 (4): 681–700.

Checinska, C. (2018), 'Aesthetics of Blackness? Cloth, Culture, and the African Diasporas', *Textile*, 16 (2): 118–25.

Chevalier, T. (2013), *The Last Runaway*, London: HarperCollins.

Chiaverini, J. (2008–19), Elm Creek Quilts Series, New York, NY: Simon & Schuster.

Christian, B.T. (1994), 'Alice Walker: The Black Woman as an Artist', in B.T. Christian (ed.), *'Everyday Use': Alice Walker*, 123–47, New Brunswick, NJ: Rutgers University Press.

Chung, H., H. Birkett, S. Forbes, and H. Seo (2021), 'Covid-19, Flexible Working and Implications for Gender Equality in the United Kingdom', *Gender & Society*, 35 (2): 218–32.

Clarke, K. (2016), 'Willful Knitting? Contemporary Australian Craftivism and Feminist Histories', *Continuum*, 30 (3): 298–306.

Close, S. (2018), 'Knitting Activism, Knitting Gender, Knitting Race', *International Journal of Communication*, 12: 867–89.

Clough, P.T. (2007), 'Introduction', in R.T. Clough and J. Halley (eds), *The Affective Turn: Theorizing the Social*, Durham, NC, and London: Duke University Press.

Coleman, R. (2020), *Glitterworlds: The Future Politics of a Ubiquitous Thing*, London: Goldsmiths Press.

Coleman, R., and J. Ringrose (2013), 'Introduction: Deleuze and Research Methodologies', in R. Coleman and J. Ringrose (eds), *Deleuze and Research Methodologies*, 1–22, Edinburgh: Edinburgh University Press.

Collins, P.H. (2019), *Intersectionality as Critical Social Theory*, Durham, NC: Duke University Press

Compton, J. (2017), 'Pink "Pussyhat" Creator Addresses Criticism over Name', NBC News, 7 February. Available online: https://www.nbcnews.com/feature/nbc-out/pinkpussyhat-creator-addresses-criticism-over-name-n717886 (accessed 21 January 2019).

Cooke, M. (2002), 'A Roundtable: Saving Brown Women', *Signs*, 28 (1): 468–70.

Cooks, B. (2014), 'The Gee's Bend Effect', *Textile*, 12 (3): 346–86.

Corbett, S. (2017), *How to Be a Craftivist: The Art of Gentle Protest*, London: Unbound.

Couldry, N. (2010), *Why Voice Matters: Culture and Politics after Neoliberalism*, Los Angeles, CA, and London: Sage.

Coulson, A., A. MacLaren, S. McKenzie and K. O'Gorman (2014), 'Hospitality Codes and Social Exchange Theory: The Pashtunwali and Tourism in Afghanistan', *Tourism Management*, 45: 134–41.

Court, K. (2020), 'Knitting Two Together (K2tog): "If You Meet Another Knitter, You Always Have a Friend"', *Textile*, 18 (3): 278–91.

Crenshaw, K.W. (1991), 'Mapping the Margins: Intersectionality, Identity Politics, and Violence against Women of Color', *Stanford Law Review*, 43 (6): 1241–99.

Cuming, E. (2013), 'Private Lives, Social Housing: Female Coming-of-Age Stories on the British Council Estate', *Contemporary Women's Writing*, 7 (3): 328–45.

Cvetkovich, A. (2003), *An Archive of Feelings: Trauma, Sexuality, and Lesbian Public Cultures*, Durham, NC: Duke University Press.

Cvetkovich, A. (2012), *Depression: A Public Feeling*, Durham, NC: Duke University Press.

Dabiri, E. (2021), *What White People Can Do Next: From Allyship to Coalition*, Dublin: Penguin.

Daly, S. (2011), *The Empire Inside: Indian Commodities in Victorian Domestic Novels*, Ann Arbor: University of Michigan Press.

Daniel, J.B. (2000), 'Function or Frill: The Quilt as Storyteller in Toni Morrison's *Beloved*', *Midwest Quarterly: A Journal of Contemporary Thought*, 41 (3): 321–9.

Dar, S., A.M. Dy and J. Rodriguez (2018), 'Is Decolonizing the New Black?', Sisters of Resistance, 12 July. Available online: https://sistersofresistance.wordpress. com/2018/07/12/is-decolonizing-the-new-black/ (accessed 12 September 2018).

Das, D. (2016), 'I Desire, Therefore I Am: South Asian Feminist Revisionism on Women's Forbidden Desires', *Hectate*, 42 (2): 102–18.

Davidson, R., and A. Tahsin (2018), *Craftfulness: Mend Yourself by Making Things*, London: Quercus (repr. 2019, New York, NY: Harper Wave).

Davis, A.Y. (2016), *Freedom Is a Constant Struggle: Ferguson, Palestine, and the Foundations of a Movement*, Chicago, IL: Haymarket Books.

Davis, T.M. (1994), 'Alice Walker's Celebration of Self in Southern Generations', in B.T. Christian (ed.), *'Everyday Use': Alice Walker*, 105–21, New Brunswick, NJ: Rutgers University Press.

Dawkins, N. (2011), 'Do-It-Yourself: The Precarious Work and Postfeminist Politics of Handmaking (in) Detroit', *Utopian Studies*, 22 (2): 261–84.

Dean, J. (2016), *Crowds and Party*, London and New York, NY: Verso.

Del Rosso, J., and J. Esala (2015), 'Constructionism and the Textuality of Social Problems', *Qualitative Sociology Review*, 11 (2): 34–45.

Deleuze, G., and F. Guattari (1987), *Thousand Plateaus: Capitalism and Schizophrenia*, trans. B. Massumi, Minneapolis and London: University of Minnesota Press.

Derr, H. (2017), 'Pink Flag: What Message Do "Pussyhats" Really Send?', *bitchmedia*, 17 January. Available online: https://www.bitchmedia.org/article/pink-flag-what-message-do-pussy-hats-really-send (accessed 21 January 2019).

Dickens, C. ([1859] 2003), *A Tale of Two Cities*, ed. R. Maxwell, repr., London: Penguin.

Dixon, C. (2014), *Another Politics: Talking across Today's Transformative Movements*, Oakland: University of California Press.

Dunn, M.M., and A.R. Morris (1992), 'Narrative Quilts and Quilted Narratives: The Art of Faith Ringgold and Alice Walker', *Explorations in Ethnic Studies*, 15 (1): 27–32.

Dunn, R. (2014), 'The Changing Status and Recognition of Fiber Work within the Realm of the Visual Arts', in M. Agosín (ed.), *Stitching Resistance: Women, Creativity, and Fiber Arts*, 43–53, Tunbridge Wells: Solis.

Dvorak, P. (2017), 'The Women's March Needs Passion and Purpose, not Pink Pussycat Hats', *The Washington Post*, 12 January. Available online: https://www.washingtonpost.com/local/the-womens-march-needs-passion-and-purpose-not-pink-pussycat-hats/2017/01/11/6d7e75be-d842-11e6-9a36-1d296534b31e_story.html (accessed 17 April 2023).

Eddo-Lodge, R. ([2017] 2018), *Why I'm No Longer Talking to White People about Race*, London: Bloomsbury.

Elsley, J. (1996), *Quilts as Text(iles): The Semiotics of Quilting*, New York, NY: Peter Lang.

Emadi, H. (2005), *Culture and Customs of Afghanistan*, Westport, CT: Greenwood Press.

Emejulu, A. (2011), 'Re-Theorizing Feminist Community Development: Towards a Radical Democratic Citizenship', *Community Development Journal*, 46 (3): 378–90.

Emejulu, A. (2018), 'On the Problems and Possibilities of Feminist Solidarity: The Women's March one Year on', *IPPR Progressive Review*, 24 (4): 267–73.

Eyerman, R. (2001), *Cultural Trauma: Slavery and the Formation of African American Identity*, Cambridge: Cambridge University Press.

Falling-rain, S. (1994), 'A Literary Patchwork Crazy Quilt: Toni Morrison's *Beloved*', *Uncoverings*, 15: 111–40.

Fanon, F. ([1952] 2008), *Black Skin, White Masks*, trans. R. Philcox, repr., New York: Grove Press.

Farinosi, M., and L. Fortunati (2018), 'Knitting Feminist Politics: Exploring a Yarn-bombing Performance in a Postdisaster City', *Journal of Communication Inquiry*, 42 (2): 138–65.

Farris, S.R. (2017), *In the Name of Women's Rights: The Rise of Femonationalism*, Durham, NC, and London: Duke University Press.

Felski, R. (1999), 'The Invention of Everyday Life', *New Formations*, 39: 13–31.

Fielding, L. (2017), 'Chicago Knitters Make Hundreds of Pink "Pussyhats" for Women's March', CBS Chicago, 17 January. Available online: https://www.cbsnews.com/chicago/news/chicago-knitters-make-hundreds-of-pink-pussyhats-for-womens-march/ (accessed 17 April 2023).

Fitzpatrick, T. (n.d.), '@covid19quilt project (2020–2021)'. Available online: https://talfitzpatrick.com/at-covid19quilt-project (accessed 9 August 2022).

Fitzpatrick, T. (2018), *Craftivism: A Manifesto/Methodology*, 2nd edn. Available online: https://www.dropbox.com/s/k42i51ng1ebiibm/Craftivism-TalFitzpatrick.pdf?dl=0 (accessed 30 November 2018).

Fitzpatrick, T. (2019), 'Craftivism as DIY Citizenship', in H. Mandell (ed.), *Crafting Dissent: Handicraft as Protest from the American Revolution to the Pussyhats*, 179–91, Lanham, MD, and London: Rowman & Littlefield.

Fitzpatrick, T., and K.-K. Kontturi (2015), 'Crafting Change: Practicing Activism in Contemporary Australia', *Harlot*, 14: n.p. Available online: http://harlotofthehearts.org/index.php/harlot/article/view/290/185 (accessed 30 November 2018).

Foster, S. (2019), 'Puns and Needles: Reactions to *The Knitting Map* in 2005', in J. Gilson and N. Moffat (eds), *Textiles, Community and Controversy: The Knitting Map*, 151–5, London: Bloomsbury Visual Arts.

Franger, G., ed. (2009), *Schicksalsfäden: Geschichten in Stoff von Gewalt, Hoffen und Überleben*, Nürnberg: Frauen in der Einen Welt.

Friedan, B. ([1963] 2010), *The Feminine Mystique*, repr., London: Penguin.

Frisby, D., and M. Featherstone, eds (1997), *Simmel on Culture: Selected Writings*, London and Thousand Oaks, CA: Sage.

Fromer, J. (2008a), *A Necessary Luxury: Tea in Victorian England*, Athens: Ohio University Press.

Fromer, J. (2008b), '"Deeply Indebted to the Tea-plant": Representations of English National Identity in Victorian Histories of Tea', *Victorian Literature and Culture*, 36 (2): 531–47.

Gajjala, R. (2015), 'When Your Seams Get Undone, Do You Learn to Sew or to Kill Monsters?', *The Communication Review*, 18 (1): 23–36.

Gauntlett, D. (2011), *Making Is Connecting: The Social Meaning of Creativity, from DIY and Knitting to YouTube and Web 2.0*, Cambridge: Polity.

Gauntlett, D. (2018), *Making Is Connecting: The Social Meaning of Creativity, from DIY and Knitting to YouTube and Web 2.0*, 2nd edn, Cambridge: Polity.

Gentile, J. (2018), 'The P*ssy Missile Has Launched: Free Speech Effects of the Women's March as Prelude to #MeToo, and with a Coda', *Studies in Gender and Sexuality*, 19 (4): 256–61.

Gerbaudo, P. (2012), *Tweets and the Streets: Social Media and Contemporary Activism*, London: Pluto Press.

Gilbert, S.M., and S. Gubar ([1979] 2000), *The Madwoman in the Attic: The Woman Writer and the Nineteenth-Century Literary Imagination*, 2nd edn, New Haven, CT: Yale University Press.

Gillis, S., G. Howie and R. Munford (2007), 'Introduction', in S. Gillis, G. Howie and R. Munford (eds), *Third Wave Feminism: A Critical Exploration*, xxi–xxxiv, Basingstoke: Palgrave Macmillan.

Gilson, J., and N. Moffat, eds (2019), *Textiles, Community and Controversy: The Knitting Map*, London: Bloomsbury Visual Arts.

Gipson, F. (2022), *Women's Work: From Feminine Arts to Feminist Art*, London: Frances Lincoln.

Glucksmann, M. (2000), *Cottons and Casuals: The Gendered Organisation of Labour in Time and Space*, Durham: Sociology Press.

Goggin, M.D. (2014), 'Yarn Bombing: Claiming Rhetorical Citizenship in Public Spaces', in C. Kock and L. Villadsen (eds), *Contemporary Rhetorical Citizenship: Rhetoric in Society*, 93–115, Leiden: Leiden University Press.

Golda, A. (2016), 'Feeling: Sensing the Affectivity of Emotional Politics through Textiles', in J. Jefferies, D.W. Conroy and H. Clark (eds), *The Handbook of Textile Culture*, 401–15, London: Bloomsbury.

Goldbard, A., and M. Smith (2017), 'The Kudzu Project: Cultural Organizing Spreads!', *U.S. Department of Arts and Culture Blog*, 21 December. Available online: https://usdac.us/news/2017/12/19/the-kudzu-project-cultural-organizing-spreads (accessed 7 January 2023).

Goldenberg, P. (n.d.), *Die Afghanin* ('The Afghan Woman'). Available online: https://www.guldusi.com/uber/p-goldenberg/tbc-afghanin.html (accessed 10 April 2023).

Goldenberg, P. (n.d.), *Verstellte Blicke* ('Disguised Views'). Available online: https://www.guldusi.com/uber/p-goldenberg/verstellte-blicke.html (accessed 10 April 2023).

Goldenberg, P. (2005), 'Aus Afghanistan zurück: Stickprojekt in Laghmani', *Guldusi*. Available online: https://www.guldusi.com/wp-content/uploads/Reisebericht_1.pdf (accessed 6 March 2017).

Goldenberg, P. (2006), 'Reisebericht 2, Stickprojekt in Laghmani (Afghanistan) und mehr', *Guldusi*. Available online: https://www.guldusi.com/stickprojekte/reiseberichte/2-reisebericht.html (accessed 13 April 2023).

Goldenberg, P. (2009), *Fäden Verbinden. Threats Unite*, Augsburg: MaroVerlag.

Goldenberg, P. (2013), 'Reiseberichte von Pascale und Margreth, Oktober 2013', *Guldusi*. Available online: https://www.guldusi.com/wp-content/uploads/7_reisebericht.pdf (accessed 6 March 2017).

Goldenberg, P. (2016a), *Gardens around the World*, Augsburg: MaroVerlag.

Goldenberg, P. (2016b), 'How Afghan Women Embroiderers from Laghmani Discover and Explore Written Language as a Communication Tool', Afghanistan Tagung, Pädagogische Hochschule Freiburg, Germany, 16–17 October.

Goldenberg, P. (2022), 'Guldusi Newsletter Februar 2022', *Guldusi*. Email newsletter circulated by Goldenberg (accessed 2 March 2022).

Gorton, K. (2008), *Theorising Desire: From Freud to Feminism to Film*, Basingstoke and New York, NY: Palgrave Macmillan.

Gould, D. (2009), *Moving Politics: Emotion and Act Up's Fight against AIDS*, Chicago, IL: University of Chicago Press.

Grattan, S.A. (2017), *Hope Isn't Stupid: Utopian Affects in Contemporary American Literature*, Iowa City: University of Iowa Press.

Graulich, M., and M. Witzling (1994), 'The Freedom to Say What She Pleases: A Conversation with Faith Ringgold', *NWSA Journal*, 6 (1): 1–27.

Greer, B. (n.d.), 'Craftivism Manifesto', craftivism. Available online: http://craftivism. com/manifesto/ (accessed 20 January 2020).

Greer, B. (2014), 'Knitting Craftivism: From My Sofa to Yours', in B. Greer (ed.), *Craftivism: The Art of Craft and Activism*, 7–8, Vancouver: Arsenal Pulp Press.

Greer, G. ([1970] 2012), The Female Eunuch, repr., London: Fourth Estate.

Grewal, I., and C. Kaplan (1994), 'Introduction: Transnational Feminist Practices and Questions of Postmodernity', in I. Grewal and C. Kaplan (eds), *Scattered Hegemonies: Postmodernity and Transnational Feminist Practices*, 1–33, Minneapolis and London: University of Minnesota Press.

Groeneveld, E. (2010), '"Join the Knitting Revolution": Third-Wave Feminist Magazines and the Politics of Domesticity', *Canadian Review of American Studies*, 40 (2): 259–77.

Groot, J. de (2013), 'How Much Is Enough Said? Some Gendered Responses to Orientalism', in Z. Elmarsafy, A. Bernard and D. Attwell (eds), *Debating Orientalism*, 192–215, New York, NY: Palgrave Macmillan.

Guldusi (n.d.), *Guldusi*. Available online: https://www.guldusi.com/ (accessed 26 January 2020).

Guldusi (2007), 'Afghanistan Inspiration, Präsentation der Werke aus dem United Kingdom'. Available online: https://www.guldusi.com/ausstellungen/afghanistan-inspiration/grosbritannien.html (accessed 12 April 2023).

Hackney, F. (2013), 'Quiet Activism and the New Amateur: The Power of Home and Hobby Crafts', *Design and Culture*, 5 (2): 169–93.

Hackney, F., H. Maughan and S. Desmarais (2016), 'The Power of Quiet: Re-Making Affective Amateur and Professional Textiles Agencies', *Journal of Textile Design Research and Practice*, 4 (1): 33–62.

Hahner, L.A., and S.J. Varda (2014), 'Yarn Bombing and the Aesthetics of Exceptionalism', *Communication and Critical/Cultural Studies*, 11 (4): 301–21.

Hall, S. (1999), 'The Work of Representation', in S. Hall (ed.), *Representation: Cultural Representation and Signifying Practices*, 13–74, London: Sage.

Hanifi, S.M.H. (2018), 'A Genealogy of Orientalism in Afghanistan: The Colonial Image Lineage', in T. Keskin (ed.), *Middle East Studies after September 11: Neo-Orientalism, American Hegemony and Academia*, 50–80, Leiden and Boston, MA: Brill.

Harding, S., ed. (2004), *The Feminist Standpoint Theory Reader: Intellectual and Political Controversies*, New York, NY, and London: Routledge.

Hardy, S.M. (2012), *A 1950s Housewife: Marriage and Homemaking in the 1950s*, Stroud: History Press.

Hartman, S. (2007), *Lose Your Mother: A Journey along the Atlantic Slave Route*, New York, NY: Farrar, Straus and Giroux.

Hartman, S. (2019), *Wayward Lives, Beautiful Experiments: Intimate Histories of Riotous Black Girls, Troublesome Women, and Queer Radicals*, New York, NY, and London: W.W. Norton & Co.

Hazlewood, S. (2017), 'Social Justice Sewing Academy {Make a Difference}', Crafty Planner, April. Available online: http://www.craftyplanner.com/2017/04/05/sjsa/ (accessed 24 August 2017).

Heath, J. (2011), 'Introduction', in J. Heath and A. Zahedi (eds), *Land of the Unconquerable: The Lives of Contemporary Afghan Women*, 1–41, Berkeley: University of California Press.

Hedges, E. (1991), 'The Needle or the Pen: The Literary Rediscovery of Women's Textile Work', in F. Howe (ed.), *Tradition and the Talents of Women*, 338–64, Urbana: University of Illinois Press.

Heilmann, A. (2000), *New Woman Fiction: Women Writing First-Wave Feminism*, Basingstoke: Palgrave.

Heinz, S. (2022), 'Making Yourself at Home: Performances of Whiteness in Cultural Production about Home and Homemaking Practices', in S. Hunter and C. van der Westhuizen (eds), *Routledge Handbook of Critical Studies in Whiteness*, 258–68, London and New York, NY: Routledge.

Hemmings, C. (2011), *Why Stories Matter: The Political Grammar of Feminist Theory*, Durham, NC, and London: Duke University Press.

Hemmings, C. (2012), 'Affective Solidarity: Feminist Reflexivity and Political Transformation', *Feminist Theory*, 13 (2): 147–61.

Hemmings, J. (2015), *Cultural Threads: Transnational Textiles Today*, London: Bloomsbury.

Hesse, B., and J. Hooker (2017), 'Introduction: On Black Political Thought inside Global Black Protest', *South Atlantic Quarterly*, 116 (3): 443–56.

Hewett, J. (2021), *This Long Thread: Women of Color on Craft, Community and Connection*, Boulder, CO: Roost Books.

Hiddleston, J. (2005), 'Shapes and Shadows: (Un)veiling the Immigrant in Monica Ali's *Brick Lane*', *Journal of Commonwealth Literature*, 40 (1): 57–72.

Highmore, B. (2002a), *Everyday Life and Cultural Theory: An Introduction*, London and New York, NY: Routledge.

Highmore, B. (2002b), 'Introduction: Questioning Everyday Life', in B. Highmore (ed.), *The Everyday Life Reader*, 1–34, London and New York, NY: Routledge.

Highmore, B. (2011), *Ordinary Lives: Studies in the Everyday*, London and New York, NY: Routledge.

Hill, H. (2022), personal email communication with author, 22 August.

Hine, C. (2007), 'Multi-sited Ethnography as a Middle Range Methodology for Contemporary STS', *Science, Technology & Human Values*, 32 (6): 652–71.

Hochschild, A. ([1983] 2003), *The Managed Heart: Commercialization of Human Feeling*, Berkeley: University of California Press.

Hood, Y. (2001), 'The Culture of Resistance: African American Art Quilts and Self-defining', *Uncoverings*, 22: 141–70.

Hooker, J. (2017), 'Black Protest/White Grievance: On the Problem of White Political Imaginations not Shaped by Loss', *South Atlantic Quarterly*, 116 (3): 483–504.

hooks, b. ([1981] 1987), *Ain't I a Woman: Black Women and Feminism*, London: Pluto Press.

hooks, b. (1991a), 'Narratives of Struggle: Conference Presentation', in P. Mariani (ed.), *Critical Fictions: The Politics of Imaginative Writing*, 53–61, Seattle, MA: Bay Press.

hooks, b. (1991b), *Yearning: Race, Gender, and Cultural Politics*, Boston, MA: Turnaround.

hooks, b. (1995), 'An Aesthetic of Blackness: Strange and Oppositional', *Lenox Avenue: A Journal of Interarts Inquiry*, 1: 65–72.

hooks, b. (2000), *Feminism Is for Everybody: Passionate Politics*, London: Pluto Press.

Hornstein, G. (2012), *Agnes's Jacket: A Psychologist's Search for the Meanings of Madness*, Ross-on-Wye: PCCS.

Huggan, G. (2001), *The Postcolonial Exotic: Marketing the Margins*, London: Routledge.

Hunter, S., and C. van der Westhuizen (2022), 'Viral Whiteness: Twenty-first Century Global Colonialities', in S. Hunter and C. van der Westhuizen (eds), *Routledge Handbook of Critical Studies in Whiteness*, 1–28, London and New York, NY: Routledge.

Ingold, T. (2010), 'The Textility of Making', *Cambridge Journal of Economics*, 34 (1): 91–102.

Ingold, T. (2016), *Lines: A Brief History*, rev. edn., Oxford and New York, NY: Routledge.

International Quilt Museum at the University of Nebraska-Lincoln (n.d.), *World Quilts*. Available online: http://worldquilts.quiltstudy.org/americanstory/identity (accessed 28 January 2020).

Ishkanian, A., and A.P. Saavedra (2019), 'The Politics and Practices of Intersectional Prefiguration in Social Movements: The Case of Sisters Uncut', *Sociological Review*, 67 (5): 985–1001.

Ivey, D. (2019), 'Reshaping the Narrative around People of Color and Craftivism', in H. Mandell (ed.), *Crafting Dissent: Handicraft as Protest from the American Revolution to the Pussyhats*, 309–17, Lanham, MD, and London: Rowman & Littlefield.

Jan-Gagneux, J., and P. Goldenberg (2014), *Out of the Kitchen: Jars, Bowls and Utensils. Coin Cuisine: De côté des ustensiles. Aus der Küche: Gefäße, Behälter und Utensilien.* Available online: https://de.calameo.com/read/0026884626ea6f8e4bb86 (accessed 6 August 2018).

Jefferies, J. (2011), 'Loving Attention: An Outburst of Craft in Contemporary Art', in M.E. Buszek (ed.), *Extra/Ordinary: Craft and Contemporary Art*, 59–82, Durham, NC: Duke University Press.

Jefferies, J. (2016a), *Crocheted Strategies: Women Crafting their Own Communities*, *Textile*, 14 (1): 14–35.

Jefferies, J. (2016b), 'Editorial Introduction', in J. Jefferies, D.W. Conroy and H. Clark (eds), *The Handbook of Textile Culture*, 3–15, London: Bloomsbury.

Jefferies, J., D.W. Conroy and H. Clark, eds (2016), *The Handbook of Textile Culture*, London: Bloomsbury.

Johnson, L., and J. Lloyd (2004), *Sentenced to Everyday Life: Feminism and the Housewife*, Oxford: Berg.

Jones, S., ed. (2019), 'Woven Textile Crafts in Contemporary Commercial Contexts: Waving not Drowning', *Textile*, 17 (2): 110–19.

Jones, T. (2018), *An American Marriage*, New York, NY: Algonquin Books of Chapel Hill.

Jong, S. de (2017), *Complicit Sisters: Gender and Women's Issues across North–South Divides*, Oxford: Oxford University Press.

Just, K. (n.d.), 'Kate Just & Tal Fitzpatrick, @COVID19QUILT'. Available online: https://www.katejust.com/covid19-global-quilt (accessed 9 August 2022).

Kabeer, N. (2000), *The Power to Choose: Bangladeshi Women and Labour Market Decisions in London and Dhaka*, London: Verso.

Kabeer, N. (2004), 'Globalization, Labor Standards, and Women's Rights: Dilemmas of Collective (In)action in an Interdependent World', *Feminist Economics*, 10 (1): 3–35.

Kauffman, L.A. (2017), *Direct Action: Protest and the Reinvention of American Radicalism*, London and New York, NY: Verso.

Kelley, R.D.G. (2002), *Freedom Dreams: The Black Radical Imagination*, Boston, MA: Beacon Press.

Kensinger, L. (2003), 'Plugged in Praxis: Critical Reflections on U.S. Feminism, Internet Activism, and Solidarity with Women in Afghanistan', *Journal of International Women's Studies*, 5 (1): 1–28.

Keskin, T. (2018), 'An Introduction: The Sociology of Orientalism and Neo-Orientalism (Theory and Praxis)', in T. Keskin (ed.), *Middle East Studies after September 11: Neo-Orientalism, American Hegemony and Academia*, 1–23, Leiden and Boston, MA: Brill.

Kettle, A., and L. Millar, eds (2018), *The Erotic Cloth: Seduction and Fetishism in Textiles*, London and New York, NY: Bloomsbury.

Khanna, N. (2020), *The Visceral Logics of Decolonization*, Durham, NC: Duke University Press.

Kimokeo-Goes, U. (2019), 'The Quilt Speaks: Crafting Gender and Cultural Norms in Hawaii', *Art/Research International*, 4 (1): 106–26.

Kiracofe, R., and M.E. Johnson (1993), *The American Quilt: A History of Cloth and Comfort 1750– 1950*, New York, NY: Clarkson Potter.

Klassen, T. (2009), 'Representations of African American Quiltmaking: From Omission to High Art', *Journal of American Folklore*, 122 (485): 297–334.

Knudsen, B.T., and C. Stage (2015), 'Introduction: Affective Methodologies', in B.T. Knudsen and C. Stage (eds), *Affective Methodologies: Developing Cultural Research Strategies for the Study of Affect*, 1–22, Basingstoke and New York, NY: Palgrave Macmillan.

Kolehmainen, M., A. Lahti and A. Kinnunen (2022), 'Affective Intensities of Single Lives: An Alternative Account of Temporal Aspects of Couple Normativity', *Sociology*, 57 (1): 3–19. First published online: https://doi.org/10.1177/00380385221090858.

Koppy, K.C.M. (2021), 'Writing Our Stories with Hooks and Needles: Literary Women's Voices in Textiles', *Cultural Studies*, 36 (5): 840–55. First published online: https://doi.org/10.1080/09502386.2021.2012707.

Krumholz, L. (1999), 'The Ghosts of Slavery: Historical Recovery in Toni Morrison's *Beloved*', in L.A. William and N.Y. McKay (eds), *Toni Morrison's* Beloved: *A Casebook*, 107–25, New York, NY: Oxford University Press.

Kudzu Project (n.d.), *Kudzu Project*. Available online: https://www.thekudzuproject.org/ (accessed 11 August 2022).

Kudzu Project (2018), 'Is Justice Blind or Turning a Blind Eye?', *Kudzu Project*, October 2018. Available online: https://www.thekudzuproject.org/single-post/2018/10/24/is-justice-blind-or-turning-a-blind-eye (accessed 11 August 2022).

Kumar, R., and H. Noori (2022), '"We Are Worse Off": Afghanistan Further Impoverished as Women Vanish from Workforce', *The Guardian*, 16 May 2022. Available online: https://www.theguardian.com/global-development/2022/may/16/afghanistan-further-impoverished-as-women-vanish-from-workforce-taliban (accessed 13 April 2023).

Kuo, H.-J. (2014), 'Revisiting Adultery: The Bodies of Diasporic Female Adulterers in South Asian Immigrant Narratives', *Contemporary Women's Writing*, 8 (2): 171–88.

Land, C., N. Sutherland and S. Taylor (2019), 'Back to the Brewster: Craft Brewing, Gender and the Dialectical Interplay of Retraditionalisation and Innovation', in E. Bell *et al.* (eds), *The Organization of Craft Work: Identities, Meaning, and Materiality*, 135–54, New York, NY, and London: Routledge.

Law, J. (2004), *After Method: Mess in Social Science Research*, London: Routledge.

Layli, P., ed. (2006), *The Womanist Reader: The First Quarter Century of Womanist Thought*, New York, NY: Routledge.

Lazreg, M. (2001), 'Decolonizing Feminism', in K.-K. Bhavnani (ed.), *Feminism and 'Race'*, 281–93, Oxford: Oxford University Press.

Ledger, S. (2002), *The New Woman: Fiction and Feminism at the Fin de Siècle*, Manchester: Manchester University Press.

Lefebvre, H. ([1992] 2004), *Rhythmanalysis: Space, Time and Everyday Life*, trans. S. Elden and G. Moore, London and New York, NY: Continuum.

Levenson, E. (2017), 'Tennessee Yarn Shop Bans "Vile" Women's March Knitters', CNN, 26 January. Available online: https://edition.cnn.com/2017/01/26/us/yarn-shop-womens-march-trnd/index.html (accessed 21 January 2019).

Lindström, K., and Å. Ståhl (2016), 'Five Patchworking Ways of Knowing and Making', in J. Jefferies, D.W. Conroy, and H. Clark (eds), *The Handbook of Textile Culture*, 65–78, London: Bloomsbury.

Literat, I., and S. Markus (2020), '"Crafting a Way Forward": Online Participation, Craftivism and Civic Engagement in Ravelry's Pussyhat Project Group', *Information, Communication & Society*, 23 (10): 1411–26.

Litvan, L. (2022), 'Trump's Hand in Shaping Supreme Court Pays Off with Roe v. Wade Decision', *Bloomberg UK*, 24 June. Available online: https://www.bloomberg.com/

news/articles/2022-06-24/trump-s-hand-in-shaping-supreme-court-pays-off-with-roe-decision?leadSource=uverify%20wall (accessed 7 January 2023).

Loomba, A. (2005), *Colonialism/postcolonialism*, 2nd edn, London: Routledge.

Lorde, A. ([1984] 2007), *Sister Outsider: Essays and Speeches by Audre Lorde*, Berkeley, CA: Crossing Press.

Love, H. (2007), *Feeling Backward: Loss and the Politics of Queer History*, Cambridge, MA: Harvard University Press.

Lowery, W. (2017), *They Can't Kill Us All: The Story of Black Lives Matter*, London: Penguin.

Luckhurst, R. (2008), *The Trauma Question*, London: Routledge.

Luckman, S. (2013), 'The Aura of the Analogue in a Digital Age: Women's Crafts, Creative Markets and Home-Based Labour after Etsy', *Cultural Studies Review*, 19 (1):249–70.

MacDowell, M. (1997), *African American Quiltmaking in Michigan*, East Lansing: Michigan State University Press.

MacDowell, M., M. Worrall, L. Swanson and B. Donaldson (2016), *Quilts and Human Rights*, Lincoln: University of Nebraska Press.

MacDowell, M., C. Luz and B. Donaldson (2017), *Quilts and Health*, Bloomington: Indiana University Press.

Madhok, S., and M. Evans (2014), 'Part I: Epistemology and Marginality', in M. Evans *et al.* (eds), *The SAGE Handbook of Feminist Theory*, 1–8, London: Sage.

Makdisi, S. (2018), 'Orientalism Today', in B. Abu-Maneh (ed.), *After Said: Postcolonial Literary Studies in the Twenty-First Century*, 179–88, Cambridge: Cambridge University Press.

Malos, E., ed. (1980), *The Politics of Housework*, London: Allison & Busby.

Mandell, H., ed. (2019), *Crafting Dissent: Handicraft as Protest from the American Revolution to the Pussyhats*, Lanham, MD, and London: Rowman & Littlefield.

Mankekar, P. (2015), *Unsettling India: Affect, Temporality, Transnationality*, Durham, NC: Duke University Press.

Mann, J. (2015), 'Towards a Politics of Whimsy: Yarn Bombing the City', *Area*, 47 (1): 65–72.

Manning, E. (2016), *The Minor Gesture*, Durham, NC: Duke University Press.

Martinussen, M., and M. Wetherell, (2019), 'Affect, Practice and Contingency: Critical Discursive Psychology and Eve Kosofsky Sedgwick', *Subjectivity*, 12 (2): 101–16.

Marx, J. (2006), 'The Feminization of Globalization', *Cultural Critique*, 63: 1–32.

Massumi, B. (2002), *Parables for the Virtual: Movement, Affect, Sensation*, Durham, NC, and London: Duke University Press.

May, K. (2018), 'Stitched Encounters: An Exploration of the Afghan–German Embroidery Initiative Guldusi', *Quilt Studies*, 19: 38–68.

May, K. (2020), 'The Pussyhat Project: Texturing the Struggle for Feminist Solidarity', *Journal of International Women's Studies*, 21 (3): 77–89.

May, K. (2023), 'Pussyhats and Women's Marches: Affective Tension in Transnational Feminism', in T. Reeser (ed.), *The Routledge Companion to Gender and Affect*, 23–31, London: Routledge.

Mazloomi, C.L. (2015), 'And Still We Rise: Race, Culture, and Visual Conversations', in C.L. Mazloomi (ed.), *And Still We Rise: Race, Culture, and Visual Conversations*, 6–11, Atglen, PA: Schiffer Publishing.

McBrinn, J. (2021), *Queering the Subversive Stitch: Men and the Culture of Needlework*, London and New York, NY: Bloomsbury Visual Arts.

McClintock, A. (1995), *Imperial Leather: Race, Gender and Sexuality in the Colonial Contest*, New York, NY: Routledge.

McGovern, A. (2022), 'Risky, Subversive, and Deviant? A Criminological Analysis of Guerrilla Knitting', *Textile*. First published online: doi.org/10.1080/14759756.2022.20 85987.

McKay, M., and M. Stewart (2005), '"The Tradition of Old People's Ways": Gee's Bend Quilts and Slave Quilts of the Deep South', *Uncoverings*, 26: 155–73.

McMillan, M. (2008), 'The "West Indian" Front Room: Reflections on a Diasporic Phenomenon', *Kunapipi: Journal of Postcolonial Writing*, 30 (2): 44–70.

McNutt, R.K. (2017), '"What's Left of the Flag": The Confederate and Jacobite "Lost Cause" Myths, and the Construction of Mythic Identities through Conflict Commemoration', *Journal of Conflict Archaeology*, 12 (3): 142–62.

Mendes, K., J. Ringrose and J. Keller (2019), *Digital Feminist Activism: Girls and Women Fight Back against Rape Culture*, Oxford: Oxford University Press.

Menon, M. (2018), *Infinite Variety: A History of Desire in India*, New Delhi: Speaking Tiger.

Metzl, J.M. (2020), *Dying of Whiteness: How the Politics of Racial Resentment Is Killing America's Heartland*, New York, NY: Basic Books.

Millar, L., and A. Kettle (2018), 'An Introduction to *The Erotic Cloth*', in A. Kettle and L. Millar (eds), *The Erotic Cloth: Seduction and Fetishism in Textiles*, 1–22, London and New York, NY: Bloomsbury.

Minahan, S., and J. Cox (2007), 'Stitch'nBitch: Cyberfeminism, a Third Place and the New Materiality', *Journal of Material Culture*, 12 (1): 5–21.

Mitchell, K. (2020), *From Slave Cabins to the White House: Homemade Citizenship in African American Culture*, Urbana, Chicago and Springfield: University of Illinois Press.

Moers, E. (1978), *Literary Women*, London: The Women's Press.

Mohanty, C.T. (1988), 'Under Western Eyes: Feminist Scholarship and Colonial Discourses', *Feminist Review*, 30 (1): 61–88.

Mohanty, C.T. (2003), 'Under Western Eyes' Revisited: Feminist Solidarity through Anticapitalist Struggles', *Signs*, 28 (2): 499–535.

Mohanty, C.T. (2013), 'Transnational Feminist Crossings: On Neoliberalism and Radical Critique', *Signs*, 38 (4): 967–91.

Monsutti, A. (2004), 'Cooperation, Remittances, and Kinship among the Hazaras', *Iranian Studies*, 37 (2): 219–40.

Morrison, T. ([1987] 1997), *Beloved*, London: Vintage.

Morrison, T. (1989), 'Unspeakable Things Unspoken: The Afro-American Presence in American Literature', *Michigan Quarterly Review*, 28 (1): 1–34.

Morrison, T. (1995), 'The Site of Memory', in W. Zinsser (ed.), *Inventing the Truth: The Art and Craft of Memoir*, 83–102, 2nd edn, Boston, MA: Houghton Mifflin.

Moss, P., and A. Maddrell (2017), 'Emergent and Divergent Spaces in the Women's March: The Challenges of Intersectionality and Inclusion', *Gender, Place and Culture*, 24 (5): 613–20.

Mulholland, J. (2018), 'Gendering the "White Backlash": Islam, Patriarchal "Unfairness," and the Defense of Women's Rights among Women Supporters of the British National Party', in J. Mulholland, N. Montagna and E. Sanders-McDonagh (eds), *Gendering Nationalism: Intersections of Nation, Gender and Sexuality*, 165–86, Cham: Palgrave Macmillan.

Muñoz, J.E. (2009), *Cruising Utopia: The Then and There of Queer Futurity*, New York, NY: New York University Press.

Myzelev, A. (2015), 'Creating Digital Materiality: Third-Wave Feminism, Public Art, and Yarn Bombing', *Material Culture: Journal of the Pioneer American Society*, 47 (1): 58–78.

Nasar, S. (2020), 'Remembering Edward Colston: Histories of Slavery, Memory, and Black Globality', *Women's History Review*, 29 (7): 1218–25.

Newmeyer, T.S. (2008), 'Knit One, Stitch Two, Protest Three! Examining the Historical and Contemporary Politics of Crafting', *Leisure/Loisir*, 32 (2): 437–60.

Nikoleris, A., J. Stripple and P. Tenngart (2017), 'Narrating Climate Futures: Shared Socioeconomic Pathways and Literary Fiction', *Climatic Change*, 143 (3/4): 307–19.

Oakley, A. (1974), *Housewife*, London: Allen Lane.

OED (n.d.), Oxford University Press. Available at: https://www.oed.com/.

O'Hare, E. (2018), 'Locals Craft their Own Brand of Activism', *C-ville*, 17 January 2018. Available online: https://www.c-ville.com/locals-craft-brand-activism/ (accessed 11 August 2022).

Ong, A. (1999), *Flexible Citizenship: The Cultural Logics of Transnationality*, Durham, NC, and London: Duke University Press.

Ong, A. (2006), *Neoliberalism as Exception: Mutation in Citizenship and Sovereignty*, Durham, NC, and London: Duke University Press.

Okumura, S. (2008), 'Women Knitting: Domestic Activity, Writing, and Distance in Virginia Woolf's Fiction', *English Studies: A Journal of English Language and Literature*, 89 (2): 166–81.

Orton-Johnson, K. (2014), 'Knit, Purl, Upload: New Technologies, Digital Mediations and the Experience of Leisure', *Leisure Studies*, 33 (3): 305–21.

Paine, S. (2006), *Embroidery from Afghanistan*, Seattle: University of Washington Press.

Parker, R. (1984), *The Subversive Stitch: Embroidery and the Making of the Feminine*, London: The Women's Press.

Parker, R. (2010), *The Subversive Stitch: Embroidery and the Making of the Feminine*, rev. edn, London: I.B. Tauris.

Parkins, W. (2004), 'Celebrity Knitting and the Temporality of Postmodernity', *Fashion Theory: The Journal of Dress, Body & Culture*, 8 (4): 425–41.

Patel, K. (2020), Diversity Initiatives and Addressing Inequalities in Craft, in S. Taylor and S. Luckman (eds), *Pathways into Creative Working Lives*, London: Palgrave Macmillan.

Pedwell, C. (2010), *Feminism, Culture and Embodied Practice: The Rhetorics of Comparison*, London: Routledge.

Pedwell, C. (2014), *Affective Relations: The Transnational Politics of Empathy*, Basingstoke: Palgrave Macmillan.

Pedwell, C. (2016), 'Transforming Habit: Revolution, Routine and Social Change', *Cultural Studies*, 31 (1): 93–120. First published online, doi: 10.1080/09502386.2016.1206134.

Pedwell, C. (2017), 'Habit and the Politics of Social Change: A Comparison of Nudge Theory and Pragmatist Philosophy', *Body & Society*, 23 (4): 59–94.

Pedwell, C. (2019), 'Digital Tendencies: Intuition, Algorithmic Thought and New Social Movements', *Culture, Theory & Critique*, 60 (2): 123–38.

Pedwell, C. (2021), *Revolutionary Routines: The Habits of Social Transformation*, Montreal, Quebec, and Kingston, Ontario: McGill-Queen's University Press.

Pedwell, C., and A. Whitehead (2012), 'Affecting Feminism: Questions of Feeling in Feminist Theory', *Feminist Theory*, 13 (2): 115–29.

Pentney, B.A. (2008), 'Feminism, Activism, and Knitting: Are the Fibre Arts a Viable Mode for Feminist Political Action?', *Thirdspace: A Journal of Feminist Theory and Culture*, 8 (1). Available online: https://journals.lib.sfu.ca/index.php/thirdspace/article/view/pentney (accessed 5 April 2023).

Pereira-Ares, N. (2012), '"The Old and Honourable Craft of Tailoring": Empowering Fabrics in Monica Ali's *Brick Lane*', in S. Martín Alegre *et al.*, *At a Time of Crisis: English and American Studies in Spain*. Available online: https://www.academia.edu/2115894/_THE_OLD_AND_HONOURABLE_CRAFT_OF_TAILORING_EMPOWERING_FABRICS_IN_MONICA_ALIS_BRICK_LANE (accessed 17 May 2018).

Pérez-Torres, R. (1999), 'Between Presence and Absence: *Beloved*, Postmodernism, and Blackness', in W.L. Andrews and N.Y. McKay (eds), *Morrison's* Beloved: *A Casebook*, 179–201, New York, NY, and Oxford: Oxford University Press.

Perry, I. (2018), *Vexy Thing: On Gender and Liberation*, Durham, NC, and London: Duke University Press.

Petrick, K. (2017), 'Occupy and the Temporal Politics of Prefigurative Democracy', *tripleC: Communication, Capitalism and Critique*, 15 (2) 490–504.

Phipps, A. (2020), *Me, Not You: The Trouble with Mainstream Feminism*, Manchester: Manchester University Press.

Pink, S. (2012), *Situating Everyday Life: Practices and Places*, London: Sage.

Pink, S., K.L. Mackley and R. Morosanu, (2015), 'Hanging Out at Home: Laundry as a Thread and Texture of Everyday Life', *International Journal of Cultural Studies*, 18 (2): 209–24.

Pöllänen, S. (2013), 'The Meaning of Craft: Craft Makers' Descriptions of Craft as an Occupation', *Scandinavian Journal of Occupational Therapy*, 20 (3): 217–27.

Pöllänen, S. (2015), 'Crafts as Leisure-Based Coping: Craft Makers' Descriptions of Their Stress- Reducing Activity', *Occupational Therapy in Mental Health*, 31 (2): 83–100.

Pollock, G. (1987), 'Feminism and Modernism', in R. Parker and G. Pollock (eds), *Framing Feminism: Art and the Women's Movement 1970–1985*, 79–122, London and New York, NY: Pandora.

Potter, R., and L. Stonebridge, (2014), 'Writing and Rights', *Critical Quarterly*, 56 (4): 1–16.

Priest, M. (2014), 'Gospels According to Faith: Rewriting Black Girlhood through the Quilt', *Children's Literature Association Quarterly*, 39 (4): 461–81.

Pristash, H., I. Schaechterle and S.C. Wood (2009), 'The Needle as the Pen: Intentionality, Needlework, and the Production of Alternate Discourses of Power', in M.D. Goggin and B.F. Tobin (eds), *Women and the Material Culture of Needlework and Textiles, 1750–1950*, 13–29, Farnham: Ashgate.

Procter, J. (2006), 'The Postcolonial Everyday', *New Formations: A Journal of Culture/ Theory/Politics*, (58): 62–80.

Pussyhat Project (n.d.), *Pussyhat Project*. Available online: https://www.pussyhatproject. com/ (accessed: 21 January 2019).

Pykett, L. (1992), *The 'Improper' Feminine: The Women's Sensation Novel and the New Woman Writing*, London: Routledge.

Quayson, A. (2000), *Postcolonialism: Theory, Practice, or Process?*, Cambridge: Polity Press.

Quinn-Lautrefin, R. (2018), '"[T]hat Pincushion Made of Crimson Satin:" Embroidery, Discourse and Memory in Victorian Literature and Culture', *e-Rea*, 16 (1): n.p.

Ramanathan, L. (2017), 'Was the Women's March Just Another Display of White Privilege? Some Think So', *The Washington Post*, 24 January. Available online: https:// www.washingtonpost.com/lifestyle/style/was-the-womens-march-just-another-display-of-white-privilege-some-think-so/2017/01/24/00bbdcca-e1a0-11e6-a547-5fb9411d332c_story.html (accessed 17 April 2023).

Ratto, M., and M. Boler (2014), 'Introduction', in M. Ratto and M. Boler (eds), *DIY Citizenship: Critical Making and Social Media*, 1–22, Cambridge, MA, and London: MIT Press.

Reckwitz, A. (2002), 'Toward a Theory of Social Practice: A Development in Culturalist Theorizing', *European Journal of Social Theory*, 5 (2): 243–63.

Reed, T.V. (2005), *The Art of Protest: Culture and Activism from the Civil Rights Movement to the Streets of Seattle*, Minneapolis: University of Minnesota Press.

Rees, K. (2018), 'Worsted, Weave, and Web: The Cultural Struggles of the Fictional Knitting-Woman', *e-Rea*, 16 (1): n.p.

Rentschler, C.A., and S.C. Thrift (2015), 'Doing Feminism: Event, Archive, Techné', *Feminist Theory*, 16 (3): 239–49.

Rhodes, S. (2015), 'Contemporary Textile Imagery in Southern Africa: A Question of Ownership', in J. Hemmings (ed.), *Cultural Threads: Transnational Textiles Today*, 206–23, London: Bloomsbury.

Rich, A. ([1978] 2013), *The Dream of a Common Language: Poems 1974–1977*, New York, NY, and London: Norton.

Richardson, B. (2018), 'Women's March Ditching "Pussyhats" because They Exclude Trans Women: Report', *Washington Times*, 11 January.

Ringgold, F., L. Freeman and N. Roucher (1996), *Talking to Faith Ringgold*, New York, NY: Crown Books for Young Readers.

Roberts, L.J. (2011), 'Put Your Things Down, Flip It, and Reverse It: Reimagining Craft Identities Using Tactics of Queer Theory', in M.E. Buszek (ed.), *Extra/Ordinary: Craft and Contemporary Art*, 243–59, Durham, NC: Duke University Press.

Robertson, K. (2011), 'Rebellious Doilies and Subversive Stitches: Writing a Craftivist History', in M.E. Buszek (ed.), *Extra/Ordinary: Craft and Contemporary Art*, 184–203, Durham, NC: Duke University Press.

Robertson, K. (2016), 'Quilts for the Twenty-First Century: Activism in the Expanded Field of Quilting', in J. Jefferies, D.W. Conroy and H. Clark (eds), *The Handbook of Textile Culture*, 197–210, London: Bloomsbury.

Rowe, L., and B. Corkhill, (2017), *Knit Yourself Calm: A Creative Path to Managing Stress*, Tunbridge Wells: Search Press.

Roy, S. (2016), 'Women's Movements in the Global South: Towards a Scalar Analysis', *International Journal of Politics, Culture, and Society*, 29 (3): 289–306.

Rudgard-Redsell, S.J. (2007), '"The Business of Her Life": Representing the Practice of Needlework in Nineteenth-Century Literature and Art', PhD thesis, University of Kent.

Russo, A. (2006), 'The Feminist Majority Foundation's Campaign to Stop Gender Apartheid: The Intersection of Feminism and Imperialism in the United States', *International Feminist Journal of Politics*, 8 (4): 557–80.

Saeed, H. (2015), 'Empowering Unheard Voices through "Theatre of the Oppressed": Reflections on the Legislative Theatre Project for Women in Afghanistan – Notes from the Field', *Journal of Human Rights Practice*, 7 (2), 299–326.

Said, E. ([1978] 2003), *Orientalism*, London: Penguin.

Salem, S. (2018), 'On Transnational Feminist Solidarity: The Case of Angela Davis in Egypt', *Signs*, 43 (2): 245–67.

Sandhu, S. (2003), 'Come Hungry, Leave Edgy: Brick Lane', *London Review of Books*, 25 (19), 9 October. Available online: https://www.lrb.co.uk/v25/n19/sukhdev-sandhu/come-hungry-leave-edgy (accessed 31 December 2017).

Sapelly, L.E. (2019), 'Spinning, Sewing, and Soliciting for the American Revolution', in H. Mandell (ed.), *Crafting Dissent: Handicraft as Protest from the American Revolution to the Pussyhats*, 47–61, Lanham, MD, and London: Rowman & Littlefield.

Scheper-Hughes, N. (2004), 'Anatomy of a Quilt: The Gee's Bend Freedom Quilting Bee', *Southern Cultures*, 10 (3): 88–98.

Schwartz-Cowan, R. (1997), *A Social History of American Technology*, Oxford: Oxford University Press.

Sedgwick, E.K. (2003), *Touching Feeling: Affect, Pedagogy, Performativity*, Durham, NC: Duke University Press.

Segal, R. (1995), *The Black Diaspora*, London: Faber.

Seigworth, G.J., and M. Gregg (2010), 'An Inventory of Shimmers', in M. Gregg and G.J. Seigworth (eds), *The Affect Theory Reader*, 1–26, Durham, NC, and London: Duke University Press.

Sennett, R. (2008), *The Craftsman*, New Haven, CT: Yale University Press.

Shamus, K.J. (2018), 'Pink Pussyhats: The Reason Feminists Are Ditching Them', *Detroit Free Press*, 12 January. Available online: https://eu.freep.com/story/news/2018/01/10/pink-pussyhats-feminists-hatswomens-march/1013630001/ (accessed 21 January 2019).

Sharoni, S., R. Abdulhadi, N. Al-Ali, F. Eaves, R. Lentin and D. Siddiqi (2015), 'Transnational Feminist Solidarity in Times of Crisis: The Boycott, Divestment and Sanctions (BDS) Movement and Justice in/for Palestine', *International Feminist Journal of Politics*, 17 (4): 654–70.

Sharpe, C. (2016), *In the Wake: On Blackness and Being*, Durham, NC, and London: Duke University Press.

Sharrad, P., and A. Collett (2004), *Reinventing Textiles: Volume 3: Postcolonialism and Creativity*, Bristol: Telos.

Sheller, M. (2012), *Citizenship from Below: Erotic Agency and Caribbean Freedom*, Durham, NC: Duke University Press.

Shove, E., M. Pantzar and M. Watson (2012), *The Dynamics of Social Practice: Everyday Life and How It Changes*, London: Sage.

Showalter, E. (1982), *A Literature of Their Own: British Women Novelists from Charlotte Brontë to Doris Lessing*, London: Virago

Singh, N.P. (2016), 'Trump and the Present Crisis', *Verso Blog post*, 5 December. Available online: https://www.versobooks.com/blogs/2993-trump-and-the-present-crisis (accessed 27 January 2020).

SJSAcademy (n.d.), *Social Justice Sewing Academy*. Available online: http://www.sjsacademy.com/ (accessed 5 July 2017).

Skaine, R. (2002), *The Women of Afghanistan under the Taliban*, Jefferson, NC: McFarland and Co.

Skeehan, D.C. (2020), *The Fabric of Empire: Material and Literary Cultures of the Global Atlantic, 1650–1850*, Baltimore, MD: Johns Hopkins University Press.

Slater, D. (2009), 'The Ethics of Routine: Consciousness, Tedium and Value', in E. Shove, F. Trentmann and R. Wilk (eds), *Time, Consumption and Everyday Life: Practice, Materiality and Culture*, 217–30, Oxford and New York, NY: Berg.

Smelser, N.J. (2004), 'Psychological Trauma and Cultural Trauma', in J.C. Alexander, R. Eyerman, B. Giesen, N.J. Smelser and P. Sztompka, *Cultural Trauma and Collective Identity*, 31–59, Berkeley: University of California Press.

Smith, M. (2019), 'The Kudzu Project: Vinebombing Virginia's Confederate Monuments', in J. Decker and H. Mandell (eds), *Crafting Democracy: Fiber Arts and Activism*, 32–7, Rochester, NY: RIT Press.

Soon, A.N.H. (2011), 'Toni Morrison's *Beloved*: Space, Architecture, Trauma', *Symplokē: A Journal for the Intermingling of Literary, Cultural and Theoretical Scholarship*, 19 (1–2): 231–45.

Spivak, G.C. ([1988] 1994), 'Can the Subaltern Speak?', in P. Williams and L. Chrisman (eds), *Colonial Discourse and Post-Colonial Theory: A Reader*, Hemel Hempstead: Harvester.

Springgay, S., N. Hatza and S. O'Donald (2011), '"Crafting Is a Luxury that Many Women Cannot Afford": Campus Knitivism and an Aesthetic of Civic Engagement', *International Journal of Qualitative Studies in Education*, 24 (5): 607–13.

Stabile, C.A., and D. Kumar (2005), 'Unveiling Imperialism: Media, Gender and the War on Afghanistan', *Media Culture and Society*, 27 (5): 765–82.

Stalp, M.C. (2007), *Quilting: The Fabric of Everyday Life*, Oxford and New York, NY: Berg.

Stalp, M.C. (2020), 'Covid-19 Global Quilt', *The Journal of Modern Craft*, 13 (3), 351–7.

Stewart, K. (2007), *Ordinary Affects*, Durham, NC, and London: Duke University Press.

Stockwell, P. (2009), *Texture: A Cognitive Aesthetics of Reading*, Edinburgh: Edinburgh University Press.

Stormer, N. (2013), 'Remembering the AIDS Quilt', *Quarterly Journal of Speech*, 99 (3): 376–9.

Strawn, S.M. (2009), 'American Women and Wartime Hand Knitting, 1759–1950', in M.D. Goggin and B.F. Tobin (eds), *Women and the Material Culture of Needlework and Textiles, 1750–1950*, 245–59, Farnham: Ashgate.

Suh, K. (2018), *DIY Rules for a WTF World: How to Speak Up, Get Creative, and Change the World*, New York, NY: Grand Central Publishing.

Sullivan, N. (2020), 'A Stitch in Time? Craftivism, Connection and Community in the Time of COVID- 19', *Museum and Society*, 18 (3): 327–9.

Sullivan, S. (2007), 'On Revealing Whiteness: A Reply to Critics', *The Journal of Speculative Philosophy*, 21 (3): 231–42.

Sullivan, S. (2014), *Good White People: The Problem with Middle-Class White Anti-Racism*, New York, NY: SUNY Press.

Sullivan, S. (2017), 'White Priority', *Critical Philosophy of Race*, 5 (2): 171–82.

Sullivan, S. (2019), *White Privilege*, Cambridge: Polity Press.

Swain, D. (2019), 'Not Now but Not Yet: Present and Future in Prefigurative Politics', *Political Studies*, 67 (1): 47–62.

Tamboukou, M. (2015), *Sewing, Fighting and Writing: Radical Practices in Work, Sewing and Culture*, London and New York, NY: Rowman & Littlefield.

Tanner, L.E. (2006), *Lost Bodies: Inhabiting the Borders of Life and Death*, Ithaca, NY, and London: Cornell University Press.

Tate, S.A., and D. Page (2018), 'Whiteliness and Institutional Racism: Hiding Behind (Un)Conscious Bias', *Ethics and Education*, 13 (1): 141–55.

Tickner, L. (1987), *The Spectacle of Women: Imagery of the Suffrage Campaign 1907–14*, London: Chatto & Windus.

Titcombe, E. (2013), 'Women Activists: Rewriting Greenham's History', *Women's History Review*, 22 (2): 310–29.

Tobin, J.L., and R.G. Dobard ([1999] 2000), *Hidden in Plain View: A Secret Story of Quilts and the Underground Railroad*, New York, NY: Anchor Books.

Trail, S., and T.D. Wong (2021), *Stitching Stolen Lives: The Social Justice Sewing Academy Remembrance Project*, Lafayette, CA: C&T Publishing.

Travis, G. (2015), *Add this Square*. Available online: https://gilliantravis.co.uk/patterns/ (accessed 24 April 2023).

Travis, G. (2016), *Letter to My Friends*, submission to Guldusi 'Message' competition. Available online: https://www.guldusi.com/en/the-various-exhibitions/message.html (accessed 12 April 2023).

Tsing, A.L. (2004), *Friction: An Ethnography of Global Connection*, Princeton, NJ, and Oxford: Princeton University Press.

Tuck, E., and K.W. Yang (2012), 'Decolonization Is Not a Metaphor', *Decolonization: Indigeneity, Education & Society*, 1 (1):1–40.

Turney, J. (2009), *The Culture of Knitting*, Oxford and New York, NY: Berg.

Turney, J. (2019), 'Stitched Up? *The Knitting Map* in Context', in J. Gilson and N. Moffat (eds), *Textiles, Community and Controversy: The Knitting Map*, 156–69, London: Bloomsbury Visual Arts.

V&A (n.d.), 'The Pussyhat'. Available online: https://www.vam.ac.uk/articles/ thepussyhat (accessed 21 January 2019).

Valenzuela, L. (1991), 'The Writer, the Crisis, and a Form of Representation', in P. Mariani (ed.), *Critical Fictions: The Politics of Imaginative Writing*, 80–2, Seattle, WA: Bay Press.

Walker, A. ([1973] 1994), 'Everyday Use', in B.T. Christian (ed.), *'Everyday Use': Alice Walker*, 23–35, New Brunswick, NJ: Rutgers University Press.

Walker, A. ([1982] 2004), *The Color Purple*, London: Phoenix.

Walker, A. ([1983] 2004), *In Search of Our Mothers' Gardens: Womanist Prose*, London: Phoenix, 2004.

Walker, E. (2020), 'The Sovereign Stitch: Re-reading Embroidery as a Critical Feminist–Decolonial Text', in A. Black and N. Burisch (eds), *The New Politics of the Handmade: Craft, Art and Design*, 217–39, London: Bloomsbury Visual Arts.

Walker, R. (2007), 'Handmade 2.0', *The New York Times Magazine*, 16 December. Available online: https://www.nytimes.com/2007/12/16/magazine/16Crafts-t.html (accessed 7 September 2018).

Walker, R. (2017), 'The D.I.Y. Revolutionaries of the Pussyhat Project', *The New Yorker*, 25 January. Available online: https://www.newyorker.com/culture/culture-desk/the-d-i-y-revolutionaries-of-the-pussyhat-project (accessed 26 January 2020).

Wallace, M. ([1978] 2015), *Black Macho and the Myth of the Superwoman*, London and New York, NY: Verso.

Wallace, M. ([1990] 2016), *Invisibility Blues: From Pop to Theory*, London: Verso.

Weeks, K. (2011), *The Problem with Work: Feminism, Marxism, Antiwork Politics, and Postwork Imaginaries*, Durham, NC, and London: Duke University Press.

Wellesley-Smith, C. (2021), *Resilient Stitch: Wellbeing and Connection in Textile Art*, London: Batsford.

Wetherell, M. (2012), *Affect and Emotion: A New Social Science Understanding*, London: Sage.

Whitehead, A. (2017), *Medicine and Empathy in Contemporary British Fiction: A Critical Intervention in Medical Humanities*, Edinburgh: Edinburgh University Press.

Williams, K.A. (2011), '"Old Time Mem'ry" Contemporary Urban Craftivism and the Politics of Doing-It-Yourself in Postindustrial America', *Utopian Studies*, 22 (2): 303–20.

Williams, R. (1977), *Marxism and Literature*, Oxford: Oxford University Press.

Wilson, H.F. (2017), 'On Geography and Encounter: Bodies, Borders and Difference', *Progress in Human Geography*, 41 (4): 451–71.

Wimpelmann, T. (2017), *The Pitfalls of Protection: Gender, Violence, and Power in Afghanistan*, Oakland: University of California Press.

WJRH (2017), 'The House that Chawne Quilt' (podcast), 31 July. Available online: http://wjrh.org/vbb/597f0f79d7d5cb000d5955e0/ (accessed 27 January 2020).

Wright, M.M. (2014), 'Transnational Black Feminisms, Womanisms and Queer of Color Critiques', in M. Evans *et al.* (eds), *The SAGE Handbook of Feminist Theory*, 327–42, London: Sage.

Yancy, G. (2014), 'Introduction: Un-Sutured', in G. Yancy (ed.), *White Self-Criticality beyond Anti- racism: How Does It Feel to Be a White Problem?*, xi–xxvii, Lanham, MD: Lexington Books.

Yancy, G., ed. (2014), *White Self-Criticality beyond Anti-racism: How Does It Feel to Be a White Problem?*, Lanham, MD: Lexington Books.

Yancy, G. (2018), *Backlash: What Happens When We Talk Honestly about Racism in America*, Lanham, MD: Rowman & Littlefield.

Yates, L. (2015), 'Rethinking Prefiguration: Alternatives, Micropolitics and Goals in Social Movements', *Social Movement Studies*, 14 (1): 1–21.

Yeğenoğlu, M. (1998), *Colonial Fantasies: Towards a Feminist Reading of Orientalism*, Cambridge: Cambridge University Press.

Yenika-Agbaw, V., and L. Mhando, eds (2014), *African Youth in Contemporary Literature and Popular Culture: Identity Quest*, New York, NY, and Oxford: Routledge.

Zouggari, N. (2018), 'Hybridised Materialisms: The "Twists and Turns" of Materialities in Feminist Theory', *Feminist Theory*, 20 (3). First published online: doi: 10.1177/1464700118804447.

Zweiman, J. (2018), 'The Project of Pussyhat', *Pussyhat Project*, 14 January. Available online: https://www.pussyhatproject.com/blog/2018/1/14/the-project-of-pussyhat. (accessed 21 January 2019).

Appendix: Interviews Conducted for Research

I obtained ethics approval for conducting these interviews from the University of Kent's Humanities Research Ethics Advisory Group.

April 2017:
Phone interview with Pascale Goldenberg from Guldusi and UK textile artist Gillian Travis, followed by a few email communications to clarify some points.

July 2017:
Skype interview with Social Justice Sewing Academy (SJSA) founder Sara Trail. Subsequently, Trail shared with me unpublished video footage of herself talking about SJSA.

August 2017:
Skype interview with quilter Chawne Kimber.

Index

www.ingramcontent.com/pod-product-compliance
Lightning Source LLC
Chambersburg PA
CBHW062029270326
41929CB00014B/2372